LATANÉ CONANT

FOREWORD BY JASON ZINTAK

NO FORMS.

NO SPAM.

NO COLD CALLS.

REVISED AND UPDATED

THE NEXT GENERATION OF ACCOUNT-BASED SALES AND MARKETING

WILEY

Published by John Wiley & Sons, Inc., Hoboken, New Jersey.

Published simultaneously in Canada.

For general information on our other products and services or for technical support, please contact our Customer Care Department within the United States at (800) 762-2974, outside the United States at (317) 572-3993 or fax (317) 572-4002.

Wiley also publishes its books in a variety of electronic formats. Some content that appears in print may not be available in electronic formats. For more information about Wiley products, visit our web site at www.wiley.com.

Library of Congress Cataloging-in-Publication Data is Available:

ISBN 9781119982876 (Paperback)

ISBN 9781119982951 (ePub)

ISBN 9781119982968 (ePDF)

Cover Design: Wiley

Cover Images: Telephone: © Spauln/Getty Images
                Clipboard: © 4kodiak/Getty Images
                Open Can: © PhotoMelon/Getty Images
                Background: © Artulina1/Getty Images

SKY10035574_081922

TABLE OF CONTENTS

FOREWORD

When Latané told me she wanted to write this book, I was excited and impressed with her ambition. I was also a bit hesitant about pulling back the curtain and showing how we operate.

After all, the philosophy and strategies in this book explain the remarkable success we've experienced at 6sense. The modern approach to sales and marketing we've embraced as a company has led to four years and counting of more than doubling our revenue, multiple rounds of investment with top-of-class valuations, and employee and customer satisfaction scores that make it clear we're staying true to who we are, even as we grow.

So you can see why I was apprehensive about spilling these secrets to the world. But helping others achieve the kind of success we've enjoyed is part of our DNA at 6sense. Yes, this book would expose the keys to our competitive advantage. But isn't helping others gain a competitive advantage core to who we are at 6sense? It quickly became clear that I needed to put my reluctance aside and encourage Latané to share our playbook with you.

If you've ever met or worked with Latané, you can probably understand why she was the right person to write this book. At first, you can't help but be drawn in by Latané's personality. She's boisterous, energetic, and engaging. She's someone people want to be around.

But the more you get to know her, the more you begin to understand her intelligence and depth. She's both sides of the coin: organized, strategic, data-driven, with an impeccable talent for plans and processes, while also being real, approachable, personable, and just incredibly *human*.

She also has a unique perspective, having been a leader in both sales *and* marketing. She knows all the ins and outs of each, and she knows how to bridge the two—to bring them together for the collective good. So Latané was just the right person to finally share the 6sense script for modern sales and marketing, and I couldn't be more pleased with how it turned out.

I think back on my own career, and I think of how different things would have been if I'd had the modern tech described in *No Forms. No Spam. No Cold Calls.* This is the roadmap I wish I'd had—from when I first started out as an eager business development representative (BDR) to when I was running sales and marketing departments as a chief revenue officer (CRO).

When I first started out as a BDR, I was so eager to win. I had a drive and a competitor's spirit, and I knew I could succeed—but like most 22-year-olds fresh out of college, I had no idea how to do it. And unfortunately, the company I worked for didn't have much of a plan for helping BDRs do their best. They pretty much handed us our lists and told us to start calling. And we did ... some with more success than others. But I think back to how much more effective each of us could have been—and how much more value we could have delivered to the company—if we had had today's tech and a book like this one.

As an account executive (AE) at my next company, it was more or less the same, just with higher stakes. It was then that I realized that as a seller, I could have really benefited from the support of a strong marketing team. But unfortunately, marketing was a complete afterthought, and collaboration between sales and marketing was essentially nonexistent. There, too, we could have been infinitely more effective—with vastly better results for the company—if we'd had modern tech and a book like this one.

It's probably no surprise given my prior experience, but when I first stepped into the role of CRO, both sales and marketing fell under my direction. I knew what I wanted to do, and I knew the importance of playing from a single sheet of music, but the right tools didn't yet exist to do it—or at least not without tons of manual labor. This book outlines the tools and processes we've since developed that would have helped me manage a revenue team so much more efficiently.

In short, *No Forms. No Spam. No Cold Calls.* is the playbook that I would have dog-eared at every stage of my career. But sellers and marketers today need it even more than I did when I was coming up. That's because the way people buy has changed dramatically in recent years, and selling and marketing to them takes much more sophistication than was needed when I was younger.

Buyers today choose to remain anonymous well into their purchase journey, and there is no single decision-maker who can easily be wooed by old-school tactics like a couple of steak dinners. Rather, today's sellers must navigate buying committees of 10, 15, or more individuals, each with their own set of distinct buying jobs to complete.

When revenue teams—and the people, processes, data, and tools involved in them—exist in silos, it's impossible to reach these modern buyers. Instead, sellers and marketers spin their wheels and have only false leads, long sales cycles, wasted time and resources, missed opportunities, inability to collaborate, and overall burnout to show for it.

In this book, you'll discover the path out of this cycle of ineffective teams and frustrated customers. Organizations that are taking this route are the ones that are thriving in our new buying environment. They're leading in their fields and garnering massive amounts of buy-in from customers and the market.

The foundation of this new approach is unified revenue technology (RevTech) with data, machine learning, and AI-based decisioning at the core. By optimizing, enhancing, and aligning capabilities across the entire revenue team—marketing, sales, revenue operations, and customer success—RevTech makes it possible for organizations to run more efficiently and effectively.

Because RevTech enables revenue teams to reach business-to-business (B2B) buyers who are actually interested in what they're selling—right at the moment when they're ready to engage—it humanizes selling in a way that wasn't previously possible. And it also helps teams focus their time and energy in the places they're most likely to be successful. Happier customers, more successful revenue teams. *Win-win.*

When you see the results that are possible with this approach, it's no surprise that more and more individuals and organizations are joining what we call the RevTech Revolution. This industry-wide movement re-envisions what's possible for B2B revenue teams:

- *A better B2B buyer experience.* One that prioritizes what the buyer needs and wants. An approach that provides the information they want, right when they need it, in service of helping them with their buying journey.

- *A better B2B go-to-market experience.* One that unifies marketing, customer success, revenue operations, and sales with shared insights and technology. An approach that tears down silos in the pursuit of informing decisions with data and eliminating guesswork to better serve customers, buyers, and the bottom line.

This movement is bigger than one company, one team, one person. It's a massive and necessary transformation of an industry, and it's well underway. This revolution asks for big change, and change requires advocates, champions, evangelists, and maybe even a few radicals. This kind of change doesn't happen because of a few process enhancements, or even better technology. It requires a movement.

Wherever you are in your career, however you serve on the revenue team, *you* can be part of the RevTech Revolution. You can change B2B selling and marketing for the better—in ways that make your customers happier and more engaged, your revenue teams more effective and fulfilled, and your companies more successful.

This book will show you how. Not just in theory, but in practice. What I appreciate most about it is that it doesn't just tell you *why* things like data, analytics, and AI are important, or how much more you can accomplish when your team is aligned on goals and metrics. It tells you *how* to get there. It lays out game plans and strategies that you can start implementing today. It's the hands-on, practical guide that we all need to step into this revolution.

You've picked up this book, which tells me you're ready to be part of this movement. And that's great news because we need you. We need you to lean into this new, better world of selling and marketing. The revolution is happening. Not in the future, but in this very moment. So I ask you: What are you going to do with it? What is your personal revolution? How are you going to make a difference?

The time for change is now. *No Forms. No Spam. No Cold Calls.* is exactly the playbook we need in this moment to get started.

–Jason Zintak
CEO, 6sense

INTRODUCTION

The original idea for this book was an initiative I called Project Bold Moves—an experiment in which we would test out a no-forms, no-spam, no-cold calls approach to the prospect experience. Our mission was twofold: (1) to figure out how to put these ideas into practice and (2) to make sure they would really work. But I always had a third part of the mission in the back of my head: To create the book you're holding right now.

That third part of the mission was inspired by another endeavor I took on around the time we started Project Bold Moves: advising companies and chief marketing officers (CMOs) on how to thrive in this new world of selling and marketing. In my work with them, I found myself repeating the same examples, sharing the same templates, and answering the same questions over and over. *How do you roll out new messaging? What about a marketecture and category design? What key things do you measure? What's the makeup of your go-to market plan?*

I kept thinking I should write it down and have it all in one place, if only to save myself the countless hours I spent digging around and emailing long explanations to everyone asking the same questions. But I also knew that what was really needed was something more comprehensive and thorough to help navigate all the changes in technology, roles, and expectations. It was time for a definitive guide to modern account engagement. I know that I would have loved to have had such a guide when I was figuring it all out. And since I once heard that you should write the book you wish you had, I decided to get started.

My goal for this book is to try to share all the things my team and I have figured out along the way, through mistakes, struggle, insights, and breakthroughs—from templates to frameworks to what to do when things go off the rails. I don't want to get bogged down in theory, since I know when I read business books, I skim those parts. After all, I'm not looking to earn a PhD; I'm just looking to do my job better.

The book I want to read tells me what works and what doesn't, and it gives me practical information that I can implement in real life. So that's the approach I take with this book. To our lawyer's dismay, I strive to provide detail and real examples, even if it have I had to divulge a secret here or there. Again, I want concrete examples to follow when I'm reading a book like this, so I took pains to provide those wherever possible. In my dreams,

I envision you highlighting, circling, and scribbling notes in the margins, just as I do with my favorite business books.

In the end, I may not succeed in including every piece of wisdom our team gleaned from the Project Bold Moves experiment, but I do believe I got a lot of the best "gold nuggets" in here. And I try to present them in a logical, practical fashion.

In Chapter 1, I confront the reality that traditional business-to-business (B2B) sales and marketing tactics and technologies deliver market-qualified leads (MQLs), but horrendous experiences for our prospects (who are future customers!). I take you through the major "a-ha! moments" that led us to Project Bold Moves, and I describe the details of how we now put prospects and their experiences at the core of everything we do.

In Chapter 2, I call on CMOs to redefine themselves as chief *market* officers— the experts who deeply understand and advocate for their markets. I share my guidance on how CMOs can differentiate themselves by owning the company's strategic plan, deepening their knowledge of the market using customer's insights, embracing the principles of category design, and becoming unifiers who enable and embody the company's culture.

In Chapter 3, I address the bones of this new approach: the customer-first tech stack. In this chapter, we roll up our sleeves and dig into the capabilities needed to deliver the insights, collaboration, and data required to deliver a truly customer-centered buying experience. With a focus on engaging accounts over leads, I walk through my five-step approach to executing account-based marketing (ABM) at scale.

In Chapter 4, I explain how we put our plan into action. I show you the behind-the-scenes at 6sense, detailing how we create a comprehensive plan to build, understand, and align on a revenue operating model, address areas that need improvement, design the right go-to-market plan, execute account-based campaigns, and build trust through relentless transparency and communication.

In Chapter 5, I hand over the mic to Mark Ebert, our brilliant CRO, who shares what it takes to be a modern sales leader. He goes deep into setting sellers up to win, new-school territory design, getting into new verticals, hiring and retaining top sellers, and so much more. It's basically a cheat sheet that will give you a peek into how Mark leads one of the most effective, successful, and happy sales teams I've ever worked with.

In the final chapter, I break down what this transformation looks like for each role on the revenue team. I call on all the difference-makers out there to mobilize and to advocate for change. I then show you the before-and-after of what your life will look like when you embrace the *No Forms. No Spam. No Cold Calls.* vision.

In my mind, I think writing this book is a natural, maybe even effortless, culmination of our grand experiment at 6sense. I figure we execute Project Bold Moves, write about it as we go, and voilà, a book is born. We will document all our learning, share it with the world, and have lots of fun along the way. I may have even argued that it would be more interesting and "not that much more work" than writing blogs. *Go team!*

Well, as it turns out, creating this book was not as easy as my rallying speech made it out to be, and writing by committee is harder than it appears. So in the end, and much to my own surprise as a woman who majored in accounting just to avoid term papers, I ended up as the author of this book. But just because my name is on the cover doesn't mean I did it alone. One of my mentors used to always say, "Good things happen to good people." I'm lucky as hell to have those good people all around me, and this book is proof of the good things that happen because of them. They support my ambitious ideas and help me turn them into reality. So this book is really the story—and the culmination of the hard work—of the entire 6sense team. I couldn't ask for a better group of people with whom to learn, make mistakes, grow, and break through to new heights of customer-driven selling and marketing.

As you know, the work we do as sellers and marketers is hard, and it's getting harder by the day. It's on us to figure it all out, without the benefit of some universally accepted textbook telling us what to do and how to do it. And while this book isn't likely to be on a university bookstore shelf anytime soon, I am hoping that the practical, real-world guidance it offers will give you a solid head start in navigating this intense, ever-changing, and opportunity-filled landscape we're lucky enough to find ourselves in.

Dedication

To the difference-makers (you know who you are). Keep breaking glass, and keep breaking through.

CHAPTER 1

A NEW ERA OF SALES AND MARKETING

We're at a crossroads in B2B sales and marketing, staring down two possible paths. We can continue with business as usual, even as we see that traditional strategies, tactics, and technologies are producing diminishing results. Or we can break through to a new and powerful future, toward a customer-driven experience fueled by meaningful account insights, big data, and AI.

It's an exciting time to be part of this world. Buyers are more sophisticated, active, and engaged than ever. At the same time, tech advances allow us to know our consumers better than at any time in sales and marketing history.

But as exciting as it is, it can also be overwhelming for us sellers and marketers to wrap our heads around all these advancements. Those smarter, more involved customers expect more from us than we've delivered in the past, and they're in control of the customer journey more so than ever before. And the amazing new tech? Well, if we don't know what we're doing with it, it can turn into an anchor keeping us stuck in one place.

It's no wonder that some sales and marketing people decide to take the easier path. I've personally felt in over my head more times than I can count, trying to leverage new tech stacks and make inroads into an industry brimming with brilliant people. But in my years in the role of CMO—first at Appirio and now at 6sense—I've had some major *a-ha* moments that have led me to choose the harder but more rewarding path—the path toward breakthroughs.

The Virtuous Cycle

At Appirio, we faced a crossroads, not unlike the one I described earlier. We could keep on going the way we had always gone—but if we did, we wouldn't see the kind of growth we knew we were capable of. So instead, we "zoomed out" to see what was unique to us—the expertise we could offer that other companies could not.

What we realized was that we had a unique understanding of culture—of how to shape the experiences of the people we worked with, both internally and externally, and how to use that for the greater good of our business.

It was the lifeblood of our company, and we knew our clients would benefit from learning our methods and philosophy too. And so we created a framework called the *Virtuous Cycle*, which helped our clients break through in their businesses by improving their employee experience and simultaneously transforming their customer experience. I believed in it (still do) and saw the payoff of really living it.

The Age of the Customer

It might be helpful to have some background on the historical context in which we developed our customer-experience-meets-worker-experience philosophy.

Over the course of the past century, business has gone through a series of evolutions. Forrester Research neatly segments the past 100 years into a series of ages that define how businesses have functioned in each era.[1]

The 20th century started with the Age of Manufacturing. This is when manufacturing-based businesses like Ford and Boeing found their foothold and eventually dominated the business world.

Fast forward to the mid-20th century, and it was no longer what you could make, but how far you could distribute that determined your success. In the Age of Distribution, a broader reach meant broader success.

Then with the advent of the Internet, we entered the Age of Information in the 1990s—that's when Amazon and Google took off, and when the stage was set for a tech-fueled future even the Jetsons couldn't have imagined. Businesses that controlled information flow came out on top.

Since 2011, we've been in the Age of the Customer. Now it's not what you make, how you distribute, or even whether you hold the reins on information flow that determine

---

1   https://www.forrester.com/report/Winning%20In%20The%20Age%20Of%20The%20Customer/-/E-RES119546

your success. It's how well you empower and engage your customers. Customers now have greater access to information than ever before, and they have radically different expectations for their customer experience. If you want to succeed in business today, you need to live up to these high expectations and deliver a truly stellar customer experience.

It's not just Forrester that champions customer experience as the backbone of success. Just take a look at all this research on how important it is today to prioritize customer experience in everything you do:

- According to a Salesforce survey, 80 percent of customers report that they value the experience a company provides just as much as the products or services.[2]

- That same survey found that people will change their buying behaviors because of customer experience—57 percent had switched to competitors who provide a better experience.

- According to Gartner, customer experience is responsible for more than two-thirds of customer loyalty—making it more impactful than brand and price combined.[3]

- Eighty-two percent of buyers expect the same treatment in business purchases as they experience in their personal lives.[4]

- B2B companies that have transformed their customer-experience processes have higher client-satisfaction scores, 10 to 20 percent reductions in cost to serve, 10 to 15 percent revenue growth, and better employee satisfaction.[5]

- Even a modest improvement in customer experience has the potential to increase the revenue of a typical $1 billion software company *by $1 billion* over three years.[6]

Clearly, customer experience needs to be front and center for any business operating today. Steve Jobs understood the importance of customer experience decades ago—even before we entered the Age of the Customer. Way back in 1997, he argued, "You've got to start with the customer experience and work backwards to the technology. You can't start with the technology and try to figure out where you're going to try to sell it." He described developing a strategy for Apple that always started with the question, "What incredible benefits can we give to the customer?"[7]

---

2   https://www.salesforce.com/blog/2018/06/digital-customers-research

3   https://www.gartner.com/document/3899777?ref=solrAll&refval=242242534

4   https://www.salesforce.com/blog/2018/06/digital-customers-research

5   https://www.mckinsey.com/business-functions/marketing-and-sales/our-insights/improving-the-business-to-business-customer-experience

6   https://www.qualtrics.com/docs/xmi/XMI_ROIofCustomerExperience-2018.pdf

7   https://www.youtube.com/watch?v=FF-tKLISfPE&feature=youtu.be

This customer-first doctrine has worked so well for Apple that more and more companies are adopting it as their guiding principle, too.

The importance of employee experience

At the same time, there's a philosophy put forth by Richard Branson that has always guided me and reflects the core of our Virtuous Cycle. It's the idea that if you treat your employees well, they'll take good care of your clients. And *that's* the key to success for your business.

In other words, according to Branson's philosophy, the *client* doesn't come first; the *employee* comes first.

That idea may seem like it's in direct contrast with the Age of the Customer argument that the most successful companies are those that put the customer first. But cultivating a level-10 employee culture is in fact the cornerstone of a stellar customer experience.

Think about it. How positive and passionate of a message will your employees convey to your customers and future customers if they're miserable, burned out, and not bought into the vision? You simply can't inspire your employees to be enthusiastic evangelists of your brand unless you treat them right.

Success has *everything* to do with how we empower, engage, and care for *both* our employees and our customers. An optimized customer and employee experience—powered by the cloud and AI-driven technologies we now have access to—can thoroughly transform a business's success.

Then ... why do we treat prospects like dirt?

When I came on as CMO of 6sense, I brought this customer and worker experience lens with me. But to be honest, at first I was so overwhelmed and suffering from such massive imposter syndrome (was I even the right person for this job?) that I immediately defaulted to what was straightforward and comfortable—the road labeled, "How It's Always Been Done."

But it didn't take long for me to look around and realize that the philosophy I'd embraced over my years at Appirio—that happy, engaged customers and employees are key to the success of a company—could be hyper-boosted at 6sense, where we had this incredible technology that allowed us to design a revolutionary approach to customer experience with deep, meaningful insights about when to engage the right accounts for the business with the right message at the right time.

So I stepped back and looked at how we could transform our approach altogether. And what I realized was that the way we were approaching our marketing activities, which was along the lines of how other companies did it, was treating future customers (aka prospects) like dirt.

We're getting in their way

The typical B2B buying process from the customer's perspective starts with the desire to do research and learn everything you can about the options out there. But guess what? Too often, our marketing process *prevents* that research in three major ways.

First, we gate our content behind forms. What's that like for you when you're the customer? You're searching for information on the best widgets, and you find what looks  like an interesting ebook—but as soon as you click "learn more," BAM—you're blocked by a form.

So suddenly you're faced with a decision: Do you hand over your email address just to learn the basics about picking the best widget, or do you move on? Keep in mind that customers know full well that filling out that form is only going to lead to problem number two ...

We annoy the hell out of them

Here comes the spam! Prospective customers know that the second they divulge their email address, they're going to start getting carpet bombed with emails. And guess what unwelcome emails are—even ones the marketing team thinks are useful and well written ... That's right, they're *spam.*

All of us wake up to overflowing inboxes because we live in a world where nearly 300 billion emails are sent *each and every day!*[8] The last thing we want is another company  harassing us daily (or multiple times a day) all because we downloaded an ebook. In fact, the problem has gotten so bad that many of us create dedicated email accounts just for the junk we know we'll be inundated with whenever we give out our email addresses. It's crazy-making, and from a business perspective, it's pretty close to useless—what's the point of creating all those nurture sequences when they're just going to end up in an inbox someone never even checks?

---

8   https://www.campaignmonitor.com/blog/email-marketing/2019/05/
    shocking-truth-about-how-many-emails-sent/

We disrupt their lives

The third way we make it difficult for our prospects to research is maybe the most egregious ... the universally hated cold call.

Picture this: You've just gotten to the office after a frantic morning of getting the kids ready, prepping for a big presentation, and surviving the school drop-off line. You're trying to pull yourself together before you head into the meeting (first thing in the morning, naturally). You're going over your notes in your head and nailing your delivery, all while making sure you don't have any of your kids' breakfast smeared across your shirt.

You finally gather your poise and walk into the conference room to give your talk, but as you walk in your phone starts ringing. You glance. Local number ... shit. Is it the kids' school? What did they do now? Or worse ... has something bad happened?

So you hurry out of the conference room, all eyes on you, and pick up the call only to hear not your kids' principal, but an unknown and gratingly chipper voice: "Good morning! This is Sally Sales. I see you downloaded our ebook on widgets. I'd love to tell you more about what our widget solution can do for you!"

Tell me: How likely are you to take a meeting after a cold call that came at the worst time and *completely* threw you off your stride? Not only did it come at the wrong time of the day, but it also came at the wrong time in your buying journey. You're nowhere near ready to set up meetings to discuss widgets—you only started researching them yesterday!

It's no wonder buyers have shifted the way they buy. They want to be treated like humans, to make purchase decisions on their own terms, and proceed on the buying journey at the pace that makes the most sense for themselves and their business. As sellers and marketers, our job is to meet buyers where they are on their journey, educate them, and help them make an informed buying decision.

How B2B buyers buy

1. *They want to be anonymous.* Buyers these days make it further than ever into the sales journey without ever revealing themselves. In fact, some research points to the fact that B2B buyers get through 70 percent of their buying process without ever speaking to a salesperson.[9]

2. *They're fragmented.* B2B buyers are no longer individual decision-makers. They're buying teams of 10 people or more. Each member of this dispersed team may

---

9   https://www.millerheimangroup.com/resources/news/
      study-half-of-b2b-buyers-make-up-their-minds-before-talking-to-sales-reps/

NO FORMS. NO SPAM. NO COLD CALLS.

own a small part of the transaction, with no one person owning the whole process. It's decision-making by consensus, and it completely changes how sales and marketing teams need to understand and speak to their buyers.

3. *They are resistant.* And no wonder, when they've been treated so poorly for so long. They know that if they give up their email address, they're going to be opening themselves up to a lifetime of harassment. All for what? An ebook? *No thank you.*

The dreaded Dark Funnel™

These three buying characteristics drive buyers into the dreaded, evil, swirling vortex we at 6sense call the Dark Funnel™. Sellers and marketers have made it so annoying to research solutions that buyers now do most of their learning away from our websites—through independent information and review sites, competitors' sites, trade publications, networking sites, and other channels we don't control.

So we're left scratching our heads and diving deeper into our old ways to try to tap into the information that's being lost. We create *more* forms, send *more* emails, and make *more* calls. Which, of course, just pushes them further into the swirling arms of the Dark Funnel.

As you can see, this approach is absolute madness from a customer's perspective. But it's not much better for our employees who are spinning their wheels and burning the candle at both ends, trying to keep up with the increasing demands for content, new tech, and endless phone calls. They're pushing that damn boulder up the hill, day after day, just to see the faintest signs of life.

And all in pursuit of what? The most useless "success" measure out there: the marketing-qualified lead (MQL).

We'll talk more about the dreaded Dark Funnel throughout this book, and I'll even show you how to shine a light into it so you can gain some game-changing insights. But for now I want to explain why we shouldn't be driving people further into the darkness in order to chase the MQL.

Why MQLs aren't worth a dime

I came from a sales background. That's my heritage. And here's a secret: I really like going to Sales Club. I also *really* like nice shoes.

You know what doesn't get you to club and definitely does not get you a new pair of Manolos? MQLs.

So MQLs have never been a thing for me. And I realize that this will sound utterly radical to a lot of marketing folks who have spent their careers chasing the MQL, but here's my take: They're not worth a dime.

Let me tell you why.

The definition of an MQL differs from organization to organization, but the basic idea is that it's someone who has engaged with marketing's efforts in one way or another. We take that engagement as an indication that we've got a prospect who's at least somewhat likely to result in a sale. Then we run them through some kind of arbitrary lead-scoring system, where we assign points or letter grades based on actions they've taken—like downloading an ebook or giving up their info at a trade show. Once they've been attributed enough points, we consider them an MQL and toss them over to sales.

The problem is that we know people will engage in our marketing efforts for all sorts of reasons. Maybe they've filled out a form to get a free ebook that we've gated—not because they're particularly likely to buy, but because they're doing some preliminary research. Or hell, maybe they're just a competitor trying to pilfer our ideas. Or maybe they're someone who gave up a badge scan at a trade show just for a chance of winning that coveted iPad. We're applying points to these nebulous displays of interest and calling it science.

Plus, we're often capturing them either too early, when they're not realistically going to engage in the buying process—or too late, when they're already inbound leads and are meeting with all our competitors too.

The truth is that the designation of MQL tells us absolutely nothing about these people's motivations or intentions, or even where they are in the buying journey. Which leaves us with lots of guesswork and very little insight.

It's no wonder so many MQLs end up on the "stuck leads" dashboard. We expect too much of them when we know literally nothing about them except their email address and maybe their name and title.

The reality is that there's commercially available tech that can fill us in on all the blanks in our MQL process. AI-based technology can tell us when accounts are in-market—not inbound. *That's* when it's time to engage.

A shift toward a customer-led digital experience

If we want to truly engage our potential customers, we need to break free of the chains of the MQL and the forms, spam, and cold calls we rely on to generate them. Instead, we need to base our sales and marketing efforts on real data and real insights.

The first step in creating this approach—one that customers actually want to engage in—is to understand that today's buyers are not like the buyers of 20, 10, or even 5 years ago.

We need to understand how modern buyers buy

Remember, modern buyers are *anonymous*, *fragmented*, and *resistant*. These three characteristics require a vastly different approach than what we've used in the past.

We need to understand the stages of engagement—and know when to act

As I mentioned, one of the reasons that MQLs are useless is that we don't know what stage they're at when they "engage" with us. We're either capturing their information too early—they're downloading an ebook when they have no real intention of buying— or too late, when they're a hot inbound that's scheduling a demo with us and 10 other competitors.

We've all seen the five stages of the buying journey:

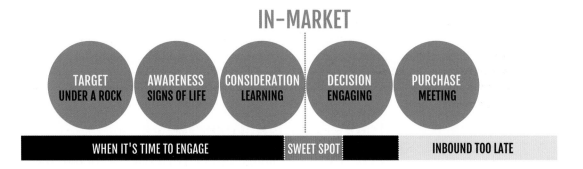

But the problem is that most marketers don't have the insight to really know what to do with these stages. Without the right technology, they have no way of knowing when a buying team is at each stage, and therefore they're not able to deliver messages that are going to connect at each given stage.

Here's how I think about the buying stages:

1. **Target.** Target accounts are essentially living under a rock. They're not actively researching products and solutions like mine, and they're showing no signs of intent.

   How to connect with accounts in the target stage: Don't. There's no reason to waste any resources on accounts that aren't even poking their heads out from under the rock.

2. **Awareness.** This is when accounts are just starting to show some signs of life. They're not researching specific brands yet, but they're searching generic keywords.

   How to connect with accounts in the awareness stage: Help them get to know you. Don't try to sell them anything. Just get into their psyche to connect their problems with the solutions you offer.

3. **Consideration.** This is where things get fun and interesting. Accounts that are considering are eager to learn.

   How to connect with consideration accounts: Make sure you're the one they're learning from. Why would you want them learning from anyone else at this point? Get your message in front of them and make it as easy as possible for them to get their burgeoning expertise from you—not your competitors.

4. **Decision.** When accounts move into the decision stage, we're at the prime time to actively engage. This is when accounts are comparing their different options and deciding which one to go with.

   How to connect with people in the decision *stage:* This is the magic window for business development reps (BDRs) to get involved, initiate call and email sequences, and try to schedule an introductory meeting. At the same time, marketing deploys campaigns and content to provide proof points, validation, and customer stories.

5. **Purchase.** In the purchase stage, prospects are ready to turn into real opportunities. They're getting into the nitty gritty of comparing solutions, scheduling meetings, and deciding which solution is the best fit for them.

   How to connect with people in the purchase *stage:* The goal here is to further deepen your level of engagement with the account and help them buy from you. While sales progresses from the first meeting to second and third, marketing provides air cover with campaigns and content that help the buyer build the business case internally that you're the best solution. This is also the time to start engaging other members of the buying team who haven't fully engaged so far.

As you can see, when you really know—from real-time data—where your customers are in the buying journey, you can find that sweet spot when they're most likely to be influenced by your messages. And that's when they're *in-market*, not *inbound*. As I said, inbound is too late. I'll dive deeper into the idea of in-market in future chapters, but for now it's just important to know that identifying in-market accounts is key to making meaningful change in your sales and marketing.

Act on real insights

Imagine that you're free from MQLs. You no longer need to waste your time relying on guesswork and delivering the wrong messages at the wrong time. So what's your new North Star?

Real insights about your accounts. Not only does this include information about their industry, number of employees, or annual revenue, but also their tech stack, who is on the buying committee, what they are researching, and (most importantly) where they are in their buying journey.

This is the kind of deep knowledge that you'll use to make your mark—with personalized content delivered over the right channel, to the right person on the buying team, and at the right time.

Suddenly, when you have these kinds of insights, your customer engagement looks entirely different. This is an example of what *truly* personalized prospective customer engagement looks like when you base your outreach on real insights—not guesswork.

A bold path forward

When you move past MQLs into an insights-driven, customer- and employee-focused approach to sales and marketing, magic starts to happen. That's what we've seen at 6sense, where we implemented this approach. We took a stance to reimagine our customer experience, stop making our employees spin their wheels, meet prospects where they are in their journey, and treat them the way they want to be treated.

For those who adopt this approach, it will lead to your next breakthrough. Without being beholden to MQLs, and with kickass technology on your side, you can fundamentally redefine the future-customer experience. Anyone who knows me knows that my approach to life is that anything worth doing is worth overdoing ... so I didn't come at this timidly. With a new initiative we termed *Project Bold Moves*, we declared that we were done with the old ways of doing things. Specifically, we took a stand against *forms*, *spam*, and *cold calls*.

It sounds crazy to ban these three pillars of sales and marketing, I know. And truth be told, not everyone rallied behind me when I proposed this overhaul. In fact, one person quit my team over it. The head of sales gave me some serious stank-eye—especially when he heard the "no cold calls" part of the game plan. In his experience, the way you create pipeline is by pounding the phones. But once he understood that I was not saying no calls—just no more wasting time on *cold* calls—he warmed up. He put his trust in me, and the rest of the team jumped on board too.

Now, the implementation of Project Bold Moves has not been perfect. We've had some hiccups and missteps, and we still have a lot of work to do. But we've learned a ton and are seeing some crazy wins that encourage us that we've chosen the right path forward.

So let me tell you more about what the "no forms, no spam, no cold calls" manifesto means to our team.

What do we mean by "no forms"?

At 6sense, we want to make it as easy as possible for our future customers to get information from us and, eventually, to buy from us. So we do whatever we can to remove friction from the buying process. But what's more friction-filled than an annoying form that pops up demanding personal info right when you're ready to learn? Forms are a total buzzkill, and they're a great way to drive potential customers away from your business—and right toward a competitor who makes it easier to access information.

At 6sense, we committed to eliminating all forms for education and product-related content. That means everything we publish is available and ungated. The only times we use forms are when we actually, honestly need a person's information to do what they want to do:

- Register for an event or webinar
- Use one of our online assessment tools
- Request a demo or ask us to contact them

Other than those times, we are 100 percent form-free. The truth is, beyond being super annoying from a customer perspective, forms are also entirely unnecessary if you're armed with good buyer intent and anonymous visitor identification tech. We're able to forgo forms because we have such great data on our side. We don't need forms in order to know what accounts are on our website. We already know. And that allows us to reimagine and redesign an amazing digital experience for customers, all without sacrificing our business goals.

So what does the customer experience look like without forms? Well, we're now completely honed in on a personalized experience on our website. When future customers visit our site, we know their account, their industry, and their business size. We know their persona. And most importantly, we know their intent keywords (i.e., what they're searching for) and where they are in their buying journey. So we can serve them up content that is most relevant to what they're researching and most effective for their stage in the buying process.

Here's an example of what one of our display ad campaigns looks like—no forms and personalized for account, persona, keyword, and timing.

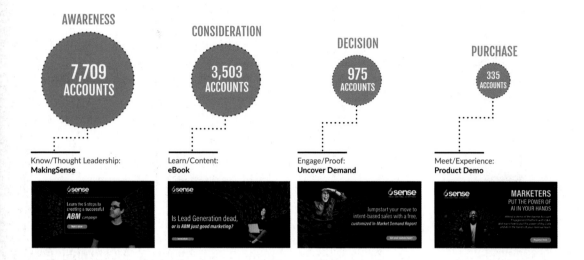

- As I said earlier, the target stage is showing no interest, so it gets zero of our dollars or effort. That's why it's not even pictured here.

- In the *awareness* stage, I just want them to be familiar with us and our thought leadership. So I connect them to a relevant episode of our video series, TalkingSense™.

- In *consideration*, I serve them up an ebook—no gate, no form—to make sure I'm the one they're learning from when they search for keywords that are important to them.

- In *decision*, I want to start to engage them and offer proof. So I offer to show them how we can uncover their Dark Funnel.

- In the *purchase* stage, it's all about getting that meeting. That's when we're encouraging them to schedule a demo.

This display approach goes hand-in-hand with our content strategy. We're creating content that people actually want and delivering it to them right when it's most useful to them. It's an intelligent, customer-driven user experience.

Content Mapped to Buying Stage and Keyword

I've explained how we use buying stage and keywords to map our display ads so we're providing the right messages to the right accounts at the right time. Well, we're able to do the same thing for visitors to our website, with our dynamic content hub. By knowing the accounts that are visiting our site—without relying on forms—we're able to tailor their experience directly to what interests them and where they are in their buying journey.

Take a look at this example. This is what the content hub looks like for someone who is interested in ABM and is in the awareness/consideration stage of the buying journey. You'll see that every piece of content they're offered is perfectly tailored to what they want in this exact moment. For another visitor—for instance, someone in a later buying stage who's interested in CDP—the content hub will look totally different.

This is what I mean when I say that eliminating forms and relying instead on deep customer insights elevates the user experience to unprecedented heights.

EXPERIENCE SPECIFICALLY DESIGNED FOR ABM & AWARENESS/CONSIDERATION

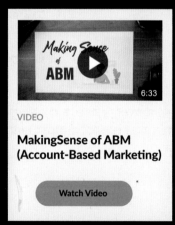

VIDEO

**MakingSense of ABM
(Account-Based Marketing)**

Watch Video

VIDEO

Aprimo: Account Based Marketing will never be the same

EBOOK

ABM is Just Good Marketing

BLOG

SailPoint Levels-Up their ABM Strategy with Intent Data

EBOOK

Compete & Win in the Age of Account Based Buying

VIDEO

Sage Intacct: How to get started in ABM

BLOG

How Today's B2B Buyers Journey Affects Your ABM Strategy

WEBINAR

Beyond ABM with Ari Capogeannis of Sage Intacct

BLOG

Ask the Expert: Meaningful ABM Awareness Metrics with Jeff Siegel

What do we mean by "no spam"?

When I said we were swearing off spam, the email-loving folks among us were mortified. But "no spam" does not mean we never send emails. It just means we don't load up people's inboxes with *yet another* email they're not going to read.

In practice, here's what that looks like. We avoid sending an email to a prospect unless we know the following:

- What they care about, based on keyword research

- Key personas in the account—in other words, who we should be trying to reach

- What stage they're at in the buying journey

Boiled down to its purest essence, our email strategy is this: If you know nothing, do nothing.

If you follow that rule—if you only send emails to people you know a lot about and who are in-market—it's nearly impossible to spam. When you deliver content you know people are interested in, right at the time when it's useful to them, that's not spam. It's just a good customer experience.

To put this into practice, we are 100 percent account-based across sales and marketing. What this means is every program follows five key steps:

We'll keep coming back to these five steps throughout the book and filling in more detail to help you understand how to implement them yourself. But for now it's just important to know that these are the backbone of meaningful and successful account engagement.

Next-level personalization

With Project Bold Moves, we've really doubled down and designed our strategy around personalizing for intent keyword and timing. The beauty of knowing intent keywords—what buying teams are searching for when they research products like ours—is that we're not guessing. We're not manually creating persona maps, which are outdated the minute the ink dries. We have a living, breathing, AI-driven dashboard telling us exactly what our accounts are searching for at any given time, and *that's* what we develop content and engagement around—and what we deliver to them. So it's more useful for our customers and less work for us. Win-win.

We use this approach across the board. For instance, our new chat bot pops up with communications tailored to persona, intent keyword, and timing. And if you happen to be a competitor visiting our site, it *just might* direct you to our careers page. So yeah, we're having fun—and connecting in a way we never have before.

As you can see, when we have real-time insights into our accounts, we're able to deliver useful content at just the right time. We're not just serving up some generic "thought leadership" pieces and crossing our fingers. We're providing exactly what our prospects need, when they need it. And that allows us to have true, trusted influence throughout the buying decision.

What do we mean by "no cold calls"?

Last but not least, the most controversial of my edicts: No cold calls. What does this look like in practice? Well, like I said, I wasn't advocating for an end to telephone usage. Calling can be really valuable—not only for pipeline building, but also for building confidence and knowledge as a seller.

So yes, salespeople *are* allowed to make phone calls under Project Bold Moves. I'm just not throwing them to the wolves. I'm not making them call people who are *cold*. I'm only giving them warm accounts to call, and I'm making sure they have all the rich information they need to be able to lead with value and have a meaningful conversation. Value is priority number one.

So under our new plan, we do not call a prospect unless we know all of the following:

- That the prospect is "in-market" for our solution
- What the prospect really cares about
- How to articulate the context of why the call is being made
- How to have a meaningful conversation and add value

One of the ways we ensure we're never calling cold is by creating something called a value card. This card is essentially a matrix, and it includes the top intent keywords and the top personas. It tells the BDR not only *what* the personas are searching for, but also why that keyword is important to them. So when the BDRs make a call, they can actually have a meaningful, helpful conversation. It's a high-value discussion, not an annoying, ill-timed cold call that pushes prospects away instead of drawing them closer.

VALUE CARDS
PREDICTIVE ANALYTICS

Predictive analytics involves any activities that leverage existing customer data to make intelligent assumptions about the activity of future customers.

HEAD OF DEMAND GENERATION

Reach the Right Buyer at the Right Time

Predictive analytics helps brands to predict buying behavior so that they can make timely, relevant offers.

MARKETING OPS LEADER

Improve Lead Scoring

Makes lead scoring an actual data-driven view of target customers.

HEAD OF MARKETING (CMO)

Focus Spending

Predictive analytics provide a more detailed view of where customers are in the buying journey and how to focus marketing spend.

REVENUE/SALES OPS LEADER

Enhance Upsell & Cross-Sell Opportunities

Predictive insights from customers who have add-on sales can be used to predict future customer growth.

HEAD OF SALES

Deal Acceleration

Advanced analytics can help identify the right leads and convert sales faster.

Dynamic territories made possible by intent data

We also implemented another key change that has made this no-cold-call philosophy not only possible, but also overwhelmingly successful. That was to shift from static, updated-once-a-year territories to dynamic territories based on customer intent.

Before implementing this change, we'd been creating territories using traditional metrics geared toward known accounts. And that was working okay, but like every business, we found ourselves pursuing some accounts that looked like the perfect fit for us on paper, but that wouldn't give us the time of day. Meanwhile our AI was uncovering accounts that were in-market— ones we knew were a great fit for us and were ready to buy—but we were leaving them on the table. Why? Because they were not on our static list of territories. So our amazing head of revenue operations, Kory Geyer, redesigned the process and implemented technology to allow us to dynamically change territories based on in-market accounts. This solution ensures our AEs have the *best* possible chance of hitting their numbers because they're always working accounts with the highest likelihood of opening an opportunity with us.

So we're evaluating and prioritizing these dynamic territories on a daily basis, and then quarterly we add and remove accounts based on intent and activity. But that doesn't mean we lose patience for the accounts that are going to take more time. In fact, one-third of our enterprise sellers' accounts are long-tail, strategic accounts that they'll continue to work on regardless of daily (or quarterly) shifts. As for the other two-thirds, we're making sure to provide *attainable* accounts—in other words, the ones that are a great fit for us and also have the highest intent scores.

For our sales team, this shift has been a boon. They're happy to have more information on timing and interest to better prioritize effort, for example, swapping out a big-name account that isn't giving them the time of day (and with our analytics, they know that the timing just isn't right) for two or three accounts that are actively engaged and interested in buying.

"The best thing is that the data we have is constantly updating, so we can constantly update our territories too," Kory explains. "Every day, we look at our accounts and prioritize them based on their intent scores. Then quarterly, we clear out the accounts that haven't shown any activity to make room for potential customers who are more engaged."

Kory Geyer
Sr. Director
Revenue Operations
6sense

And these dynamic territories have been even more successful than we hoped they'd be. In aggregate, we had 103 percent quota attainment after implementing dynamic territories—which is unheard of in an industry whose average attainment is between 75 and 85 percent for a business of our size.

Let's talk results

Well as I said, we're having fun. But we're doing a lot more than that too. Project Bold Moves is totally working. We've tracked our conversions, and we've seen a big boost in conversions and new business win rates after taking this approach. Every quarter has been a beat and a raise, and we're doing it with industry-leading customer acquisition costs.

Everyone is happy—especially our BDRs. Now that BDRs have real insights into the composition of the buying team, each person's current level of engagement, what they care about, and when to time their outreach, they're blowing their goals out of the water.

Before we started Project Bold Moves, we used TOPO's BDR benchmarks based on our industry and size and determined the amount that each BDR should reasonably be able to bring in per month. We were hovering right around that amount, but I was baffled because I felt like we should be meeting it easily. (Truth be told, I felt like we should be crushing it.) But we weren't … until we ditched the forms, spam, and cold calls.

After six months, we were easily doubling the pipeline per BDR per month. Now, a year later, the system continues to deliver. And on the employee experience side, we've had zero percent regrettable turnover among BDRs. In fact, three BDRs have been promoted.

But the best part for me is when we get emails like the one on the following page.

This is what customer-led engagement looks like—customers who are so pleased with how we've treated them that they actually take the time to call us out as examples for *how companies should market and sell*!

As we hoped and expected, our numbers have gone up. But more importantly, we have happier, more engaged customers and happier, more successful employees. And that's what these breakthroughs have been about all along.

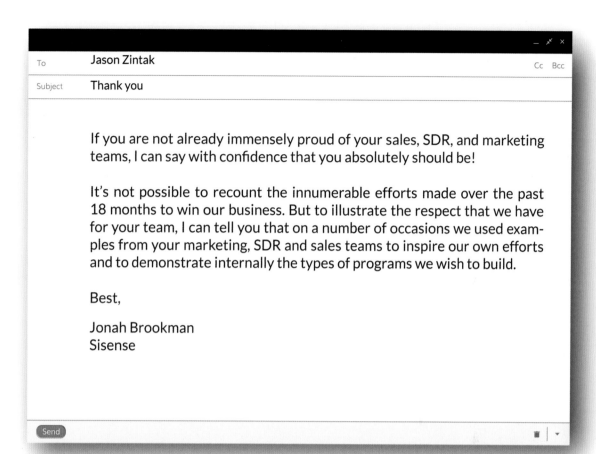

To   Jason Zintak   Cc Bcc

Subject   Thank you

If you are not already immensely proud of your sales, SDR, and marketing teams, I can say with confidence that you absolutely should be!

It's not possible to recount the innumerable efforts made over the past 18 months to win our business. But to illustrate the respect that we have for your team, I can tell you that on a number of occasions we used examples from your marketing, SDR and sales teams to inspire our own efforts and to demonstrate internally the types of programs we wish to build.

Best,

Jonah Brookman
Sisense

CHAPTER 2

IT'S TIME FOR CMOs TO PLAY OFFENSE

In Chapter 1, I laid out my case for why it's time for a wholesale re-visioning of how we approach the customer experience. This bold new approach eliminates some of the sales and marketing stalwarts—specifically forms, spam, and cold calls. But more importantly, it treats customers (and future customers) as humans instead of faceless dots in a pipeline.

Meanwhile, I've been traveling the country meeting with groups of CMOs and talking to them about this idea. As I did in the last chapter, I tell these folks about the results they can expect from implementing this customer-centric approach: bigger deals, faster cycle times, increased pipeline, and lower customer acquisition costs. And I make it clear that this isn't just some pipe dream. This is a plan that we've implemented aggressively, and we've seen how effectively it works.

The reaction is always the same: palpable enthusiasm. When people hear about this new way of approaching sales and marketing, they get *riled*. Heads are nodding. There's a chorus of *Uh-huh*s and *Hell Yeah*s whenever I talk about how broken our system is ... and lay out my plan for how to change it. When I talk about the successes I've seen at 6sense with this approach, they're champing at the bit to see it work in their own organizations.

What I'm saying is, they are ON BOARD. Like, 100 percent ready to carry the banner of this Brave New Sales and Marketing Order.

Until ...

They realize they're going to be the ones who are going to implement it. And then, without fail, those *Uh-huhs* turn to *Nuh-uhs*. The *Hell Yeahs* become *Hell Nahs*.

"My board will never go for this!"

"My CEO will think I'm nuts!"

"My head of sales *lives for* cold calls. No freaking way she's getting behind this."

I've heard every single one of those objections from CMOs around the country. To be clear, these are smart, capable, established, and, frankly, personal-hero-type CMOs, but they don't feel like they have the political capital to say to their CEOs and boards:

"Hey. I understand these *really important things* about our market. And we need to make these *really important shifts* in our approach so we can give the market what it wants. And by giving the market what it wants, we are going to see X, Y, and Z results."

And honestly, I wish I could tell them, "Don't worry about it! Just remind them that you're the expert on your market. Your CEO (and your board, and your sales team …) will trust you!" But I can't say that. Because the truth is, CEOs actually don't trust their CMOs, by and large. In fact, a global survey by Accenture revealed that two out of three CEOs don't believe their marketing leads possess the business acumen or leadership skill their role requires.[1]

The Incredible Shrinking CMO

Maybe that's why more and more prominent companies like Johnson & Johnson, Hyatt, and Uber are eliminating the role of CMO altogether. Meanwhile, other companies are layering their upper management so that the CMO now reports to another C-level, like the chief revenue officer, taking the CMO out of the board room—and out of the highest-level business decisions—altogether.

These trends are bad for CMOs, obviously. The lack of perceived value turns career success into an uphill climb for marketing leaders. In fact, of all the C-suite titles, CMOs have the shortest tenure, and it's getting shorter year over year. In 2016, the average CMO tenure was 4.1 years. In 2020, that dropped to just 3.5 years. And in the tech sector, it's even shorter, with the average CMO exiting (or being shown the exit) after just 3 years, according to an analysis by organizational consulting firm Korn Ferry.[2]

Carein Fleit, Korn Ferry's leader of Global Marketing Officers Practice, puts this trend in perspective: "Short CMO tenure is a reflection of a lack of understanding of how powerful this role can be in terms of driving business outcomes."

---

1   https://www.accenture.com/us-en/insights/consulting/cmo

2   https://www.kornferry.com/about-us/press/age-and-tenure-in-the-c-suite

I couldn't agree more. Which leads me to my next point: Suppressing the power of the CMO, burying marketing under sales, or removing the CMO from the "room where it happens" isn't only bad for CMOs themselves—it's bad for business.

The truth is that for marketing and sales to *both* succeed, each one needs to function with authority and focus. That's not possible when marketing is treated as a subsection of sales rather than as an essential and independent part of the business.

I have a unique perspective on this, having seen it from both sides. Before I was in marketing, I was in sales. And I've seen what it looks like when marketing is run as a part of sales. In short, it simply doesn't work. The demands of sales are completely, and necessarily, different from those of marketing. Sales needs to keep its eye on month-to-month or—with longer cycles—quarter-to-quarter goals. The focus is forever on the next deal, and when that one comes in, the deal after that. There's not enough room to step back and get the headspace to think long term about the overall market.

And again, that's smart for sales departments. But it doesn't work for marketing, which requires a broad and deep understanding of the market as well as long-view strategic insight and planning. So when sales and marketing find themselves in the same department, marketing often gets ignored or goes on autopilot.

Kate Bullis
Managing Partner
SEBA International

I've spoken to so many other people who have seen the same issues when sales and marketing compete for focus. 6sense CEO Jason Zintak (JZ) used to have marketing and sales bundled together—but he changed that when he realized marketing was getting the shaft.

I have another friend who is a killer sales executive and was thrilled when she gained leadership of both sales and marketing. She was so enthusiastic about the synergies she'd create by having the two departments together, under her wing. But the reality was that instead of the alignment she was expecting, she saw exactly what JZ and I have observed: That giving proper attention to the fast-moving demands of the sales department made it impossible to give marketing the support and attention it deserved.

So why are so many companies combining sales and marketing? Some would say laziness—that CEOs want to cut their number of direct reports—but I think it goes deeper than that.

Kate Bullis, managing partner at executive search firm SEBA International, explains that at the core, the CMO is responsible for three things: brand, experience, and growth. But companies that layer marketing under the blanket category of "revenue" are selling themselves—and their CMOs—short.

That long game is key, and for a lot of companies, it requires a rethinking what a CMO is.

New Rule: No More Verbing

It's easy for CMOs to find themselves immersed in activities and tasks—creating content, churning out MQLs, publishing press releases, launching products. And it makes sense, since these are all things that need to happen for marketing to be successful. But all these activities and tasks are the reason it's so hard for CMOs to prioritize their efforts in order to make their greatest impact within the organization.

A survey by the Empowered CMO Network found that CMOs believe they should be spending less time on these day-to-day activities and more time on bigger-picture endeavors.[3] By spending more time managing down into their teams (where vice presidents should be taking the lead), CMOs are failing to keep tabs on the market, and making the inroads necessary within the C-suite and board to gain their trust, respect, and understanding, it's important that they're not bogged down in marketing activities.

According to Bullis, CMOs often find themselves crushed by the weight of all this *verbing*, due to a lack of understanding about marketing at the highest levels. "Failure often boils down to the vision, the support, and the value that a CEO places on marketing and what he or she expects it to be. Is it about pretty logos and product pushing? Advertisements and billboards? Or is it about what the brand stands for, building engagement or declaring a category? How about dominating a market? CEOs need to evolve and elevate their understanding of the value of marketing and the CMO."

Maybe it's because CMOs have an *-ing* title—chief market-*ing* officer—that people expect them to *verb* all day long. But the truth is that an empowered CMO isn't wrapped up in these day-to-day marketing activities, any more than the CFO spends his or her day running payroll.

So just like we don't call the CFO the chief financ-*ing* officer, Bullis argues (and I'm with her!), we should stop calling the CMO the chief marketing officer and think of them as the chief *market* officer instead. What do I mean by that?

The chief market officer

- **Owns the seat at the table that understands the market.** The CMO is your company's expert in what your customer wants today and will want in the future.

- **Translates that understanding into alignment.** First and foremost, that means alignment between sales and marketing. Because while the two need some healthy separation, they can't be siloed—they need seamless alignment, and the CMO is the one to create it. Beyond sales and marketing alignment, the CMO is also the lynchpin when it comes to alignment between the executive team and the entire company.

- **Delivers market-leading experiences for customers.** Which is exactly what the plan I'm proposing in this book will accomplish.

Now of course, before a CMO can pull off that last bullet point, it's essential to be able to accomplish the first two. So whether you're a CMO or whether you work with CMOs, I'm going to challenge you to re-evaluate what *you* believe the role of a CMO should be. If your company's CMO doesn't have a seat at the table, and if they are not trusted to be

---

3   https://www.empoweredcmo.com/

the voice of the market within your organization, you're playing from behind when you really need to be playing offense.

Time to Play Offense

So what does it look like to play offense? It means taking ownership—and I argue that it's CMOs who need to be the ones to do it. Bullis agrees: "I want the CMOs and anybody in marketing to put a stake in the ground and say, 'This is what marketing is.' **It's *the market*. Think of yourself as an advocate for the market on behalf of your company.**"

The good news is that, while some CMOs are struggling to advance their mission in companies that don't yet understand their worth, it's not that way everywhere. In fact, many forward-thinking CEOs are embracing and empowering their CMOs to be the voice of the market. That was reflected in a survey from McKinsey & Company that found 83 percent of global CEOs believe marketing can be a major growth driver.

According to this report, the CMOs who are able to deliver on this promise have something in common: They're *Unifiers*:

> These CMOs are masters at fostering cross-functional collaboration. They ensure that marketing has a clearly defined role in the eyes of C-suite peers; they adopt the language and mindset of other C-suite executives; and they articulate how marketing can help meet the C-suite's needs. They also establish mutual accountability and a shared vision with other executives. Sought after by peers for advice, they have a seat at the table when critical decisions are made, have broad profit-and-loss (P&L) responsibility, and are often involved in defining the company's strategy. As a result, their budgets are more likely to be protected during a downturn, and they enjoy a 48 percent longer tenure. Unifiers may be born or made. Aside from inherent leadership abilities, the organizational and cultural conditions for creating Unifiers can be established by the CEO.[4]

When a company has a Unifier as a CMO, growth is inevitable. In fact, according to the McKinsey study, high-growth companies are *seven times* more likely to have a Unifier-type CMO.

The first step in becoming that empowered Unifier is taking a stand and saying, "This is what a CMO is." In other words, *define or be defined*.

---

4   https://www.mckinsey.com/business-functions/marketing-and-sales/our-insights/
    marketings-moment-is-now-the-c-suite-partnership-to-deliver-on-growth

From my experience and the challenges I've faced as a CMO, a general manager, a sales leader, and a go-to-market adviser, I've seen a few key areas where CMOs can differentiate themselves:

1. Strategy
2. Customer Insights
3. Category Design
4. Culture

If you can show up in these four areas, I believe you can make the shift from chief marketing officer to chief *market* officer. I want to share some examples and frameworks that have been helpful to me in making this shift. My hope is they'll help you too, as you master each of these four critical aspects of marketing leadership.

1. Strategic Plan

In my view, the first (and arguably most important) way a CMO can set themselves apart is to own the company's strategic plan. I'm not talking about inspirational posters on a wall. I'm talking about a living, breathing, time-bound plan of what the company must do to win.

There are many ways to approach strategic plans, and for every company you talk to, you'll get a different idea about how to best do it. I've seen companies create a high-level, multiyear visions in which each person is assigned a bunch of objectives and key results (OKRs).

And I know that can work for some companies. If it works for you, go for it! But in our industry, three years is an eon. I need to use a framework that keeps my eyes on the future that's reasonably within grasp. When I'm planning strategy, these are the questions I'm asking myself:

- What are we going to do in a year? In a quarter?
- How do those priorities transfer across the organization?
- How do we get teams inspired?
- How will we measure whether we are on track?
- How do we change the business for the better every day?

In my experience, V2MOM can be a great tool for developing a well-articulated, focused, and prioritized plan. I personally use it and love it, and I've seen it used successfully not just at the places I've worked, but at other companies I really respect as well.

I'll tell you more about this framework in just a minute, but first let me tell you why I love it so much. From what I've seen—and trust me, I'm as guilty of this as anyone!—without a solid, commonly agreed-upon plan, we work a ton but accomplish very little. We see thousands of fires everywhere, but we don't have any guideposts to figure out which ones need to be put out (and in which order).

The V2MOM gives us those guideposts, and having it in place makes it so much easier to make day-to-day decisions with big-picture strategy in mind. The fact is, in a world of finite resources, there is an opportunity cost to every *yes*, since it necessarily results in a *no* elsewhere. If you're making those choices based on anything other than your guiding strategy, you may have unintended consequences. You may have a higher-than-anticipated customer acquisition costs. Your brand may get diluted. You may see more attrition because your team is overworked and overstressed.

A solid strategic plan can prevent that. For me, the V2MOM is a great framework for creating that plan.

V2What?

Marc Benioff developed the V2MOM framework and used it to launch Salesforce. The company continues to use it for organizational alignment. V2MOM stands for

- Vision,
- Values,
- Methods,
- Obstacles,
- Metrics.

It's a framework that allows you to create a roadmap to identify, assign, measure, and track priorities for your organization and your team. Since its success at Salesforce, V2MOM has become the strategic framework for many companies, both in the Salesforce ecosystem and the tech world in general.

I've successfully used V2MOM at multiple companies to focus our energy on the initiatives we identify as the most important to our overall strategic vision. Over time, I've adapted it slightly to meet my needs and the needs of my team.

> [V2MOM] is the core way we run our business; it allows us to define our goals and organize a principled way to execute them; and it takes into consideration our constant drive to evolve. ... It is challenging for every company to find a way to maintain a cohesive direction against a backdrop that is constantly changing, but V2MOM is the glue that binds us together.
>
> ~ Marc Benioff / Behind the Cloud

Here is how I use the V2MOM: At the beginning of every year, the leadership team helps shape the V2MOM, so it isn't just me telling everyone what to do and how to do it. We create the Vision and Values together. I challenge the team to make our V2 bold and aspirational because V2MOM isn't for maintaining the status quo; it's about changing the business for the better.

We then commit to what we are actually going to *do* to achieve the vision. These are the *methods*. The methods are time-bound (typically quarterly), and they are hyper-prioritized. That means Method 1 gets more attention than Method 2, Method 2 takes priority over Method 3, and so on. The team and I rank the methods together so that we all understand the priority of each.

Then we move on to the final two letters—O and M—but I have made a slight tweak there. I'm not a big fan of focusing on obstacles, so I've replaced *obstacles* with *owner*. Each method has a clear owner driving it—not a team, not a duo, but one person. This part is critical because if multiple people own a method, no one truly owns it.

Metrics are the last part. Like *owner*, they are also associated with a method. Metrics need to be clear so on a weekly basis you can deem them red, yellow, or green. I typically like to assign three or four metrics per method. Any more than that and the method will always be stuck in the yellow zone.

A key element of the success of a V2MOM is that *everyone* knows what's happening with it. We make our V2MOM completely transparent. The entire company understands what we are working on and why, and can see how we are tracking. This makes it easy for everyone to see what makes sense for their team to work on and what doesn't, using metrics to back it up. Importantly, it is just as much about what is on the V2MOM as what is not.

what we'll achieve

THE FiVE-0 PLAN

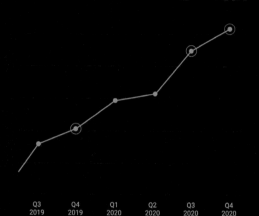

DELIVER A CUSTOMER PROVEN ACCOUNT
ENGAGEMENT PLATFORM THAT UNITES
REVENUE TEAMS

| Q3 2019 | Q4 2019 | Q1 2020 | Q2 2020 | Q3 2020 | Q4 2020 |

how we stay on track

VALUE BASED

EASE OF USE

PROCESS DRIVEN

FAMILY

FUN · ACCOUNTABILITY · MINDFULNESS · INTEGRITY · LOVE · YES, AND...

how we get there

1 SCALE OUR GROWTH CULTURE

2 DELIVER INCREDIBLE CUSTOMER EXPERIENCE

3 CREATE A MOVEMENT

4 ADOPTED & LOVED PLATFORM

5 ENABLED ECOSYSTEM

6 DEFEND & ENHANCE OUR TECHNOLOGY MOAT

7 CONQUER NEW SEGMENTS

Putting Your V2MOM to Work

The sidebar on page 38 lays out how to create a V2MOM for your organization. Once you and your executive team have agreed upon your V2MOM, you can also create separate V2MOMs for all the functional teams. Each of these plans should ladder up to the organization's global V2MOM to ensure alignment across all teams.

Now that you have your V2MOMs developed and signed off on, don't go tinkering with them. That doesn't mean you ignore them, but it *does* mean that you don't jump in and shift your priorities as soon as you hit a bump in the road. If you do, you're negating the entire purpose of the V2MOM.

You will, of course, need to review, revisit, and revise with a frequency that makes sense for your business and industry. At 6sense, we adhere to this schedule:

- Every two weeks: Provide updates on all V2MOMs—departmental and organizational—to the whole company on the all-hands call.

- Every six months: Do an overall status update on all V2MOMs. Were the goals too aggressive? Not aggressive enough? Now's the time to either remove some methods or add new ones if you're killing the ones you've already committed to.

- Every year: Create a new V2MOM for the coming year.

Some companies—like Salesforce and Appirio—take the V2MOM even further and have each employee create one to clarify their own priorities. If you've really mastered V2MOM at an organizational level and within your functional teams, you might want to give that a try as well. Be careful, though, not to let these personal V2MOMs stray from the overall team and company priorities. Again, the purpose is to create overall alignment, and that can't happen if individuals are going rogue.

How to Create a V2MOM for Your Organization

Ready to start identifying, prioritizing, executing, and measuring high-impact goals for your organization? Here's how to get started.

First, get on the same page about what a V2MOM is designed to do. It should

- Set out a clear goal and specify and prioritize what is needed to achieve that goal.

- Drive alignment across the company.

- Build momentum, passion, and the right mindset.

- Identify the capabilities needed for success.

Now, get started thinking about each element of the V2MOM.

This formula works for creating a V2MOM in various situations. In Chapter 5, we'll dial in and take a look at how to structure your V2MOM if you want to implement the big changes we're laying out in this book.

VISION

Ask yourselves:
WHAT DO YOU WANT?

YOUR VISION SHOULD

- Be aspirational
- Be time-bound
- Highlight what's new or different
- Show visible success

VALUES

Ask yourselves:
WHY IS THIS IMPORTANT?

YOUR VALUES SHOULD

- Embody your beliefs and guiding principles
- Be prioritized to highlight highest principle
- Provide a good gut check

METHODS

Ask yourselves:
HOW ARE WE GOING TO DO IT?

YOUR METHODS SHOULD

- Outline actions and inspiration
- Be prioritized to help make decisions
- Be measurable

OWNER

Ask yourselves:
WHO WILL DRIVE EACH METHOD?

YOUR OWNERS SHOULD

- Have sole responsibility for the progress of each method
- Call upon other resources as needed
- Report regularly on progress
- Be passionate about the method and what it will deliver

METRICS

Ask yourselves:
HOW WILL WE KNOW IF WE'RE SUCCESSFUL?

YOUR METRICS SHOULD

- Have a specific impact (done is not a great metric)
- Answer the right questions
- Be listed in consumable chunks
- Be easily reportable

CASE STUDY
TRANSFORMATION AND ALIGNMENT
THANKS TO V2MOM

Clearly I'm a big fan of the V2MOM framework for strategic planning. But it's not just because I've had success with it personally. I've also seen how it has helped my peers and colleagues, like Isabelle Papoulias, CMO of sales enablement platform Mediafly.

Before implementing V2MOM, Mediafly was facing the same challenges so many fast-growing companies face: Leadership wasn't on the same page, goalposts were constantly shifting, communication was tanking, and tensions were running high.

Mediafly was at a pivotal moment in terms of growth and change, and Isabelle realized that if they were going to succeed, the whole company—starting with the leadership team—would need to get hyper-focused on priorities. They'd need to ramp up their strategy, discipline, and account-ability across the company in order to work toward common goals. She recognized that to do that, they would need a clear plan that everyone agreed upon.

She found what she was looking for in the V2MOM. She started by roll-ing out a V2MOM for the marketing team, but the CEO was so impressed with the results that he decided to adopt the same framework for the whole company. So now each department has its own V2MOM, and they all ladder up to the corporate V2MOM.

The company has fully embraced V2MOM as a tool for strategic planning, and it has transformed their accountability and alignment. "It provides two forms of alignment," Isabelle explains. "There's alignment within my team, and there's alignment with the leadership team."

In two weekly meetings—one with her marketing team and one with the leadership team—the V2MOM serves as the living, breathing status document. In each meeting, everyone gives a status update for any areas of the V2MOM that they own. This keeps everyone clear on progress and keeps individuals accountable for the methods they own.

"That's the Bible," Isabelle says. "That is the document that we go through together, and it's not complicated. It's very action-oriented."

The Results

Thanks to the new culture of accountability facilitated by the V2MOM, Mediafly has become the hyper-focused, strategically prioritized organization Isabelle knew it could be. "As an organization, we have shown tremendous growth. We have seen exponential growth in pipeline and significant growth in revenue since implementing V2MOM. It's undisputable."

Introducing V2MOM had another benefit Isabelle hadn't anticipated: It cemented her role as a visionary leader within the company. She gained a lot of respect as a CMO by placing a stake in the ground and saying, "I see a problem with the organization. It's not just about marketing; it's company-wide. And I'm going above and beyond my role to deliver a strategy to fix it."

"That, in and of itself, was a pivotal moment in my career," Isabelle says.

"I wasn't looking for a 50-page PowerPoint deck of strategery," Papoulias says. "I was looking for very tangible, quantifiable goals and an action plan that would keep my team marching to the same drumbeat."

ISABELLE PAPOULIAS
CHIEF MARKETING OFFICER
MEDIAFLY

2. Customer Insights

With a strategic plan in place—and the structure with which to achieve it—it's time to get to the heart of the job of the CMO: To deepen knowledge and understanding of the market. And that requires a mastery of customer insights. This is an area that surprisingly few marketers have a true handle on. While most have a general understanding of their market, many don't have the in-depth knowledge necessary to use customer insights to propel real business growth.

And to be honest, it makes sense that it's difficult to get a deep understanding of the market, since we know that so much of the buying journey happens anonymously. Remember, B2B buyers get through 70 percent of their buying process without ever talking to a salesperson.[5] Without real insights, marketers are forced to rely on tools like persona interviews and guesswork.

Just think about the genesis of most revenue plans. They're not built around your customer's needs or an understanding of who your actual market is. In fact, most plans are developed from a spreadsheet—either to build up to a quota or to grow a certain percentage from last year. And to be clear, those are key factors to consider, but they don't tell the whole story.

Unfortunately, this approach is so ingrained in the brains of most marketers and sales teams that it can be hard to change. And the truth is you'd never want to delete spreadsheet-based drivers from your planning—they're essential to the overall picture. But the key is to revisit them from a customer-first perspective, layering market factors into the plan as well. With a better understanding of your customer and your market, you can gain control over how you meet the goals set forth in your revenue plan.

Before we get into how to do that, I want to decode two commonly used terms we'll be using:

- **Total addressable market (TAM).** This is the entire universe of opportunities available to you—every potential customer for your solution.

- **Ideal customer profile (ICP).** When you narrow down your TAM to the companies that are a perfect fit for your solution, you have your ICP. These are the prospects and customers you want to focus the majority of your top-tier sales and marketing resources on. They're the ones who are most likely to buy, most likely to be profitable, and most likely to be successful using your solution.

While most companies know who their TAM is, you'd be surprised to know how many don't know their ICP—or how much variation there is in the understanding of ICP among executives within the same company. A clear, consistent picture of your ICP is absolutely essential—and it's the CMO who needs to own the job of identifying and

---

5   https://www.millerheimangroup.com/resources/news/
     study-half-of-b2b-buyers-make-up-their-minds-before-talking-to-sales-reps/

NO FORMS. NO SPAM. NO COLD CALLS.

communicating who the ICP is. I'm so bullish on this that when a group of future marketers at Northwestern University wanted my advice on what to ask during a job interview, I told them to ask the interviewer if they know their ICP. If they don't? My advice is to *run*.

So how do you get a clear understanding of your ICP? Well, you could workshop it. But that's not the best way, because it's not based on real data—or if data are used, they're historical data. That gives you a view of the past, but it's not the best representation of future demand. Workshopping will get you a lot of opinions about who everyone *thinks* your ICP is. But you won't really know with certainty.

Instead, you need to play offense. Don't gather opinions and mash them up into some generic customer profile. Use all the tech tools at your disposal—including artificial intelligence and big data—to gather historical patterns and identify which accounts resemble accounts you've had the most success with in the past. (These insights have the added bonus of helping you uncover your Dark Funnel.)

With these types of insights, you get to see not just which customers are an ideal fit for your solution, but also which ones are in-market to further refine your ICP. That gives you what Ed Breault, CMO of Aprimo, coined the IICP—the in-market ideal customer profile, and the TAIM—total addressable in market. These two metrics represent your commercial opportunity right now. Your TAIM is your total commercial opportunity right now—every company you could try to sell to that's in the right stage of the buying journey. The IICP lets you get even more precise—it's the best, most likely to be won, commercial opportunity. Armed with this level of insight—knowing the IICP and the TAIM—your sales and marketing teams have the highest odds of winning because you know they're targeting not only the best opportunities, but they're pursuing them at exactly the right times.

For Breault, this more refined customer insight gives him a new level of influence in the boardroom. "As marketers we're always asking, and my board of

"Data wins in the boardroom," he says. "Whoever has the data can tell the best story. It's proven, it's substantiated. I'll get the nod of the board, of my boss, the CEO to go in a direction of change. So TAIM is our new boardroom strategy planning metric."

Ed Breault
CMO
Aprimo

directors and CEO are always asking, 'What's the total addressable market? What's that total possible opportunity out there?'" he says.

"And we do that analysis. But is it a commercial opportunity? Meaning, are they in-market right now?" Breault says. "The economics of winning come into play whenever you only go after what's in-market versus the total. You can't go after everything and continue to be very precise and targeted. The idea is to load up all the resources you have to go after the most winnable market opportunities."

Breault recalls walking into the boardroom with a 6sense report showing all the opportunities with the highest intent scores. Arming himself with this precise, in-market data totally transformed the dynamics of the boardroom. "Data wins in the boardroom," he says. "Whoever has the data can tell the best story. It's proven, it's substantiated. I'll get the nod of the board, of my boss, the CEO to go in a direction of change. So TAIM is our new boardroom strategy planning metric."

This data-backed approach doesn't just help to motivate change. It also counters the idea that sales and marketing teams are less valuable now that so much of the buying process happens in the Dark Funnel—because now we're able to shine a light on the Dark Funnel and see what's happening in there at every stage. "We in marketing and sales have this thing called disintermediation," Breault says. "What does that mean? You're no longer needed. But if you've got that data that I had in the boardroom—and I can see intent, low engagement—I can start to influence."

At 6sense, we are laser-focused on in-market opportunities because it prevents us from wasting resources going after anyone and everyone who looks like a potential customer. Instead we tailor our marketing to the accounts that show intent and engagement and are at the sweet spot in the buying journey. We do this by using a combination of AI-powered behavioral and fit scores to determine exactly where each account is in the buying journey, allowing us to segment accounts by buying stage. This means we can invest appropriately for each stage, rather than hitting everyone with a one-size-fits-all approach.

Developing your IICP doesn't just give you the confidence to know you aren't wasting time and money with your marketing efforts. It also makes it possible to create a great prospect experience that doesn't rely on forms, spam, and cold calls. If an account is in your IICP, it's much less likely that your communication will be perceived as spam or cold calls, because you're only communicating with customers who are eager to receive the information you're providing. It's the key to delivering the right message, to the right account, at the right time. To me, this is putting marketing back where it belongs—as close to the customer as possible.

3. Category Design

Sometimes it feels like everyone in the organization is "on the marketing team." Because we're all exposed to marketing in our everyday lives, we are biased to believe that we understand marketing—whether or not we have any marketing background or expertise. Which means that CMOs are often fielding opinions and suggestions from people who don't actually know anything about understanding and harnessing the market.

I'll be honest: For marketers, it can be super annoying to be constantly peppered with not-so-subtle suggestions about how we should do our jobs. But also? It's totally our fault. When we've failed to create structure, alignment, repetition, and great assets, what we create instead is a vacuum. And guess what happens in a vacuum? It gets filled with random stuff.

Playing offense means creating a solid strategy and doing the work to get everyone on the same page. And when you do that, you'll gain trust. You'll give off the "I've got this handled" vibe, and people will stop trying to come up with their own marketing plans for you.

I saw this when I first started as CMO of 6sense. One of my first challenges was to get everyone on the same page with the positioning of our company. We had outgrown the old way of talking about what we did, and it was time to re-establish ourselves in our space.

Start with your brand

Positioning, of course, starts with brand. While product category and point of view may change, you need consistency in what you stand for. This must be pervasive across the brand—from your look and feel to how you write and what you invest in. You need guideposts to keep you deliberate in creating and bringing your brand to life.

When I took this on at 6sense, I knew I needed company-wide input and buy-in at the front end, so I wouldn't be fielding criticisms and the virtual suggestion box on the back end. So I set out to assemble a team with representation from across the company. I wanted to make sure that, as we developed our new messaging, we were considering all aspects of our solution and soliciting different perspectives on what would resonate with prospects, customers, and employees. It was important that we had the personas in the room that were doing the jobs of the people we were trying to reach.

My pie-in-the-sky vision was that we would emerge from whatever crucible we created in that room with our category point of view and the most powerful, all-encompassing, emotionally connecting single line of copy to describe what we do.

Well, it didn't unfold quite as neatly as I envisioned, but in the end we accomplished what we set out to do. Here's how we did it:

- **We collected feedback from customers, influencers, and employees** by asking them, "What are the top three words that come to mind when you think of 6sense?"

- **We picked the right people for the workshop.** This is critical. You want collaborators—not people who just want to be the loudest voice in the room. Pick collaborators who are open to change but offer perspective and include a mix of levels and roles. Optional: Give your group a catchy name. I called mine The Tiger Team.

- **We asked everyone what their favorite brand is, and why.** This gave us insights into what sort of messaging and positioning resonates with our target audience.

- **We kept going until we got it right.** We went round and round (and round) to find the perfect words to describe 6sense. While it got frustrating or discouraging at times, the process worked. We didn't walk out of the collaboration with an actual tagline, but we had the insights we needed so our creative team could come up with "the one."

- **We listened to feedback, but I owned the final decision.** When we finally came up with the perfect words to describe 6sense—*Know everything. Do anything.*—I knew we had the one. Did anyone object? Sure. But as CMO I knew I was the voice of our market, and this was what would resonate best.

The big lesson through this process for me was that it wasn't just about creating a tagline or summing up 6sense. It was about how we "make it a thing"—which means bringing the idea to life, not just coming up with pretty words.

So we took this thing we made, and we brought it to life. At our sales kickoff, we used this new messaging as a catalyst for the changes we'd be making as a company. We had fun with it too, creating the "6sensei" character—the brilliant salesperson/marketer who knows everything and does anything. With video clips, costumes, bobbleheads, messaging, and imagery, we made it easy for our stakeholders to truly feel this new messaging.

Develop a strong category point-of-view

One of the books that has had a huge influence on how I view my role as CMO is the book *Play Bigger—How Pirates, Dreamers, and Innovators Create and Dominate Markets.* If you haven't read it, you really should. It's a brilliant framework for how to break out of the old game of winning by beating the competition and how to break into the space where real change happens: In defining, designing, and eventually dominating your own new market category.

The book talks a lot about point of view and the challenge of aligning and unifying differing points of view within an organization. It's hard work, to be sure, but in my experience it's doable. Let me tell you a bit about what has worked for me, and you can see if there are any lessons in there that may be helpful to you.

When I took over marketing at Appirio, we were a company in the midst of an identity crisis. We had gone all-in on crowdsourcing development—probably before its time. We had over-rotated on partnerships that did not pay off and gone down market with an enterprise sales model, which left us with upside-down customer acquisition costs.

Bottom line? We needed to get back on track and reclaim our space.

Around that time, I happened to read an article that changed my life.[6] It was about the five essential elements of a great sales pitch. This article gave me the framework to codify what I'd been preaching for years: Better doesn't sell; *different* sells. By really digging in and identifying these five elements, you end up not only with a totally on-brand sales narrative, but also a clearly defined company point-of-view. Based on these ideas, I created a workshop designed to lead people through creating a great sales narrative.

At a high level, this is what the framework looks like.

THE FIVE ELEMENTS OF A GREAT SALES NARRATIVE

THE BIG TREND
The undeniable shift in the world that created both (a) big stakes and (b) huge urgency for change.

NAME THE ENEMY
Name the customer's challenges in relation to moving from the old world to the new.

THE PROMISED LAND
Present a teaser vision of the happily-ever-after that will be achieved.

CAPABILITIES ARE KEY
Position capabilities in the context of transitioning from an "old world" to a "new world."

PROOF   Present evidence of our ability to deliver happily-ever-after.

Source: Medium "The Greatest Sales Deck I've Ever Seen" by Andy Raskin. https://medium.com/the-mission/the-greatest-sales-deck-ive-ever-seen-4f4ef3391ba0

---

6   https://medium.com/the-mission/the-greatest-sales-deck-ive-ever-seen-4f4ef3391ba0

I suggest workshopping this framework to come up with your company's great sales narrative—time to bring back the Tiger Team! After you've developed your killer narrative, it's time to repeat, evangelize, and enable.

Map your message

Part of being a category king is conditioning the market to think like you. That starts with your own team and permeates out. So in building a unified message that embodies your sales narrative, you need to integrate the new messaging into every single marketing asset you have—each web page, LinkedIn profile, email communication, brochure—you get the idea.

But that message needs to be consistent across the board within the organization—not just in your writing. The way we do that is by using the sales narrative we've just created to build a message map. A message map is a tool that makes it easy for everyone in the organization—from content writers, to salespeople, to the CEO—to anchor their messages around the centralized, consistent themes we've determined to be our most effective messaging strategy.

"From a brand perspective, consistency is really important," explains Michael George, our vice president of brand and digital experience at 6sense. "Not only from the visual perspective of the brand, but the words need to follow a hierarchy. So when we talk about any particular thing that we do, a feature of the software, or an advantage we have, or a benefit for our customer, we're not making up new ones every time we write. We're anchoring and rooting those in a common set of messages that we want to deliver."

The message map facilitates this consistency by tracing specific language to the story we want to tell—and it always ladders up to the main, overarching message of our brand.

Spinning off the work you did in creating your sales narrative in the previous section, here's how to create your message map:

- State the large industry shift that's going on and what your solution offers that every potential customer is trying to achieve. This is what you want your top-level message to be, from a brand messaging and positioning standpoint.

- Name the ways your customers struggle to evolve to that shift.

- List the challenges that your customers face as a result of each of those struggles.

- For each listed challenge, identify the ways your solution helps your customers meet the challenge.

- Finally, establish what sets your solution apart from others your potential customers could choose from.

Here's an example of what a completed message map looks like.

THE INDUSTRY SHIFT
Big, relevant, undeniable change in the world

EVERY COMPANY IS TRYING TO ACHIEVE THIS The undeniable shift in the world that creates both (a) big stakes and (b) huge urgency

EACH TAKES A UNIQUE PATH....

THE CURRENT STATE
What is current progress toward reaching future state?

Some companies are stuck in the past, unable to change.

Some companies have made progress.

Some companies have embraced the industry shift.

BECAUSE OF THIS SHIFT, AND INABILITY TO ADAPT, COMPANIES ARE LIKELY FACING THESE CHALLENGES...

THE CHALLENGE
Most companies experience at least one of these

Not generating enough X

Inability to prioritize budget /resources

Inability to scale/grow

Misalignment of team/goals

OUR SOLUTION SOLVES THIS BY ENABLING YOUR ORGANIZATION TO

OUR SOLUTION
Product/Solution name

MAJOR CAPABILITY	MAJOR CAPABILITY	MAJOR CAPABILITY	MAJOR CAPABILITY
Feature/ Benefit	Feature/ Benefit	Feature/ Benefit	Feature/ Benefit
Feature/ Benefit	Feature/ Benefit	Feature/ Benefit	Feature/ Benefit
Feature/ Benefit	Feature/ Benefit	Feature/ Benefit	Feature/ Benefit
Feature/ Benefit	Feature/ Benefit	Feature/ Benefit	Feature/ Benefit

WHAT SETS US APART
Our differentiators

WHAT SETS US APART FROM OTHER SOLUTIONS

DIFFERENTIATOR #1	DIFFERENTIATOR #2	DIFFERENTIATOR #3	DIFFERENTIATOR #4	DIFFERENTIATOR #5	DIFFERENTIATOR #6

The message map is a structured storytelling tool that maps specific language to your story—and it always keeps your team focused on the big picture. "What this forces us to do in our communication is to elevate that conversation," Michael explains.

This is important at every stage of the conversation, but it has an especially big impact when account executives are pitching to potential clients. With buying teams now including 8 or 12 people (or more), it's only natural that each one will enter a pitch meeting with their own functional concerns. People on the marketing team may want to ask about filling up the pipeline and meeting demand numbers. Someone on the sales team may just want to talk about cross-channel communication. The guy from the ops team may be asking about metrics. All those are important, but they're not the story we want to tell in a pitch. We want to stay focused on that top-level message—the big-picture value we deliver—and use our capabilities and features to reinforce that message.

"If we don't establish at the company level what the value is to the organization, versus any one of these individual values, we keep our discussion small," Michael explains. "Part of selling is getting people to understand there's a higher-level value at the organizational level. When we get that kind of buy-in, it's a whole different sales game."

Michael emphasizes that the message map is essential if you want to arm your sales people to have these higher-level conversations. It's not that they're resistant to elevating the conversation. It's just that without the framework to do it, they get backed into the "How does it work?" conversations. With the message map, they can take that question and pivot it to the "why" instead of getting stuck in the "how" and "what."

If it sounds like the message map is overly dogmatic or prescriptive, it's really not. "The idea is that if you're going to talk about something, anchor that back to the core theme and message," Michael says. "I wouldn't say everybody's using it 100 percent of the time, but it has helped our teams, especially new folks, attach to and understand how we get back to that. It's not about imposing discipline for discipline's sake. It all comes back to consistency. And when you think about brand and position and messaging, it's just that repetitive consistency that really makes a difference."

Develop Your Marketecture and Category Blueprint

Until this point, we've talked about owning your market, nailing your messaging, getting real with branding, building your point-of-view, and other things that marketers love to geek out about. What we haven't talked about is the product itself. But when it comes to building your company's "marketecture"—you know, the stack slide or graphic that is supposed to show what you do in some super-brilliant fashion—you can't do that without really digging into the nuts and bolts of your solution.

On the surface, that doesn't sound like a daunting task. After all, your product is your entire reason for being, right? And your job is to help your market understand how awesome it is. But the truth is, integrating with the product team to develop your super-brilliant stack slide can be a real challenge.

Let me start by saying that I love agile development. But the nature of agile development can make it hard to get product teams aligned with marketing priorities. Instead of big, bold moves like we're pushing for in marketing, agility-focused development teams release small updates all the time. Incremental improvement is essential from a product perspective, but it's tough to get customers and potential customers jazzed about little things.

What's more, product teams are organized based on skill sets. So that's how the capacity plan is organized—not necessarily by order of what is a module or what would be a release. Whereas marketing wants to see a roadmap for where the product is going, the product team organizes around feature lists.

Aligning the two teams and creating something that tells your story in the best light calls for a shift in perspective. Instead of coming up with a marketecture that represents a current snapshot in time, you need to create a vision for the future—a tool that customers, investors, future customers, and your team can look at and understand where you're headed as a company. It's not a roadmap of how we were going to get there, but a picture of the promised land.

This change in perspective was a major epiphany for us at 6sense, and it was just what we needed to start thinking big picture. Here are some of the guiding principles that helped us and that might help you too.

- **Don't get lost in the weeds.** *Play Bigger* taught me to decouple the "product roadmap" and category design from the marketecture. We're looking for something much more far-reaching than a product roadmap or marketecture; we're looking to build a category blueprint. Think about creating big buckets of capabilities that customers will need to reach the promised land. That doesn't mean you don't include details. You do. But think in terms of future functionality, partnerships, potential acquisitions, etc.

- **Don't think of the category design as a sales asset.** Err on the side of simplicity rather than trying to include every IP differentiator, what each feature means to each persona, and so forth. This is not the pitch explainer video and every use case in one.

- **Be sure to quantify.** We worked with Mediafly's Tom Pesilo to help us quantify the value of going from status quo to the promised land. This is critical to unlocking budget and answering, "Why now?"

- **Include partnerships and potential mergers and acquisitions.** Make this a vision for the category, not a description of what you do today.

- **Never waste a deadline.** This work could have gone on and on for years, but I gave us a deadline. There was a customer conference coming up, and I (wink, wink) put this in the agenda so we'd be forced to have the POV and category blueprint done before then.

Category design is a *huge* undertaking, but by developing your brand, your category point of view, and your marketecture, you can do it with vision and strategy—two things that empowered CMOs bring to the table.

ROADMAP

- Product Development Plan
- Includes new features and enhancements
- 3-6-month view

MARCHETECTURE

- Easy-to-digest visualization of your product's capabilities today
- Bubbles features up into capabilites customers need
- Nontechnical language
- 12-18-month view

CATEGORY BLUEPRINT

- Visualization of the future of the category
- Shows your capabilities **and the supporting ecosystem**
- Inspires what is possible
- 18-24-month view

SALES

Get into more deals earlier
Increase win rate

MARKETING

Increase pipeline
Optimize spend

CUSTOMER SUCCESS

Increase up/cross sell
Reduce customer churn

UNCOVER DEMAND	PRIORITIZE ACTIONS	ENGAGE BUYING TEAMS	MEASURE RESULTS
Proprietary Intent Network	Accounts In-Market	Sales Alerts	Campaign Analytics
Company Graph	Account & Contact Scoring	Display Advertising	Profile Analytics
3rd Party Profile Data	Sales Intelligence	Omni-channel Integration	Engagement Analytics
Dynamic Segmentation	Next Best Actions	Web & Content Experiences	Value and Model Metrics

EMBEDDED CDP | AI–DRIVEN ORCHESTRATION

As of Summer, 2020

PRODUCT VISION:
6SENSE ACCOUNT ENGAGEMENT PLATFORM

UNCOVER **DEMAND**	PRIORITIZE **ACTIONS**	ENGAGE **BUYING TEAMS**	MEASURE **RESULTS**
Proprietary Intent Network Company Graph Third-Party Profile Data Dynamic Segmentation	Accounts In-Market Account & Contact Scoring Sales Intelligence Next Best Actions	Sales Alerts Display Advertising Omni-Channel Integration Web & Content Experiences	Campaign Analytics Profile Analytics Engagement Analytics Value and Model Metrics

6SENSE TODAY

THREE-YEAR VISION

EMBEDDED CDP | ALL-DRIVEN ORCHESTRATION

As of Summer, 2020

4. Culture

The next, and final element that every great CMO needs to enable and embody is culture. The CMO needs to be the cheerleader not only for the brand and category, but for the company as a whole. A Unifier-type CMO *lives* for this role. We're born to rally people together around a common goal.

In Chapter 1, I talk a lot about my belief that you can't deliver a great customer experience without providing a great employee experience. And it makes sense that the CMO would be passionate about both. After all, experience, brand, and growth are the CMO's biggest responsibilities—and culture is the magic that inspires teams to create industry breakthroughs.

A great culture fosters a sense of community that binds people behind a single purpose, a mission that can create a once-in-a-career high for employees, partners, and customers. When the culture is right for an industry breakthrough, the "team" putting in the extra effort includes all three groups with little distinction between who wants who to succeed more.

You can find lots of resources that discuss the benefits of creating a great culture, but most fail to offer concrete, tangible ways to actually develop and reinforce the kind of culture I'm talking about. So I want to finish this chapter by offering examples of some of the specific things I've done or seen work well.

It all starts with leadership

A company's leadership sets the tone for the whole organization, so if you're not aligned and all on each other's side at the C level, you're not going to get very far in terms of creating a positive culture throughout the company. That's why the most important thing you can do as an executive is to embrace the idea of First Team.

This is a concept I learned from Chris Barbin, my old CEO. He told me to think of the leadership team (your peers) as your First Team—the ones you champion *first*, the ones you build up and support *first*, and the ones you align with *first*, before trying to align the organization.

When you see your fellow executives as your first teammates—not as competition for resources or as adversaries, which is too often the case among executives—you'll see the benefits flow throughout the organization. A healthy, united First Team makes it possible for the unifier-type CMO to create a culture that permeates every team and every department within the company.

Help your salespeople love their jobs

My favorite week of the year is our Field Kickoff (sometimes called sales kickoff or commercial kickoff). It's the week of the year when we get all our field-facing commercial teams together for what essentially amounts to the world's best pep rally. It's a chance to get everyone on the same page in terms of brand, messaging, and culture so we can start the year with excitement and enthusiasm.

To me, Field Kickoff is more like a big family reunion—but the best kind, not the kind with mushy potato salad and that annoying uncle who won't stop talking about his bunions. We have an absolute blast at Field Kickoff, laughing, eating great food, having fun, and presenting awards to the people who really shone in the past year.

But beyond the fun, Field Kickoff also serves an irreplaceable business function. It's our big chance each year to get sales and marketing seamlessly aligned and to remind us all that we're on the same team—including the leadership team.

When done correctly, Field Kickoff sends a strong signal to the entire company that the First Team stands behind common goals and strategies for go-to-market, messaging, metrics, and key assets. It's a solid reminder that we're all working together for the success of the whole team.

Field Kickoff sets the tone for the upcoming year—and everyone coming out of it should leave feeling totally prepared to fully execute on their goals.

Cultivate a culture of transparency

Trust is essential to a positive and productive company culture. And the foundation for that trust is honesty, openness, and transparency. Even in organizations in which leaders are transparent with each other, they're often not extending that same level of openness throughout the organization. That's a mistake.

One of the reasons I love the V2MOM is that it keeps everything transparent. It lays out a clear, timebound vision and detailed plan to bring it to life. It's critical that your plan—whether it's V2MOM or something else—is openly communicated to all levels. That means talking a lot about not only the plan itself, but also progress.

Transparent communication means no happy talk. No blowing smoke. Give people the real information—good and bad. They're grown-ups. They can handle it. Plus, they're on your team because they're awesome. They can help problem-solve. When we talk about transparency throughout the organization, this is where the rubber meets the road. It's easy to be honest with the rest of the C-suite about the state of the company. But can you extend the same level of trust to each employee throughout the organization?

Live your values

You've done the hard work of defining your V2MOM and your point-of-view. Now be sure to live it. Be the change you want to see in your organization. The movement you're creating starts with you. Be ready to learn and grow in the same way you're asking the rest of your organization to. Leading by example is the best way to get everyone excited to join you.

Go Forth and Transform

It's time for a bold new approach to how we market and sell our solutions. It's time to start treating our customers the way we want to be treated. And to do that, we need to understand our market, our companies, and ourselves in ways we never have before.

This new approach requires a new type of leader—an empowered, Unifier-type CMO. Whether you're a CMO or someone who works with one, this chapter gives you the game plan you need to make sure your marketing is transforming your company in all the right ways.

Of course, there's more to it than what we could include in a single chapter, and future chapters will build on the essential responsibilities of the CMO with dissections of things like how the CMO shows up in the boardroom and how to create, understand, and report on a revenue operating model. But this chapter should provide some good tools for creating the kind of change our industry needs today.

CHAPTER 3

BUILDING THE CUSTOMER–FIRST TECH STACK

In Chapter 2, we took a step back from the nitty-gritty of our bold new plan to talk about who is best suited to champion it. And as you read, I'm quite passionate about the fact that CMOs are the perfect people to lead the charge. It's clear to me that it's time for us—the chief market officers—to transform how we treat our prospects (aka future customers). It's time for us to pivot to playing offense and establish ourselves as the experts who will pave the road to a new, more effective approach to customer engagement. *(Imagine my impassioned fist-shake here!)*

To be clear, I know that the changes I'm describing in this book aren't small or easy. But I also know that they're 100 percent necessary if we're serious about treating customers differently and reaping the benefits that come from putting customers first.

In theory, customer-first sales and marketing isn't a difficult idea to get behind. After all, who's going to defend practices that piss off our customers and prospects, right? For me, as I've explained, the customer-first approach starts with **no forms, no spam, and no cold calls**—because we know that those practices don't just drive people crazy, but they also drive them deeper into the Dark Funnel™. And that makes it even more challenging to know when they're in-market and ready to engage.

So we know the risks of providing a bad customer experience. And I explained in Chapter 1 what a crappy customer experience looks and feels like. But when we flip the script to define how to provide an *awesome* customer experience, we get a wide range of ideas and no real consensus on how to do it. We might realize we need to use more personalization, customize content by persona, and focus on delivering value with every interaction. Or we might look to improving our websites, implementing a chatbot, and reaching customers across channels other than email.

All of those tactics can be effective. But they're all piecemeal, which can result in a lot of work (and sometimes a lot of guesswork) and not much reward. What's missing is an overarching strategy for improving customer experience based on insights and knowledge. And that's often missing because sales and marketing teams don't know where to start when it comes to understanding the key capabilities needed to truly deliver on customer-first experience.

The truth is that we *can* light up the Dark Funnel™. We *can* identify the exact moment accounts move in-market. And we *can* determine exactly what our prospects are interested in—without making them fill out annoying forms. All of that results in the engaging and positive customer experience we're trying to achieve. But the trick is you need the right technology to make it all happen—and that's where a lot of teams fall short.

In this chapter, we'll roll up our sleeves and talk about exactly what capabilities you need in your tech stack to gain the kinds of insight, collaboration, and data in order to provide a truly customer-centered buying experience.

The business case for customer-first sales and marketing

Before we get all techy, though, I want to ground us in the *why* behind all these efforts. Yes, being nice to your prospects is an admirable cause. But we're not just doing this to be nice. We're also doing it because it's good for business—and for the bottom line.

Remember how much I love Club trips? And fancy shoes? Well you've got your personal financial goals too, and regardless of what they are, they rely on the success of your organization.

So all these efforts are not for our health. They're not just for the feel-good factor (though it does feel good to provide a kickass customer experience). They're designed to achieve the goal everyone is ultimately focused on: growing revenue and doing it predictably. In other words, we're continually reimagining and improving our customer experience *because* our goal is predictable revenue growth.

But the sad fact is, while we're all after predictable revenue growth, only 18 percent of organizations met more than 100% of their revenue goals in 2019.[1] So clearly there's work to be done, and improved customer experience is key for improving those numbers.

Here's why: A buyer's experience with your brand spans from their first touchpoint to customer success and renewals. A thoughtful, comprehensive experience yields solid,

---

1   https://hub.6sense.com/welcome/state-of-predictable-revenue-growth-report

NO FORMS. NO SPAM. NO COLD CALLS.

quantifiable rewards across the journey—from accelerated decision-making in the early stages to increased customer loyalty after the ink has dried.

Accounts > Leads

A primary hurdle to overcome in providing a customer-first experience is recognizing a key way in which buying has changed. We know that there are now 10 or so people involved in every big B2B buying decision. So a key step that many companies take when seeking to identify and target the right customers—and to connect with them in the right way at the right time—is to make the switch from lead-based marketing to account-based marketing (ABM).

ABM emerged as *the* hot new trend in marketing, with the promise that it would rescue us from the unpredictability and frustrations of the lead-based world. ABM of course necessitates a shift to an account-centric approach, where knowledge and insight about an account are used to create targeted, highly personalized outreach. And the good news is that this shift puts us one step closer to a customer-first approach, because now we're talking about accounts, people, and personalization rather than leads, volume, and conversions. So all good, right?

But even after making the switch to ABM, many companies struggle to reap the rewards. We know that lead-based marketing doesn't surface the best leads, yet nearly 60 percent of account-driven organizations are still most focused on generating leads (MQLs or SQLs) despite the role an ABM strategy plays in their marketing mix, according to "The State of Predictable Revenue Growth," a report we recently conducted with Heinz Research.[2] Why? Because even with an account-based focus, 50 percent of respondents believe their lead scoring processes don't even surface the best leads accurately or consistently.

And for good reason. Simply shifting focus from lead-based to account-based isn't enough to ensure sales and marketing is working the *right* leads—those from accounts that are in-market and ready to engage. This is where intent data and predictive modeling earn their pay (two key capabilities we will talk about later). How do we know? We commissioned Forrester Research to conduct an independent Total Economic Impact™ (TEI) study to evaluate the potential financial impact of marketing with these types of insights.[3]

Forrester analyzed multiple 6sense customers both before and after using 6sense to generate and work MQLs. They found that leads from accounts identified as being in-market had a 75 percent higher MQL-to-opportunity conversion rate, a 40 percent higher close rate, and 50 percent higher contract values than MQLs identified

2   https://hub.6sense.com/welcome/state-of-predictable-revenue-growth-report

3   https://hub.6sense.com/welcome/forresters-total-economic-impact-of-6sense-report

without in-market insights. The proof of focusing on in-market accounts is undeniable, but breaking old habits is hard.

So sales and marketing leaders often fall back on their old, comfortable ways—even though those are proven not to work—and they end up with the same old results. Just take a look at content gating as an example. Ever since marketing crowned content as king, we've been trying to lure prospects out of the Dark Funnel™ by gating the content we think they need in order to make an informed decision. The thinking has been that a prospect will step out of the shadows and give up their anonymity in exchange for some exclusive, or even relevant, content. But as we know—and as I explained in detail in Chapter 1— B2B buyers aren't willing to sacrifice their anonymity to access information that is ubiquitously available online.

Why is it that even with this knowledge, gated content still persists? Sure, it makes sense that it's still front and center in lead-based marketing, but how do we explain the fact that even 53 percent of <u>account-driven</u> companies continue to gate their content?[4] I'd argue that it's because they don't have the tools needed to make an account-based approach work—so without content gating, they can't identify or learn about their accounts.

Where ABM falls short

Now I don't want to give the impression that ABM is a recipe for disappointment. It's not. In fact, it's a step in the right direction if you want to escape the lead-based marketing grind.

The problem is that while plenty of marketers see positive results from ABM, the results have been inconsistent. And that's in part because it's really difficult to scale. Ask 10 people what you need to do ABM at scale, and you'll likely get 20 different answers.

So even with ABM, digital marketing teams continue to struggle to target the best accounts and orchestrate consistent, engaging experiences across channels that meet their ideal buyers where they are on the customer journey. At the same time, sales teams lack the account data and territory alignment they need to engage the best accounts.

That disconnect shows up in various ways in organizations that are trying to implement ABM strategy:[5]

- Nine in 10 account-driven organizations say that orchestrating their ABM program across multiple channels and tools is challenging.

- Half of all marketing and sales leaders are not confident that their data enables them to either make strategic account-driven decisions or to meaningfully engage prospects at all.

---

4   https://hub.6sense.com/welcome/state-of-predictable-revenue-growth-report
5   https://hub.6sense.com/welcome/state-of-predictable-revenue-growth-report

- Most sales and marketing leaders lack a singular view of their accounts, including their in-market readiness as well as what they care about, and 50 percent of sales and marketing leaders lack confidence in the structure and alignment of their sales territories.

- Sixty-four percent of organizations implement ABM as at least half of their entire marketing mix, yet more than one in three account-driven organizations don't even know which messages will best engage target accounts, what channels to reach them through, or which accounts to prioritize in the first place.

In short, even sellers and marketers who are fully on board with the philosophy of ABM feel overwhelmed when it comes to actually implementing it. They have to wade through a vendor marketplace filled with hype and confusion. Nearly every sales and marketing tech company out there hails ABM—making massive, too-good-to-be-true promises about how it will revolutionize your sales and marketing practices (and results!). But that's where most of them stop. They don't give a clear roadmap for how to make it work for your business, what specific results you should expect, how you'll know if it's working, and what other solutions you might need to stitch together to make it all happen.

That's what we're going to do in this chapter.

My own turbulent ABM journey

I hope I've made it clear that I'm not some marketing guru who does no wrong. I've had more than my fair share of ups and downs and eff-ups in my seven years as a marketing leader. And if a year of marriage counseling taught me anything, it's that sharing experiences is way more valuable than spouting off advice. So with that in mind, I'll go ahead and tell you that my first attempt at ABM was a colossal failure. I was exactly like the marketers I described in the last paragraph—totally on board with the ABM philosophy and ready to jump in with both feet. I had read the hype, and, shame on me, I bought it all. I was convinced that if we adopted an ABM strategy, it would soon be raining pipeline, deals would be huge, win rates would be off the charts ... and we'd all be packing our bags for the Club trip. (Can you tell I really love Club?)

Instead, here's what happened. We followed the advice of aligning with sales for account selection. We looked at accounts on which we'd done well previously and collaborated with the sales team to come up with a list of 25 accounts we were sure we could win. But what we ended up with wasn't our most winnable target accounts. What we got instead was a hodgepodge of everyone's individual priorities instead of a cohesive and strategic selection of accounts.

I now fondly call this the "potluck dinner" approach to account selection.

Because here is what really happens. Marketing says they are doing ABM, and everyone wants in on the action. So everyone brings *something*. The top rep gets to bring the biggest dish—let's call it the sushi platter—since he has the best success. That random geo that complains a lot gets to bring an account, because you want to throw them a bone. So there's your cheese ball (which, of course, no one is going to eat). Each RVP gets some accounts—oh look! That's 10 desserts. What about your lookalike analyst? Sure, she yields some accounts, so let's invite her too. Oh and here she comes with her grocery store veggie platter. Yum.

You look at your banquet table and wonder ... *What kind of a meal is that?*

But you're stuck with the potluck you've got, not the potluck you want. So we took our 25 mismatched accounts and again followed the standard ABM advice: Personalize! So we set to work creating content, web experiences, direct mail—you name it, we did it. And since the accounts were all over the place, we went after each of them with a fully customized, personalized approach. What we designed for each account was gorgeous! Real award-winning work. But we were spinning our wheels, for two big reasons: First, the potluck approach had not yielded the right accounts. Second, this boutique approach to customer experience was *way* too labor intensive. So we called it off.

BREAKTHROUGH

I had some big breakthroughs from this ABM flop. First was that it's impossible to do ABM without the right technology. My team had told me at the start that we needed to up our tech game. They even did research and brought me a bunch of recommendations for what we needed. But I thought we could start without it and prove out the ABM theory first before diving into the technology piece. I was wrong. The fact is the success or failure of account-based sales and marketing hinges on selecting the best accounts. And it's impossible to do that without the right technology. My second breakthrough was this: In order to be cost-effective, ABM must be scalable and repeatable. Again, that's impossible without the right technology.

Even if most ABM pilots fare better than mine did, sooner or later, a lot of organizations come to my same conclusion. It's why people have created double funnels (as if one funnel is not enough). It feels way too hard or unattainable to do account-based everything.

Back to basics

Without clear definitions of what ABM entails, the technical capabilities it requires, and how to successfully scale an ABM program, many companies will stay on the ABM struggle bus. In order for ABM to be successful—and in order to achieve predictable revenue growth—it needs to uncover a complete picture of customer demand, provide rich account insights and meaningful metrics to sales and marketing, and have comprehensive orchestration capabilities that meaningfully engage buyers. It also requires sales and marketing to align on the full funnel rather than operating in silos.

In short, successfully implementing ABM comes back to that five-step process I introduced in Chapter 1—and each of those five steps can only work if you have the right technology. These steps are fundamental to any account-based strategy, so let's go over them again, but this time with an eye toward the tech needed to make them happen.

STEP 1 — SELECT THE BEST ACCOUNTS

We know we need to start with the best accounts. But half of all sales and marketing leaders only somewhat agree (or don't agree at all) on their target account list, and one in three account-driven organizations lack a defined strategy to select their target accounts.[6]

Maybe that's how so many of us end up with potluck-style account lists. What we need to do is select accounts based on data—not opinion and personal preference.

---

6   https://hub.6sense.com/welcome/state-of-predictable-revenue-growth-report

And we need to be looking at the right things. As we discussed in Chapter 2, that means we need to pick the accounts we can successfully sell to—the ones that are in-market and most likely to buy. Whether you call it your total addressable in-market (TAIM), target account list (TAL), or ideal in-market customer profile (IICP), you need to know your best targets.

The data we use needs to be reliable, but according to a B2B marketing survey from Forrester Research, only 12 percent of B2B marketers have confidence in their data.[7] So we need better data than what most organizations are currently working with. And specifically, we need to select accounts based on real buyer intent and activity data that's in the Dark Funnel™. We also need to model out the buyer journey that leads to a closed/won opportunity based on previous behavior, which takes data crunching power we don't have without the right technology.

STEP 2 KNOW ABOUT THEM

Once we've selected the accounts, we need deep insights into them—beyond their industry, number of employees, annual revenue, etc. It means understanding their tech stack, who is on the buying committee, what they are researching, and (most importantly) where they are in their buying journey. But collecting that kind of account data can be difficult, time consuming, and expensive without the right tech.

STEP 3 ENGAGE THE RIGHT WAY

ABM relies on understanding your buyer personas and ICP in order to create compelling, personalized content delivered over the right channel, at the right time. From display to direct mail to BDR cadences to website experience, everything needs to be personalized by account, persona, and, most importantly, timing. But only 48 percent of respondents to the State of Predictable Revenue Growth survey believe they can deliver personalized content experiences—maybe because it requires so much technology to make it happen.

The kind of engagement we're talking about requires predictive analytics to understand where accounts are in the buying journey and what they care about. Which means we need to be able to glean insights from millions of signals to understand buying patterns and predict when an account is ready to engage.

---

7   https://www.siriusdecisions.com/blog/what-can-customer-data-platforms-do

Without the right tools in your tech stack, you're going to fall back on manual coordination, detailed project plans, and dedicated teams ... and soon you'll discover that you're simply not able to implement top-level account-based engagement at scale.

STEP 4

 **COLLABORATE WITH SALES**

And no, this does not mean simply inviting them to the potluck. Collaborating with sales means sharing the same set of data, being aligned on goals and priorities, and knowing when they should engage with accounts for maximum success. If you're using spreadsheets, weekly calls, handoff processes, or outdated information, you're not going to have real collaboration. The same is true if you have multiple systems to track, report, and manage your sales and marketing efforts. I'm telling you, when sales and marketing achieve real collaboration, magic starts to happen. But to get there, you need the right technology so everyone is on the same (unbiased) page.

STEP 5

 TRACK REAL STUFF

Marketing teams typically have the MQL. (I've told you my opinion on those, but for now they persist, so we need to talk about them.) We typically separate MQLs from unqualified leads using some kind of lead-scoring system, often based on points assigned to actions a person might take, such as reading an email, downloading an ebook, or filling out an online form. Once the prospect has tallied up enough points, they are considered an MQL and thrown over the wall to sales. Not only is that a subjective measure of a person's intent, but it only accounts for one of potentially 10+ individuals participating in a complex B2B sale. Not to mention it provides zero insight at the account level with regard to intent, engagement, or where they are in their buying journey.

Instead, we need to be tracking and reporting on things that actually matter and affect deal velocity and pipeline acceleration, such as new accounts engaged, new personas engaged, opportunity rate, and account win rates. Knowing which accounts and personas are engaging can open a whole new prospecting pool that you didn't know existed.

An orchestrated path forward

These five steps toward account engagement can truly transform the way you do business—as I saw personally once I implemented an account-based strategy the right way. When you have the right tools, it's absolutely possible (and scalable) to deliver amazing prospect experiences. Predictable revenue growth is achievable when you nail account engagement. It just takes something more than ABM. It takes orchestrated account engagement.

DESTINATION:
PREDICTABLE REVENUE GROWTH

ORCHESTRATED ACCOUNT ENGAGEMENT
Sales and marketing use AI to align on the best accounts to target, and then seamlessly deliver engaging experiences throughout the customer journey.

ACCOUNT-BASED MARKETING
Marketing targets campaigns to select accounts to proactively generate leads.

LEAD-BASED MARKETING
Marketing generates and nurtures leads for sales.

"BY 2025, B2B DEMAND GENERATION EFFORTS WILL FOCUS PREDOMINANTLY ON ACCOUNTS, NOT LEADS."
—FORRESTER

Now, let's take a look at the technology that's required to make that orchestrated, scalable, and repeatable account-based approach possible so you can say goodbye to forms, spam, and cold calls for good.

Time to get Techy

The *no forms, no spam, no cold calls* philosophy is transformational, and as you will find in Chapter 4, it reliably delivers revenue results, *but* there are some very specific capabilities needed to make it happen. This is where the rubber meets the road—and it all starts with core capabilities. There are 13 essential things your tech stack must be able to do, and I'll outline them in the following sections.

But what about all the tried-and-true technology in our tech stacks, like our beloved marketing automation platforms (MAPs)? Back when we were all wearing mom jeans, flannel shirts, and Doc Martens, MAPs were the hottest marketing tech out there, but the unfortunate reality is that (like those late-90s outfits) they haven't kept up with the times.

Sure, MAPs still deliver valuable functionality, like automating our customer onboarding nurture programs and delivering our monthly newsletters, but they're simply not built for the modern customer journey. As I mentioned earlier in this chapter, 50 percent of organizations report that their MAP's lead scoring capabilities do not accurately surface the best leads, and only 40 percent of organizations report that their MAP's journey mapping capabilities are effective in helping them create engaging customer journeys.

Add to these shortcomings the fact that MAPs simply lack most of the essential capabilities modern sales and marketing teams need to identify and reach buyers today (which we cover later in this chapter), and it's plain to see that additional technologies are needed to meet and effectively engage buyers as they proceed along their journeys.

ONE MODERN PLATFORM

Lead-based orchestration, manual scoring	Account-based orchestration, AI-based scoring
Marketing to sales handoff	Blended responsibility
Email-based	Multi-channel
Generic, unpersonalized	Targeted to the right person at the right time
Linear, seller-led journey	Adaptive, customer-led journey
Built for the known	Designed to uncover the unknown

Eleven capabilities may sound like a lot to add to your plate—and it would be if you had to reinvent the wheel for each one. But the fact is every capability I recommend here is available, either a la carte or with a comprehensive platform. So take your time and evaluate different solutions for your tech stack, making sure you have all your essential capabilities covered. Getting it right with step one makes step two (and beyond) that much easier as you grow and scale your program.

1. Customer Data Platforms

Customer data platforms, or CDPs, are the modern marketer's solution to managing big data. With buyer journeys, channels, and campaigns getting increasingly complex, we're generating (and relying on) more data than ever before to do our jobs. And it's not easy to mash together data from 10 or more different platforms in order to better understand our customers, what they care about, and where they are on their buying journey. (Remember, we're putting the customer first now, so it's important that we know more about them—without making them fill out forms or open emails!)

The whole idea behind CDPs is to break down data silos, de-duplicate and normalize records, and, ideally, cleanse data along the way so we end up with a single source of rich, accurate account data that we can take action on. And CDPs are definitely built to do that. The problem is that standalone CDPs take a boatload of work to implement and integrate (think multi-quarter implementation timelines), so they generally don't make sense for all but the largest and most complex businesses.

But that doesn't mean smaller businesses don't have similar needs to aggregate and manage their own big data. Consider all the types of data businesses of any size need to be able to capture, integrate, and normalize in order to put the customer first:

- Firmographic and technographic account data from internal systems and third-party sources

- Buyer intent data from first-, second-, and third-party websites

- Known and anonymous website traffic data

- Email, call, calendar, and meeting data from customer relationship management (CRM) and marketing automation platform (MAP)

- Opportunity data from CRM

- Digital ad campaign metrics like accounts reached and results

- Psychographic data

- Market intelligence data

Depending on the nature of your business, the list could go on. The point is that all businesses generate and rely on lots of big data today, and it's essential to have a single source of truth in order to gain deep insights about accounts—whether that's via a standalone CDP or one that's embedded into a more comprehensive solution.

By combining, cleaning, and organizing this critical but disparate data, we can then extract meaningful trends and insights to guide decisions. I think of it as an Alexa for my business. For example, if we're considering hiring a new AE in Canada, it takes me just a few clicks to understand our TAM, identify trends in that market, and even zero in on the specific in-market accounts we might assign to the rep. This type of analysis would have taken a colossal amount of work in the past.

Additionally, with a single source of truth for all of my critical account data, I can slice and dice the universe of accounts into audiences with similar attributes—whether that's by industry, location, buying stage, intent, engagement, or a combination of factors—to conduct segment-specific analysis or run targeted campaigns. In the world of account-based selling and marketing, everything starts with the data.

CDPs aren't the sexiest topic, but they're truly the foundation for the other 10 core capabilities we cover in the following pages. And once we layer in intent data, company identification, AI-driven predictions, and dynamic segmentation, the Dark Funnel™ is truly lit, and the critical step of account selection becomes a breeze.

2. Intent Data

We've talked about the fact that today's customers remain anonymous until late in the buying journey. Instead of raising their hands and identifying themselves, they instead hang out in that dreaded Dark Funnel™ and conduct their own research until it's too late for us to have much influence. This is one of the biggest challenges for sellers and marketers today. Nobody (myself included) wants to fill out a form only to end up on yet another email list—or worse still, be on the receiving end of cold calls. It's just easier to remain anonymous until you're sure you want to talk to a vendor. We all do it.

Intent data offers a path forward for sellers and marketers trying to hit their numbers in this new, anonymous world because intent solutions are designed to capture buying signals from both known *and* anonymous buyers. In other words, it doesn't matter whether an account or contact showing intent already exists in your CRM or other systems. The whole idea is that we're lighting up our Dark Funnel™ and uncovering the entire universe of buyers we might want to sell to.

Intent signals can come from multiple sources, and there are several different types of intent. The largest source of first-party intent signals is typically from buyers browsing your company's website. And if you have multiple websites (for instance, a primary "front porch" website as well as a separate help center site), intent can be captured from all of them. Other first-party intent signals include data from CRM and MAP, like buyers interacting with marketing campaigns, opening emails from sales reps, and attending meetings.

Second-party intent data comes from sites you don't own, but whose content and conversations are about your company. Think review sites like TrustRadius, Capterra, and G2. Knowing that someone is researching your company, your category, or even your competitors can be an interesting signal. It may or may not indicate intent to buy, but it's a piece of data that can add to your overall understanding of a potential customer's buying journey.

Third-party intent data encompasses the research being done elsewhere on the web—not on your site or a review site. It includes specific keyword and topical research that you know to be significant signals from the prospects most likely to purchase your product. Third-party intent data are important at all stages of the customer journey, but particularly early on since they point you toward potential customers who may not have even visited your website yet. That's the stage when they're educating themselves on the problem they have and the solutions that exist—and that's when you want them to start thinking about your brand.

Intent is generally captured only on relevant websites based on a set of customer-defined keywords, categories, or topics.

It's also helpful to have what we call *pre-intent* data, which signals that a buyer may be entering the market at a predictable future point. Based on historical data, AI can make predictions about what companies will buy and when. These predictions are based on three types of data:

- Technographic data. We live in a connected world, especially when it comes to technology. By understanding a company's tech ecosystem, including their current tech stack, what integrates with what's already in that stack, and when they're up for contract renewals, we can predict not only what they'll be in market for, but also when.

- Psychographic data. Buyers have conversations across the web that can give us insights into their pain points and their plans for fixing them. By combing through vast amounts of content across the web—including annual reports, web pages, social media, and more—AI can sort through all the chatter to pick up on important psychographic data that can inform our marketing and selling.

- **Market updates.** Certain market changes can be significant revenue moments because we know that even if buyers are not in market yet, they might be as a result of a big change. These moments can include new product launches, relevant hires, funding updates, acquisitions, events, and more.

Regardless of the exact method used, it's critical that you are able to capture first-, second-, and third-party intent signals, as well as pre-intent signals—and that you get them from as many sources as possible. You never want to miss a signal, and the more data points you have, the more you can create and engage audiences with relevant experiences, as we'll discuss in the next sections.

These signals give you visibility into the accounts you should be selling to—those that are showing buying intent today or are going to be entering the market for what you offer at a predictable future time.

But just as importantly, these signals help you understand what, specifically, your customers care about. Whether you're analyzing a segment of accounts or a single account, knowing which keywords or topics they're researching gives you a significant advantage when it comes to crafting campaigns, creating content, and developing outreach strategies. And when you know exactly what an account or group of accounts care about, you can easily develop resources that help your team market and sell, like value-based messaging, topical sales cadences, and highly relevant content and ad copy.

It takes the guesswork—and personal opinions and biases—out of the equation. For instance, I think CDPs are about the least exciting thing in the world. They're the *last* thing I want to write about or create content about. But our intent data shows it's a top keyword for us, so I put personal preference aside and dove in. I know our customers and potential customers are interested in it, so we produced a ton of content to meet that need. This serves as a great reminder to me that we really have to check ourselves—and intent data makes it possible to do that.

Intent data are also a critical input to most of the other capabilities we'll talk about later in this chapter, like AI-driven predictions, personalization, and sales insights. If we don't know what buyers are doing and what they care about, we can't predict where they are on the buying journey, personalize their experiences, or give sales reps insights into their journey with our brand. Like CDPs, intent data are foundational.

The catch with intent data is that you need to be able to easily store and glean insights from it, which stems back to our last section on CDPs. And this is not a small amount of data we're talking about; intent data can constitute billions of rows of prospect activity data each month from across the B2B web, including search engines, industry trade publications, blogs, forums, and communities.

The other trick with intent data is that you need to be able to accurately match those buying signals to accounts and personas because it does you no good to know that 100 unknown companies are anonymously researching the keyword "widgets"; you need to know *which* companies are conducting that research. And this leads us to the next core capability.

3. Account Identification

With today's buyers remaining anonymous through 70 percent or more of the purchase journey, it's impossible to reorient ourselves toward customer-first experiences if we don't have visibility into who our B2B buyers are and what they care about. Capturing first- and third-party intent signals is the first step in that process, but before we can go any further we need to know who they are.

Matching anonymous intent signals to accounts is fundamental for an orchestrated account engagement strategy because the quality and success of your campaigns is directly tied to the quality and completeness of your account data.

I want to pause here for a minute to point out that this is an area where we need to be cognizant of the current regulatory environment. Between GDPR, CCPA, and other pending legislation around the world, sellers and marketers have to be more careful than ever with personally identifiable information (PII). You as the "controller" of your PII (personal data from your web pages or CRM) need to ensure you've followed the appropriate steps to share the data with your solutions providers, including obtaining "consent" where required. And similarly, you should expect that your account identification solution provider have in place the appropriate safeguards to process your PII and source third-party intent data in compliance with applicable privacy laws.

With the appropriate safeguards in place, intent providers will match an intent signal to an account. For example, we may know from intent signals that Acme Industries is conducting research on widgets, what keywords were viewed, when the research was conducted, and other relevant account-based insights. The intent signal doesn't identify anonymous visitors at the "person" level, but only surfaces account-level activity.

So now that we know what we can and can't do when it comes to identification, let's talk about how it works. The most common (and obvious) way to match intent to an account is via the IP address, but mobile advertising IDs and cookies can also be used for matching.

BREAKTHROUGH

This was another breakthrough: For every percentage point drop in your account-matching capabilities, you're sacrificing hundreds if not thousands of accounts that you could target with campaigns and outreach—accounts that are in-market for your solutions today and may be a strong ICP fit. That's just leaving money on the table.

However it's accomplished, account matching is critical because it's part of how we light the Dark Funnel™; otherwise, we're just left with a bunch of anonymous intent and still need forms for buyers to (fingers-crossed) identify themselves. But we know that in order to put customers first and help them buy from us, we have to be able to ungate our content with the confidence that we aren't losing out on critical information needed to engage accounts. We *want* those early funnel buyers to learn from us without any friction.

It almost goes without saying, but the accuracy of match rates is also critical. If an account is misidentified—say, Acme Industries is conducting the research but your tech stack thinks it's Beta Company—you'll end up wasting precious time and budget pursuing the wrong account. Plus, there's nothing worse than personalizing a message or experience based on incorrect information. Acme Industries isn't likely to convert or engage if they visit your website only to see the chatbot, content hub, or other elements personalized for their fierce competitor, Beta Co.

As you investigate adding account identification to your tech stack, be mindful of both the comprehensiveness and accuracy of account matching capabilities. Check out the tips in the sidebar on page 74 for more information.

4. AI-Driven Predictions

In the past few sections we've spent a lot of time talking about capturing and storing big data. The whole reason we need this data is to better know and understand our customers. When we have deep insights into our current and future customers, we can deliver incredible experiences that put them first, and that in turn help us improve revenue success.

Putting Account Matching Vendors to the Test

When it comes to evaluating account identification solutions, the best way to determine the accuracy and completeness of their capabilities is to put them to the test. Literally.

One of the most common ways to test vendors is to provide a list of known IP addresses and ask them to report back to you the corresponding accounts. Of course, in order to run a test like this you'll need a long list of IPs for which you already know the accounts, and the longer the list the better for evaluation purposes. Anything less than a few thousand IPs is too small of a dataset to be meaningful, so for many companies this isn't a feasible way to compare vendors.

Another way to test vendors is to place their JavaScript tags on your website for a predetermined period of time (typically around a week) and ask each vendor to report back on match rates and accounts visiting your website during that period. This approach works well if you're comparing vendors with different approaches to account matching, such as one vendor that matches only based on IP and another that uses multiple data points to match accounts.

Either way, the key is to conduct an apples-to-apples comparison that challenges vendors to deliver the best possible results from the same dataset, which will help you to determine which vendor is the best fit for your stack.

But a CDP filled with big data doesn't give us deep customer insights on its own. For that we need AI and machine learning to analyze historical and real-time behavioral data, understand which signals are relevant, and predict future outcomes.

However, a CDP *is* critical to AI and machine learning because predictive models rely on really large amounts of data—the more data, the more accurate the predictions. With account and person-level data coming from multiple systems, it's vital to continually merge, master, cleanse, and de-duplicate those records so that AI can accurately score the complete dataset, not just the most recent interaction.

So what does this look like in practice? The easiest way to think about AI and predictive capabilities is to break it down into four essential predictive models, each of which provides a different level of insight into customers. You'll remember some of these ideas from Chapter 2, but now I want to outline the tech capabilities you'll need to bring them to life.

Predictive Model #1: ICP Insights/Account Fit

The first model is all about understanding your ICP—and not just what you *think* your ICP is. AI can analyze your historical opportunity data and determine the patterns and characteristics that truly comprise your ICP (often things that don't occur to humans analyzing the data), and it continually refines this picture as your data, company, customers, and market change.

ICP models often uncover insights that can transform a company's business, like alerting you to a new vertical market that nobody had ever considered selling into. Of course, that doesn't mean that you *have to* start selling into additional industries, and you can always add filters to your account fit model in order to fine tune your ICP. (Later in the chapter, we'll talk more about this in the Data Segmentation section.)

With an accurate model of your ICP, you can then apply it to any account or segment of accounts to better understand what your next move should be. If an account is a poor ICP fit, it's probably not worth investing time and budget, whereas a strong-fit ICP account is one you likely want to consider pursuing.

Predictive Model #2: Contact Fit

The second model focuses on lead or contact fit, so this one is all about how well different personas match the typical buying teams involved in your opportunities. For example, a manager in finance might be a hugely important persona for your team to engage and influence, while a director in sales or marketing is not.

This model is incredibly important because in order to put customers first, we have to look beyond the account to the individual roles within it that are researching and engaging with our brand. Ideally, this model understands the key personas (e.g., CMO or vice president of marketing) that your sales and marketing team typically engages with and that consume your content during the sales process. As you'll see in the next model, understanding the makeup of—and engaging with—the entire buying team is critical for account-based success.

Combining this contact-level score with ICP and account buying stage predictions helps your revenue team understand not only which accounts to prioritize and when to time outreach, but also which contacts to engage so their time and budget generate the highest return on investment (ROI).

Predictive Model #3: Contact Engagement

The third model is also related to the lead or contact level, but here we're focused on how an individual contact's engagement with your sales and marketing tactics compares to that of previous buyers. This model provides buying center analytics that enable your team to understand which contacts are engaged, how and when they engaged, and where you have whitespace (no activity). And with a complete picture of the buying center, you can engage the right contacts at the right time, and also fill any gaps in your database with net new contacts.

Think of this model as a replacement to traditional point-based scoring in marketing automation. Rather than humans deciding on the importance (and corresponding score) of individual activities, AI continually analyzes patterns in the data and determines what's most relevant.

Predictive Model #4: Identifying In-Market Accounts

The fourth model is all about identifying accounts that are in-market and understanding where they are on the buying journey. Is a buyer just getting started with their journey, conducting preliminary research and identifying potential solutions to their problem, or are they researching vendors and getting ready to issue an RFP? Knowing where a buyer is on their journey enables sellers and marketers to time campaigns and outreach and ensure that they're providing relevant support and information at each stage that helps buyers move forward.

This model establishes a typical pattern of behavior specific to each of your company's products, and then looks for matches to those patterns in the behavior of accounts. And when combined with the other three models, this model enables you to understand the complete picture of the commercial opportunity available to your company *right now*. Not only do you know which accounts are the best fit for your business, but you know exactly where each one is on the journey, who's on the buying team, and how engaged they are with your brand. And this enables your sales and marketing teams to prioritize how, when, and why they work accounts.

Predictive Model #5: Account Reach

The fifth model, account reach, measures the quality, quantity, recency, and diversity of outreach activities on a given account compared to previously won opportunities. It paints a picture of whether we're reaching all the significant personas we should reach, whether we're engaging via multiple channels, and how recent the outreach is.

With the Account Reach score, you can increase your team's efficiency by flagging accounts with high intent but low levels of outreach so you know where best to spend your time and resources for the best ROI. You can also learn from previous open/won opportunities by seeing what types of outreach to which personas has historically yielded the best results. The big idea is that you want to make sure that when accounts are showing intent, you're doing the right amount of outreach to get a meeting and opportunity.

5. Data Enrichment and Acquisition

Between all the different types of data we've already covered, it's hard to believe that there could possibly be a need for even more—but for segmentation you will want to further enrich your data with *third-party data sources*. But before we get to the *why*, let's cover the *what*. In short, third-party data is generally a catchall term for several types of data relevant to every business:

- Firmographic data, like an account's industry, location, revenue, and size
- Technographic data, like platforms and other technology an account has invested in
- Contact data, like title, phone number, email, and address

While you may have SOME of this in your CRM and MAP, if you are like most sales and marketing teams, it's full of holes and ages quickly. This is why you want to refresh your data constantly with third-party data. Now, I fully understand that it sounds a little crazy to hear that you need to acquire even more data that will eventually be stale and useless. But stay with me as we move back to the *why* question.

Remember that the stack we're building includes intent data to pick up anonymous buying signals, account identification capabilities to match those signals to accounts, and AI-driven predictive capabilities to help us identify the right accounts and contacts to pursue. What happens if we uncover a major account that matches our ICP perfectly and is in market to buy, but that doesn't exist in any of our systems of record? Or what if it does exist in CRM, but we have only one contact created, and it's based on years-old engagement? Or what if we have tons of contacts on the account in CRM, but we have no idea whether that data are still accurate?

No matter which of these cases we're dealing with, we need to enrich our database with accurate information before we can unleash our sales team with outreach campaigns geared toward key personas. That's where third-party data providers come in.

It's important to understand if your platform comes with data, how much, and how many types—and whether it can dynamically enrich and acquire records in your systems (like CRM) at exactly the time your team needs it. Best-in-class account-based tech stacks use voting algorithms to determine which data to use when enriching records, and that removes the guesswork (and manual effort) from the process.

To be clear, I'm not suggesting anyone should begin purchasing lead lists or enriching every account currently in CRM. What I *am* advocating is targeting your data acquisition budget toward enriching and refreshing data on the right accounts at the right time. And with the right tools in your tech stack, this type of strategic, targeted data acquisition can happen automatically as soon as accounts hit certain thresholds of predictive scores, fit matches, or other criteria.

Now that we have all this data, predictions, and a CDP to aggregate and cleanse records, let's figure out how to make use of it.

6. Data Segmentation

With a CDP chock full of rich account, contact, intent, and predictive data, we need a way for sales reps and marketers to easily slice and dice it into meaningful audiences for analysis and activation. This is where segmentation comes into play.

Unlike some of the other capabilities covered in this chapter, data segmentation will likely be a feature within a platform or system that covers one or more other capabilities. In other words, you can usually get data segmentation capabilities from vendors that specialize in CDPs, intent data, and orchestration. However, I'm calling it out as a separate capability because it's vitally important for your sales and marketing team to be able to quickly build target audiences—and also because there are several key requirements to keep in mind as you consider segmenting the data within your CDP.

The first requirement for data segmentation is that it should be entirely self-service. Sales and marketing users must be able to create segments on their own rather than submitting requests to a data science or services team. If the process is slow and cumbersome, your team can't be agile in meeting customers where they are on their journey with timely campaigns and outreach.

Second, the segmentation process must be simple. Users should be able to create segments with just a few clicks—and without going through hours of training. Nothing kills adoption like a cumbersome, non-intuitive process, and you'll also likely see configuration errors that result in poor customer experiences if it's overly complicated.

Next, the segmentation process should be fast. Remember my Alexa metaphor from the CDP section above—and my example of quickly understanding in-market accounts in Canada before hiring a new AE? Data segmentation is how we get quick answers to these types of business questions, and it shouldn't take more than a few moments for a new segment to be available for analysis and use. If users have to come back later after configuring a new segment, you can bet adoption and usage will suffer.

Segmentation needs to be endlessly flexible too. Users should be able to build segments using any combination of filters on technographic, firmographic, intent, behavioral, and predictive account data. For example, it should be easy to create a segment for all manufacturing accounts in the central region that are a strong ICP fit, are in the consideration buying stage, are actively researching the keyword "widgets," and haven't been to the website in the past 45 days.

And last but not least, users must be able to create both static and dynamic segments. A static segment might be created based on your current customer list, a list of accounts registered for an upcoming event, or all accounts with closed-lost deals in the last quarter. No matter the source, a static segment can be useful for analyzing or targeting a fixed audience as well as creating look-alike lists.

Dynamic segments, on the other hand, use filters to continually refresh a list of accounts based on any criteria. In the previous example, two of our segment filters are based on account behavior (researching a specific keyword and not visiting our website in the past 45 days). If we use this segment to target accounts with a campaign designed to generate website visits, we'll want to remove any accounts from the campaign as soon as they *do* visit the site. With dynamic, continually updated segments, we don't have to worry about whether our segment data is up-to-date because it's updated automatically.

As we'll cover in the next sections, segmentation capabilities are indispensable for giving your sales and marketing teams access to insights about specific audiences and also for seamlessly orchestrating engagement across channels as buyers move through the purchase journey.

7. Orchestration

Moving further up in our tech stack, it's time to start putting all of our data, predictions, and segments to work, because ultimately our goal is to deliver meaningful, timely experiences to customers. And that requires the ability to seamlessly engage the right buyers from the right accounts with the right message at the right time—and do so across every channel at scale.

The problem is that this level of orchestration is impossible with traditional marketing automation and journey mapping tools. Those legacy tools were designed for linear, one-size-fits-all journeys, and they require us to guess at the timing and path buyers might take. But the reality is it's impossible to perfectly map the ideal journey for our buyers, even if we lock the whole department in a conference room for the rest of the year. With 10 or more buyers across thousands of accounts—plus hundreds of different tactics, messages, and assets to leverage—it's easy to see why the complexity is too great. There aren't enough whiteboards, sticky notes, and dry erase markers on the planet to cover all the options.

Unfortunately, ignoring the customer journey isn't an option either. We simply need to embrace the fact that buyers are in control of the purchase journey today and that each person on the buying team will take his or her own unique journey. And if we want to put customers first, we need to up our technology game to truly meet them where they are and deliver great experiences.

Orchestration really begins with the dynamic data segmentation we discussed in the last section. This is a core way our solution is architected to allow tactics and personalization to fire based on buyer behavior, which is not static—it changes all the time.

Remember, our intent and account identification capabilities are lighting the Dark Funnel™ to expose the whole universe of accounts we could potentially sell to, but we want to focus on the best accounts. AI-driven predictions help us understand where to focus our resources, and segments are how we organize those accounts into meaningful groups to analyze and engage. So let's put 'em to work engaging.

Depending on the size of your sales and marketing teams, you might have dozens or even hundreds of segments—some for ongoing use (like your dynamic ICP segment), some for use in a specific window of time (like a segment of accounts attending an upcoming conference), and some just for quick analysis (like how many manufacturing accounts in Kansas meet your ICP, and what keywords they're researching). The orchestration layer of your tech stack is what takes these segments and does something with them to engage target buyers.

Examples of actions we might orchestrate for accounts within a segment could include the following:

- Automatically serving a dynamic display campaign
- Personalizing the website with industry-specific elements
- Alerting sales reps by Slack or email when one of their accounts is showing increased engagement
- Customizing content hub experiences with company logos and industry-relevant content
- Recommending content based on buying stage or intent keyword
- Automatically acquiring missing buying center data from third-party sources
- Adding accounts to other systems like CRM, MAP, or a sales engagement platform
- Sending a gift or other direct mail to key personas

Unfortunately, orchestration is easier said than done; as I pointed out earlier, our research revealed that orchestration is a challenge for 9 in 10 organizations.[8] So it's critical that the orchestration layer in your tech stack seamlessly connects with other systems, from display advertising and web personalization to third-party data providers and sales engagement tools.

Of course, there's initial setup required as your orchestration layer comes online, but the idea is that most campaigns are "always on" and require zero day-to-day tweaks and adjustments. This frees your team to get creative and productive in other ways, whether that's running a competitive takeout or creating different multi-channel campaigns each quarter based on trending keywords.

One of the key reasons orchestration is so crucial is that it seamlessly weaves together personalized content, campaigns, and actions based on real-time data and predictions about your buyers—who they are, what they care about, and where they are on the journey. Let's take a deeper look at one of the ways orchestration can engage buyers.

8. Display Advertising

© marketoonist.com

---

8   https://hub.6sense.com/welcome/state-of-predictable-revenue-growth-report

Digital display advertising is one of the most important channels for reaching B2B buyers. Which makes sense, considering most buyers conduct anonymous research online well into the buying journey. If someone is researching my company, product, or competitors on the Internet (and if I know about it, thanks to my intent and account identification capabilities), display ads are an ideal way to introduce my brand, associate my solutions with the problem they're trying to solve, and invite them to learn from me as they proceed on their journey.

As everyone knows, it's possible to reach potential buyers with ads just about anywhere across the Internet, whether they're checking news and weather sites or posting an update to social channels like LinkedIn. Regardless of the specific site on which an ad appears, the key is to make it relevant, timely, and personalized based on all the data and capabilities we've been talking about. To that end, there are several key requirements to keep in mind as you consider account-based display advertising solutions.

First, it's important that your display advertising solution be entirely self-service. It's good to have the option of managed services, but a self-service solution enables you to save on budget, and also means the platform is simple and intuitive enough for anyone to use. There's just no reason your display capabilities should be the domain of a single person or team within the organization, or that it should take days to launch a campaign. My field marketing team launches their own display campaigns, and I've personally launched display campaigns while hanging out in the Admiral's Club before flights.

Second, it's critical to hyper-target ads to the right accounts, so your display solution needs to integrate with your orchestration layer and leverage the dynamic segments your team builds. The whole idea here is that you're fishing with a spear rather than a net. You only want to invest your time, budget, and energy in the accounts that are a good fit and in-market to buy. The old "spray and pray" approach simply doesn't deliver relevant and personalized messages that help us put the customer first—nor does it result in a strong ROI.

In addition, your team needs to be able to experiment with multiple campaigns running simultaneously with some hitting a handful of accounts while others may be targeting thousands. The point is flexibility and the ability to target ICP accounts in a customized and creative way all the time. I'm an ideas person. I want to be able to experiment and test new ideas quickly, invest more in what's working, and kill what isn't. Should we test the funny Valentine's Day campaign? Hell yeah! What about going all-in on a particular deal and providing air cover? Let's do it! My philosophy is "limits suck," and there are enough of them out there. My display capacity shouldn't be one of them. In Chapter 4, I'll walk you step-by-step through what this flexibility enables in terms of agile campaign planning and execution—but for now just know that it's transformative.

It's equally important to engage the right personas within target accounts. If the vice president of finance isn't part of the typical buying team, there's no reason to spend precious budget on ads geared toward that role. Similarly, it's crucial to speak to the unique needs and concerns of the personas that do matter, so you might have two campaigns targeting the same segment—yet delivering different creative and messaging for diﬀerent personas within those accounts.

Third, you need to be able to use this targeting across advertising channels like social. Ensuring that your brand safety standards are embedded wherever your ads are served is table stakes. Beyond that, you want to make sure that you can use your business audiences across advertising channels, whether that's targeting specific types of publications, contextually advertising, or using your audiences across social channels like Facebook and LinkedIn.

And finally, you need to be able to monitor success and continually refine campaigns, but metrics like click-through-rate just aren't as relevant in this new world. So in addition to traditional display metrics, we also need to be mindful of new metrics like view-through rate, accounts newly engaged, accounts with increased engagement, and pipeline and revenue impact of ads. Additional metrics include which personas a campaign reached, new personas reached, and personas with increased engagement.

In short, display advertising is critical to warming target in-market accounts and taking the buying team on a journey without forms, spam, and cold calls.

It's unlikely that account-based ads alone will generate instant conversions, and that's okay. Because the goal of account-based advertising is to educate and engage buyers in order to help them proceed on the buying journey and, ultimately, move into the decision and purchase stages of the journey where our sales team begins outreach. And with warmer accounts that are familiar with and learning from our brand, it's easier to ramp new AEs and set them up for success when they pick up the phone and call future customers.

9. Email

With all the advances we've seen in marketing and sales technology, one place we've been stagnant is how we deal with emails. How long have we been stuck at the "Hello [FirstName]" stage of email personalization? And how long have we been stuck in the linear path of decisioning based on rudimentary measures like whether an email was opened or a link was clicked?

Too long.

A world of possibilities is now opening up to marketers and sellers that goes far beyond standard MAP and mail merge capabilities.

That's thanks in part to the major leaps in machine learning and natural language processing that have occurred in the past couple of years—specifically with the advent of GPT-3 (short for the third version of Generative Pre-trained Transformer). With massive datasets from which to learn, GPT-3 processes input and then generates shockingly intelligent language in response.

t of email, that enables us to seriously up our game. We can now automate
e responsive and conversational. AI can manage the timing and pacing of
ds, understand responses, and then make smart decisions about how to
route, respond to, and multithread—and when to get sellers or marketers involved in
threads.

For instance, if we send an email and get a "Sorry, I'm not the right person," response,
the AI understands that, crafts an appropriate response, and then loops in the correct
person. Or if an email kicks back an out-of-office reply, the AI can pick up on the person's
return-to-office date and send a follow-up then.

Next-generation email capabilities have GPT-3 baked in. Not to replace humans,
but to lighten our lift and allow for personalization at scale. Instead of writing emails
from scratch, we can provide a prompt and let the AI do the rest. AI can also leverage
real-time data like intent, technographics, psychographics, and market insights to
inform the emails it drafts, bringing together a universe of signals to create relevant,
timely campaigns. We can, of course, approve or make changes before sending, and the
AI can learn from that too.

Of course, even with next-gen email, some old rules still apply. It'll still need to sync up
with your CDP. You'll still need to make sure you're not sending spam. But this new technology will make it possible to have much more conversational, relevant, and well-timed
interactions without much more effort.

10. Personalization

Just like display ads, personalized web and content experiences are vital for engaging
with B2B buyers. And they go together well. Imagine a perfect-ICP-fit account that
suddenly starts showing buying intent, yet our predictive models tell us that they've
just started their journey. There's no point in sales calling or emailing now because
they're still learning, so instead we target them with display and invite them to learn
from us with content tailored to their current buying stage and the keywords they've
been researching.

If our ad strategy is successful, we eventually get them to click or view-through to our
website, content hub, or landing page. But what then? If we're truly serious about putting the customer first, this is when we put our best foot forward by personalizing their
web or content experience based on all the rich data we have in our CDP.

Remember, our goal is to generate predictable revenue growth. We know that the best
way to make that happen is by putting the customer first. And that means we're going to
meet them where they are on their journey and help them learn by offering curated content and experiences with no forms in the middle. And who needs forms anyway when
we have first-party intent signals? When they come a-knocking at our door, this is our
time to shine and begin building a relationship.

Now, there are a lot of ways we can approach this experience, from customizing imagery based on industry to recommending content based on the buying stage to throwing the account's logo on top of the page with a welcome message. There's a delicate balance—you want to add value to every interaction, but you don't want to seem creepy. On that front, it's best to start with more generalized levels of personalization (like industry, company size, buying stage, and location) and experiment as you work your way up.

Personalization doesn't have to (and shouldn't) stop at web and content experiences. Targeted, personalized experiences should be the bread and butter of every organization focused on a customer-first approach—and should extend to every channel: email, direct mail, advertising, web, content, sales engagement, chat, and so on. Depending on how you choose to build and grow your tech stack, some of these capabilities may come later, so be sure to think about how data will move between systems (hint: open APIs are essential) to enable personalization and targeting at scale.

Remember, personalization isn't a parlor trick—it's about being helpful.

Here are some of the ways my team uses personalization to deliver great customer experiences:

- **Chat:** Our chatbot knows who's visiting the website, so it initiates conversations and recommends content based on an account's buying stage and interests. And if they're ready to talk, we immediately connect them with someone who knows about them and can help—the account owner.

- **Content hub:** Every marketing team is a content engine, but unless you're Netflix, nobody is binging on your content. The best way to make use of your content is by curating personalized experiences for buyers based on data. And when it comes to great content experiences, less is more. Think a curated tasting menu rather than the Cheesecake Factory mega menu. By serving up content personalized for our visitors, our content hub has three times better time-on-page than industry average.

- **High-value offers:** Free trials, discounts, and other special offers can help boost engagement with late-stage buyers, but offering those kinds of deals to every web visitor can bring all the window shoppers to your door—and bog your team down. However, with web personalization linked to our dynamic segments, we ensure that high-value offers are extended only to accounts for which we want to offer high-touch experiences.

When your tech stack has the capability to facilitate personalized web and content experiences, you bring customer experience to a whole new level. It's no longer just about having a few versions of your website or content for different verticals. Now you're recognizing accounts and providing the exact digital experience that's most useful for them, based on all that rich data like intent, buying stage, and more.

11. Sales Insights

As I said at the beginning of this chapter, revenue is the goal we're all after, and every company is on a journey to grow revenue in a more predictable and repeatable way. I also outlined the five steps of an account-based strategy, and this capability is all about step four: collaborate with sales.

In short, the goal of sales insights is to enable sales reps to prioritize the leads, accounts, and contacts they spend their time on, and also to ensure that their outreach is timely and relevant to customers. And to do this, we need to give sales reps direct access to the data and predictions delivered by the other key capabilities in our customer-first tech stack. But of course this doesn't mean inundating reps with all the data in our CDP; the insights delivered to reps must be relevant, intuitive, easy to access, and inspire action.

The challenge with sales insights is that it's difficult (if not impossible) to get sales reps to use yet another platform or tool, no matter how great it is. It can be hard enough to get reps to fill out all the fields on an opportunity record. So asking reps to log into the account engagement platform the marketing team uses is almost certain to be met with resistance.

The best way to deliver sales insights to reps is to do so where they spend the bulk of their time: within your CRM or sales engagement platform. This way, anytime a rep looks at one of their accounts, they can quickly see critical information like the current predicted buying stage, the keywords the account has been researching, the level of account engagement over time, and the complete buying center, including which contacts have been engaged and which have not.

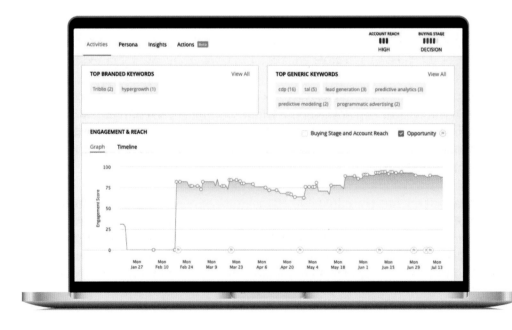

These data points can also be stored in custom fields on account and contact records to enable your operations team to build dashboards and reports that help reps understand where they should spend their time on a day-to-day basis. Every single sales rep at 6sense—from BDRs to our most senior enterprise account executives—starts their day with a prospecting dashboard that shows which of their accounts are in the decision or purchase buying stage and how many days they've been there. These dashboards also enable sales managers to identify unassigned accounts showing buying intent so we don't miss potential opportunities as a result of account assignment.

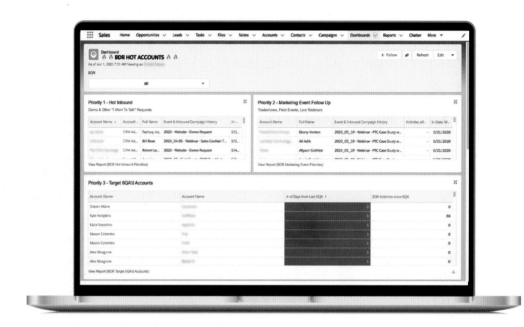

Knowing which accounts to prioritize and having insights about them is super important, but our sales team takes it a step further by using AI to recommend the next best action a rep should take to increase engagement with an account. For example, the AI recommends specific contacts for a rep to add to the sales engagement platform and begin outreach, and even offers suggested talking points based on the contact's interests and behavior. It also recommends new contacts to add to CRM to flesh out the buying center, enabling reps to acquire relevant data with a few clicks. In other words, this helps reps both know and do everything they should in order to deepen relationships with the accounts they're working.

When sales reps and managers have instant, easy access to these kinds of insights—and when marketing is looking at exactly the same data and insights—alignment between sales and marketing comes naturally. Everyone understands which accounts and contacts are most valuable and why, how, and when they've engaged with the brand, and where they are on the buying journey. With this level of alignment, it's finally possible to put customers first and orchestrate engagement with the best accounts for the business.

12. Analytics

The 12th and final key capability in our customer-first tech stack is all about measuring success. Again, we're moving to a customer-first approach because it's the best way to generate predictable revenue growth, but we can't assume that reorienting ourselves toward customers is going to result in immediate success. We need to continually measure, test, optimize, and improve.

Account-centric measurement capabilities in your tech stack will make it that much easier to start baselining and improving results, which you will learn I'm really big on in the next chapter!

As I mentioned in the display advertising section earlier, there's a built-in disconnect between some of the traditional metrics sales reps and marketers are used to (like cost-per-click and click-through rate) and the reality of how we need to connect with customers and sell today. It's not that these legacy metrics are totally irrelevant; it's just that they don't paint a full picture of how accounts are engaging with our brand. And this is because we've switched from fishing with a net to fishing with a spear, so our ad spend is now highly targeted to the accounts and personas we care about.

NO FORMS. NO SPAM. NO COLD CALLS.

Additionally the account engagement tech stack I described over the past sections is all about using big data and AI to uncover the best accounts and engage with them, so other legacy metrics like MQLs, SQLs, and SALs are suddenly no longer relevant. And believe me, I understand the heart palpitations that may cause. As I said in Chapter 2, I've had this conversation with hundreds of CMOs over the past 18 months, and many get nervous when I tell them they should ditch the metrics they've grown up with.

But think about it. If we know what accounts and contacts are doing as a result of our intent and identification capabilities, and if we can predict what those signals mean to our business using AI-based models, and if we can understand who they are and what they care about due to our limitless segmentation capabilities ... well then, we simply don't need to arbitrarily score leads anymore based on clicks, form fills, page views, and downloads.

Here are a few ideas to help you start thinking about the new kinds of metrics and analytics that will change the way you think about sales and marketing alignment—and how you measure success.

Legacy Metrics	Account Engagement Metrics
CTR (Click Through Rate)	VTR (View Through Rate)
CPC (Cost Per Click)	CPR (Cost Per Result)
Number of Impressions	Number of Accounts Reached
Number of Clicks	Number of Accounts Engaged
Number of Leads	Number of ICP Accounts
MQLs	Number of Accounts In-Market
Pipeline Attribution	Conversion of Accounts In-Market to Pipeline and Revenue
Conversion Rate	Account Engagement Score
Page Views	Relevant Content Consumed
Contacts Reached	Buying Team Engagement
Number of Leads Processed	Account Velocity Through Buying Stages

One of the leaders on my marketing team often talks about how he was one of the first users of Pardot (waaaay pre-Salesforce acquisition) and was a big fan. But he remembers the first time he set up a lead scoring model, and it was as finger-in-the-wind as you could imagine. *Hitting our pricing page is worth a solid 5 points. And surely downloading our ebook is worth 10 points. And SURELY if you have a score of 50 points you're an A+ lead.*

He was guessing. But we're now in the world of knowing. And when we know everything, we can do anything to meet our buyers where they are, deliver amazingly engaging experiences, and help our companies deliver predictable revenue growth. But we need the right account-centric analytics to help point us in the right direction.

We'll get even deeper into analytics in Chapter 4 when exploring revenue operating models, which ultimately are all about measuring and improving success—from tracking and improving average deal size to boosting win rates, amping deal velocity, and generating more renewals and upsells.

13. Pipeline Intelligence

Pipeline is the lifeblood of any revenue organization. Simply put, if you want to future-proof your revenue, you need to get right with your pipeline. In a recent survey, 88 percent of CMOs said pipeline or closed-won business were their most important metrics. Sadly, only 25 percent of those CMOs said they hit their pipeline targets most or all of the time.

That disconnect has a serious impact not only on business performance, but also on our credibility and alignment with our sales counterparts.

After all, sales leaders have long had the tools to accurately manage and predict revenue. They've had the formal processes and tech that allows them to manage opportunities throughout their entire funnel and forecast with a high degree of precision.

Marketers, on the other hand, have had to deal with disconnected data and a lack of tech capabilities both in forecasting and measuring pipeline. That's beginning to change with new technology that provides pipeline intelligence to marketers as well as sellers.

This tech uses AI to allow us to do three important things: plan, track, and forecast pipeline. Let's dig into each of those a bit.

Plan: How much pipeline do we need to generate and by when?

Marketers need a fast, reliable way to generate pipeline plans that we can trust—and that our colleagues trust as well. Spreadsheets can only get us so far. The right tech can help us build these plans from booking targets based on actual conversion rates and sales cycles. It also makes it possible to intelligently balance pipeline production across GTM segments and plan for multiple possible scenarios. For example, it could allow you to test out how much pipeline you'd need to meet your revenue goals if you were to change out your GTM segment mix.

Track: How is your performance stacking up against your plan?

New pipeline intelligence technology gives us more control over hitting our goals than we've ever had. It makes pipeline key performance indicators (KPIs) visible at a glance so we can track performance and make sure it's matching up with our plan. It also allows us to drill down and see our performance by go-to-market (GTM) segment, product, channel, and campaign so we can adjust targets and tactics, thereby addressing pipeline gaps before it is too late to fix them.

This real-time visibility into pipeline performance elevates our interactions with our counterparts in sales, allowing us to have data-driven conversations and stay aligned throughout the entire pipeline journey.

Forecast: Get ahead of performance gaps and know which levers to pull to hit goals

This is where the latest tech really puts marketing on the same level as sales when it comes to pipeline planning. Forecasting qualified pipeline based on AI models, using real-time and historical performance, has the potential to totally change the game for marketing leaders.

It's one thing to know where you are and where you've been, but it's infinitely more valuable to be able to predict where you're going. AI can take into account both trends and current realities to produce far more predictable forecasts than humans can ever do on their own. With a precise understanding of how much pipeline you're likely to generate, you eliminate surprises and guesswork. So if you're not on track to meet your number, you can adjust and act before it's too late.

CASE STUDY
HOW PTC TRANSFORMED BUSINESS
WITH THE RIGHT TECH STACK

I'll be honest with you: All this tech talk can be overwhelming, even for me. But if you want to really identify and engage with customers at scale, there's simply no way around it: You need the right technology.

Our friends at PTC understood that when they decided to totally overhaul their tech capabilities in an initiative they dubbed the Revenue, Orchestration, and Intelligence (ROI) Engine. PTC is a global software company that transforms how companies create, operate, and service products. They came into this endeavor with a mature and successful sales and marketing team, including a dialed-in, data-driven marketing ops team. But they realized that with all the new technology available these days, marketing was under unprecedented pressure to deliver even better, more provable results. They could no longer rest on their laurels—relying solely on their amazing content and killer events—now *everything* they did needed to drive revenue.

Their marketing ops team recognized that the key to doing that (and doing it at scale) would be to tackle their tech stack. They knew that small, incremental changes weren't going to cut it if they wanted to maintain a competitive advantage in their industry—just as I discovered with my first attempt at ABM. They had to go big if they wanted to remain relevant and achieve the kind of revenue growth they were after.

"You see the writing on the wall," explains Saima Rashid, former vice president of Field Analytics & Insights. "You either make the leap, or you don't. And by not making the leap, we would—as a marketing org—be left behind."

The first step Saima and her team took when undertaking this ambitious venture was to identify the gaps in their existing technology. They had all the standard solutions that most companies have—a CRM, a MAP, and so forth—and they were using it with a high level of sophistication. But they didn't have any technology that covered intent or helped them operationalize. They also didn't have a way to identify anonymous accounts, which meant they were leaving lots of opportunities on the table.

"We need to know who is out there doing research who we do not know about today, because you can't just continue mining the same pool of customers that you've always gone after," Saima explains. "The whitespace was a huge piece we wanted to solve for. That included, obviously, anonymous web visitors, but also, who is doing research on the Internet, across the board, and may not know about us?"

The second gap they wanted to fill was the ability to prioritize accounts by knowing which accounts are ideal-customer matches and are in-market—in other words, the accounts most likely to buy.

And as a customer-centric company, they wanted to be able to connect and engage with their ideal prospects through the right channels, at the right times.

They knew that to do this, they'd need technology that would align sales and marketing and provide end-to-end visibility of the digital thread, so they set to work researching their options. After an exhaustive search, they landed on three solutions that would work together to fill all the gaps in their tech capabilities:

- 6sense would identify VIP accounts and their activities, while also uncovering high intent whitespace accounts they needed to be engaging with.

- Drift, a conversational marketing platform, would allow direct engagement to PTC's B2B buyers through a chatbot, creating the right connections at the right time.

- People.ai would integrate the sales team's outreach and activities into PTC's CRM, showcasing a proven pathway of what's working, enabling them to assess deal health and leverage best practices for future efforts.

The combination of these three solutions now empowers the PTC sales and marketing teams and allows them to be smarter and faster in their outreach—and also to best deliver value with every single interaction.

CASE STUDY *continued*

A new era of customer engagement

With their new tech solutions PTC has been able to truly deliver on the customer-centric approach they want to provide. "With every single interaction, we're moving away from just telling prospects about our products, which is what we used to do," says Mariana Cogan, former SVP Digital Marketing Strategy & Operations at PTC. Now, with deep insight into who they're talking to, and with the tools to personalize at scale, Mariana says, "Every line they read has value for them. Every asset that we provide, every image they see, lets us connect at the human level."

So hitting these key tech capabilities has strengthened PTC's customer-focused approach. But it has also had more measurable effects, including on that key metric we're all centered on—revenue. Let's take a look at the new day in the life at PTC:

- They're identifying net-new large whitespace, high-intent accounts and adding them to their CRM.

- They're having thousands of live, high-value conversations via their chat bot.

- They're adding net-new engaged contacts to their MAP and CRM in real time.

- They're generating pipeline.

- They're winning awards. In fact, they were recognized by Sirius Decisions as the 2020 program of the year for marketing operations.

Those results are beyond impressive. And what's more, this technology is surfacing information that's empowering employees across the sales and marketing team to take greater ownership—and have more success in their jobs.

Even junior reps have the confidence to go into these accounts and feel like they're bringing real value. "It's changed the mindset of how they approach prospecting or even working inbound leads, because they know the interest is there," Saima explains. "They're taking this competitive advantage that the tools have given them, and there's been a real shift in the way they approach their jobs day to day."

Reminder: We're doing this for a reason

Okay, that was a lot of information, and your eyeballs hurt, but I promise *it's worth it!* And remember what I said early in this chapter—we're not doing all this hard work for our health, and we're certainly not doing it for the feel-good vibes we'll get from a beautiful tech stack. We're doing it because it's key to achieving that all-important goal we're all after: predictable revenue growth.

The path to predictable revenue growth is quite a journey—and old lead-based technology isn't going to get you there. You need a shift in both your thinking *and* your tech stack so you can buckle up and get ready to reach a level of sales and marketing that's been unattainable until now.

Now, are you ready to take this thing for a spin? In the next chapter, I'll show you how technology, process, and customer experience come together to create the real business results we've been talking about.

CHAPTER 4

OUR BOLD NEW VISION IN ACTION

In the first three chapters of this book, I laid out my vision for a revolution in sales and marketing—a future with *no forms*, *no spam*, and *no cold calls*. I hope I fired you up about playing offense and forging your path as a leader within your organization. We also drilled down into why we're doing this—not for the accolades, but for the holy grail of results: predictable revenue growth. I've talked about the journey you'll need to take to achieve these outcomes, and in the previous chapter, I broke down all the specific processes and tech capabilities you need to make it happen.

Now that we have that solid foundation built, it's time to roll up our sleeves and put our bold new vision into action. So how exactly do we do that? I've boiled it down to six steps:

1. Align on a revenue operating model.

2. Find the red.

3. Design your go-to-market plan.

4. Execute using the five-step account-based formula.

5. Inspect what you expect.

6. Communicate and repeat.

I'll spend this chapter breaking down each of these steps so you'll have a detailed, repeatable process for creating truly customer-first, account-based, insights-driven sales and marketing programs.

Step 1: Align on a revenue operating model

If what we're after is revenue, and specifically reliable revenue that increases (aka, predictable revenue growth), it makes sense that we would need to start by defining our revenue operating model.

At a high level, a revenue operating model is a framework for how you're going to make money. I like to call it a revenue *operating* model (rather than a revenue model) because this isn't a set-it-and-forget-it endeavor. What you're creating is a living, breathing plan. You make assumptions, and you operate against those assumptions. So as you learn more and assumptions change, your plan has to adapt accordingly. If a conversion rate decreases, you have to increase inputs, for example. If upsells are performing better than expected, you can double down there. So I use the term "revenue operating model" to highlight the fact that we're not carving a plan in stone and blindly adhering to it; it informs how we operate, and how we operate, in turn, informs the model.

A revenue operating model is not an MQL goal or an SQL goal. It's an in-depth plan that details what you need to achieve at each stage of the marketing, sales, and customer success cycle. It requires you to evaluate your past experiences for things like cycle time, win rates, and average deal size, and using these, you build your "pipeline quotas." You'll start by doing this at an aggregate level before drilling down into more granular detail.

The reason it's important to dial in on a revenue operating model—and to align on it across the revenue side of the organization—is that it makes sure we're all focused on a common goal, and we all understand the underlying dependencies on how to get there (more on this in Step 2: Find the Red). It ensures as a marketer you are not just throwing MQLs over the wall and "crushing your numbers" while overall the company is not meeting its plan. Too often, I've seen marketers abdicate responsibility for revenue success to sales instead of taking ownership of hitting revenue goals.

It's clear that if we want to get the entire team engaged in creating predictable revenue growth, it's crucial for sales and marketing teams to align on goals, data, and metrics. A siloed approach sets even the most sophisticated strategies and tactics up for lackluster results. That's why it always surprises me to learn that a lot of organizations aren't even tracking the metrics they need to create and stick to an effective revenue operating model.

But that's what we found in our research, even among organizations that have embraced ABM. Not even half of account-driven organizations track these account-based metrics that are vital when creating a useful revenue operating model:

- 49 percent track account win rate.
- 47 percent track accounts in-market.
- 42 percent track deal velocity.

The nuts and bolts of creating a revenue operating model

At both 6sense and Appirio, I've been lucky enough to create our revenue operating models with Kory Geyer, our head of revenue operations (you might remember him from Chapter 1). He's brilliant not just at interpreting data and using it strategically to meet revenue goals, but also at explaining the whole process to the rest of us. So I sat down with him again for this chapter to go through the nitty-gritty of what we need to do in order to complete Step 1: Align on a Revenue Operating Model.

Before building out your revenue operating model, you need to look at historical data to determine some key metrics, including your average transaction cycle time, win rate, deal size, and the amount of pipeline you create at each stage in the marketing funnel. Determining how the averages are calculated depends on the types of deals you do. For transactional-type deals, Kory recommends doing a three-month average. For long-cycle deals, you can look at your data for the past 12 or even 18 months to determine the averages you'll use to make assumptions in your plan. We typically look back six months. The details of how the calculations are made matter and need to be articulated. If your CFO calculates win rates one way and you are building a plan another, you'll run into problems. So make sure to get on the same page before you start.

At that point, you apply what you know to your current goals and your marketing and sales journeys. Looking at the amount of pipeline you've historically had at each buying stage and the revenue you've attained with those numbers, it's simply a math exercise to determine how many accounts you'll need at each buying stage in order to achieve your current revenue goals.

Now that you know what you need to hit at each buying stage, you can use these goals to inform your marketing strategy. To do that, you need to segment out to your different marketing channels like inbound, outbound, events, digital, etc., again looking at historical data for how those channels have performed and extrapolating what will be possible in the future quarter.

At 6sense, our data shows that 80 percent of our revenue comes from what we call "6QAs," or 6sense–Qualified Accounts. These are accounts that meet our ideal customer profile and have just hit a critical tipping point: Based on the predictive scores we discussed in Chapter 3, we determined that the account just moved from the "consideration" stage into the "decision/purchase" stage in the buying journey. Our results show that this is the most effective time for sales to engage. We are constantly backtesting this, and it consistently proves to be true. So based on our revenue plan, we can determine how many 6QAs we need for BDRs to work per month in order to generate our target amounts of pipeline for sales.

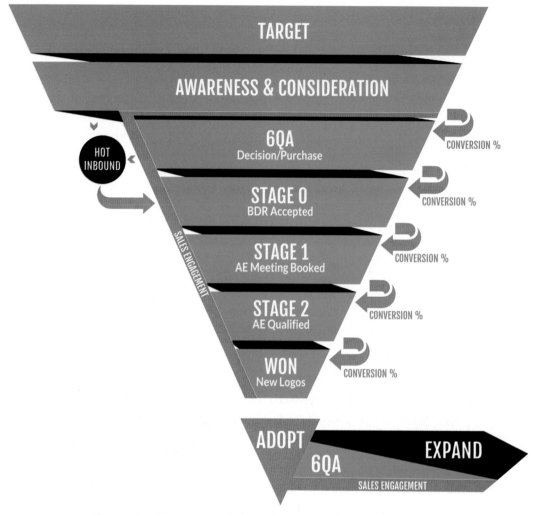

Our account-based funnel shows how we move our ICP accounts from target, through our marketing funnel, and into sales.

For the purposes of this conversation, I want to give you a visual of the opportunity stages we use (not to be confused with buying stages, which are pre-pipeline).

Here's an example of how we use our revenue operating plan to determine quotas. You'll see we start with our conversion rates for each stage, our average deal cycle, and our average sale price. We also know the percentages that come from each of our channels. So we can then map it out with monthly quotas for each of our opportunity stages.

SALES OPPORTUNITY STAGES

	STAGE 0 CALENDARED MEETING	STAGE 1 UNDERSTAND PAIN & PRIORITY	STAGE 2 AGREEMENT ON EVALUATION PLAN	STAGE 3 SOLUTION VALIDATION	STAGE 4 CONFIRMATION	STAGE 5 CONTRACTING & REDLINES	STAGE 6 CLOSED WON
	PIPELINE	PIPELINE	QUALIFIED PIPELINE	BEST CASE	BEST CASE	COMMITTED	CLOSED
DURING STAGE	1 Prospect pre-qualification 2 Meeting set	1 Pains Documented 2 Identify project champion	1 Broader buying team validates pains & priorities 2 Decision Criteria Identified 3 Decision Process Identified	1 Execute go-forward plan 2 Proposal Review 3 Close Plan Discussions begin	1 Confirm VOC 2 Close Plan dates are mutually agreed to 3 Contracting & Procurement Process Begins	1 Final Pricing is agreed to 2 Set up as approved vendor	1 Ring the bell 2 Win Review 3 Internal Kickoff 4 External Kickoff
EXIT CRITERIA VERIFIERS TO ADVANCE TO THE NEXT STAGE	1 Meeting is accepted by Prospect	1 Meeting set with broader buying team 2 Decision timeline established	1 Go-forward plan agreed to 2 Budget & Priority has been discussed	1 Selected as Vendor of Choice	1 Close Plan dates are agreed to 2 Both Legal teams begin reviewing contracts	1 Sales to Customer Success Handoff 2 Signed contract	N / A

CALCULATING MONTHLY PIPELINE TARGETS

	Q1-2020	Q2-2020	Q3-2020	Q4-2020	Q1-2021
BOOKINGS TARGET	$40,000,000	$45,000,000	$55,000,000	$60,000,000	$65,000,000
S2 PIPE CREATED GOAL	$150,165,184	$183,535,224	$200,220,245	$216,905,265	n/a
S0s CREATED GOAL	4,004	4,894	5,339	5,784	n/a
S1s CREATED GOAL	3,003	3,671	4,004	4,338	n/a
S2s CREATED GOAL	1,502	1,835	2,002	2,169	n/a
DAY 1 OF QTR S2 GOAL	$119,599,262	$134,549,170	$164,448,985	$179,398,893	$194,348,801
S2 GOAL 6 WEEKS PRIOR	$76,407,579	$85,958,526	$105,060,420	$114,611,368	$124,162,315

CREATED MONTH	IMPACT MONTH	TARGET			
		S2 PIPE	# OF S0S	# OF S1S	# OF S2S
Feb-20	May-20	$50,055,061	1,335	1,001	501
Mar-20	Jun-20	$50,055,061	1,335	1,001	501
Apr-20	Jul-20	$50,055,061	1,335	1,001	501
May-20	Aug-20	$61,178,408	1,631	1,224	612
Jun-20	Sep-20	$61,178,408	1,631	1,224	612
Jul-20	Oct-20	$61,178,408	1,631	1,224	612
Aug-20	Nov-20	$66,740,082	1,780	1,335	667
Sep-20	Dec-20	$66,740,082	1,780	1,335	667
Oct-20	Jan-21	$66,740,082	1,780	1,335	667
Nov-20	Feb-21	$72,301,755	1,928	1,446	723
Dec-20	Mar-21	$72,301,755	1,928	1,446	723
Jan-21	Apr-21	$72,301,755	1,928	1,446	723
		$750,825,918	20,022	15,017	7,508

BOOKING TO PIPE CONVERSION & AMOUNT CHANGE AFTER OPENING

S2 TO WON CONVERSION	30%
AMOUNT CHANGE AFTER OPENING	99.9%

STAGE 0–2 CONVERSION, DEAL CYCLE TIME, & AVG SELLING PRICE

STAGE 0 TO 1 CONVERSION	75%
STAGE 1 TO 2 CONVERSION	50%
DEAL CYCLE STAGE 0 TO 7 DAYS	90
AVERAGE SELLING PRICE	$100,000

Benefits of a solid revenue operating model

With all this information, you can build out your sales capacity plan to determine necessary headcount for sales and BDRs/SDRs. It also gives you the information you need in order to build your marketing activity plan so you know what you need to do in a given quarter to hit your targets.

One of the benefits of having your goals planned out to such a stage- and channel-specific level is that if there's a disruption to one of your channels—oh I don't know, maybe a pandemic that brings all events to a grinding halt?—you can now look at your revenue operating model and say, "We were supposed to have X accounts at Y buying stage coming in from events, so how do we pivot and get those numbers up in other channels?"

When you start at the very top with big data at your side telling you where to focus all the way through your marketing and sales processes, it has a multiplicative effect on conversions all the way through that funnel. And that has a tremendous effect on ROI. At 6sense, since we have predictive models (a necessary capability, as I outlined in Chapter 3), our revenue operating model game is significantly upgraded and way more predictable. We use AI and big data that are tested, proven, and proven again. That means guesswork—and made-up lead scoring—don't enter into our predictive equation.

This is an important concept as it explains one of the more controversial points in this plan: that MQLs need to go away. I understand that MQLs feel predictable since you have a lot of historical data on them. And the truth is that once you do away with them, you may actually end up with fewer accounts that are predicted to be in-market or at that magical 6QA stage. But that's okay, because the accounts you'll be working with will be much higher quality than MQLs, and they'll have a far better likelihood of closing.

Another point I want to make: Depending on your organization size and structure, you may need to have more than one revenue operating model. For instance, at 6sense we started out with one revenue operating model. But then we added a commercial segment, which has a totally different deal size, velocity, and selling motion than our enterprise segment. To align with our sales motions, we now add a new revenue operating model for each new segment we introduce.

That's Step 1. And while it may seem basic, you'd be surprised at how many organizations don't do it. And as you can see, it's critical if you want a data-driven and aligned plan to meet revenue goals. Once you have this nailed down, you can move on to Step 2: Find the Red!

Step 2: Find the red

We marketers often fall into the trap of adding more and more to our collective plate—more campaigns, more initiatives, more exciting ideas that we just can't wait to put into practice. It's what we all love about marketing because it's invigorating, creative, and *fun*. But we need to focus that energy on the places the business needs us the most.

If we want predictable revenue growth, we need to follow the revenue operating model and look for shortcomings so we can keep improving. This is what I call "finding the red"—in other words, looking for spots in the plan that either aren't performing or are at risk of falling short.

This concept will be familiar to the sales folks out there. I learned it back when I was in sales, and we would do deal reviews to determine the probability of successfully closing a deal. What I learned is that the best salespeople don't tell you all the reasons their deal is going to close; they tell you all the reasons it *isn't*. They look at their deals and see a minefield of "red flags"—or everything that could possibly go wrong. You might think that sounds like a negative, but as a sales leader, I loved the red. I taught my reps that bringing the "red" forward was a GOOD thing. Red means you're thinking ahead. Red means that we can look to fix it before it happens. And the more granular you can get in identifying your red flags, the better.

Now, as a marketing leader, I coach my team to do the same. In fact, it's key across the revenue team—we must always look for the red. And that means that more is not always the answer. More campaigns, more events, more initiatives—those are all too often geared toward filling our pipelines with useless MQLs and not focused on the ultimate goal: revenue. But the reality is that marketing can and should have an impact at all stages of the revenue operating model. If we're not set up to increase net new pipeline, or partner co-sells, or any other element of our revenue operating model, that's a red flag. We need to identify it, bring it forward, and address it.

This is why understanding the revenue operating model and aligning focus areas in conjunction with strategic plan (V2MOM), customer insights (IICP), and category vision are absolutely critical to success.

Where should you be looking?

Clearly it's important to find the red in your revenue operating model. Benchmarks can be a great place to start. Insight Partners has some great ones on their website, and I also love all of TOPO's benchmarks. But I've found the best benchmark is yourself. Start baselining and set your sights to improve. So where exactly do you look? Well here's a visual of all the places we look in our account-based funnel to find holes, gaps, leaks, or any place we could do better. In each of these stages, we ask, "What can we do to improve this specific conversion rate?"

FROM → TO		GOOD PLACES TO "FIND RED"
AWARENESS & CONSIDERATION	6QA	ICP Web traffic, ICP Engagement, VTR, SOV, AR Mentions, Accounts Reached, CTAs, Segmentation, Creative, Content, Keywords, Predictive Model Metrics
6QA	MEETING	ICP Engagement, Conversion Rate & Velocity Stage 0, 1s, Cadences, CTAs, SLAs, Web/Content Experience, 6QAs Worked, Bot Conversations
MEETING	PIPELINE	Conversion Rate & Velocity, 1,2, Aging Reports (stuck stage 1s), Gong Calls, Nurture Cadences, Worked Opps Accounts, Web/Content Experience
PIPELINE	CLOSED / WON	Win Rate Compete & Non-Compete, Cycle Time, ACV, Engagement Trend, Persona Map, Aging Reports (stuck stage 2s), Gong Calls, Product Demo, Sales Materials, Win/Loss Calls, Competitive Intel
CLOSED / WON	ADOPT & GROW	Net & Gross Retention, Time to Go Live, Usage, Adoption By Use Case, Personas Engaged, Relationship Map, Value Metrics, NPS

I like the way the consulting company Winning by Design encourages people to find the red. They challenge sales and marketing folks to answer the question, "How can you double your revenue?" The obvious answer is to double your number of leads. But a better answer echoes what I've been arguing for in this book: You double your revenue by improving the prospect and customer experience. You identify the most critical moments for them and ask yourself how you're performing in those critical moments. Are you performing magically? If not, that's your red. And if you're able to perform even 10 percent better at each of those critical moments—and therefore up your conversion rate at each stage—you can double your revenue without bringing in a single new lead. Again, more is not always the answer.

Digging into conversion rates

One good place to look for the red is in your sales velocity. Generally speaking, if you want to grow your revenue, you need to increase your sales velocity. Chris Codelli, the director of sales and marketing at Marlin Operations Group, Inc., explains how he uses the sales velocity formula to calculate the rate at which an organization is closing business—and how the formula itself helps identify opportunities for improvement.

Chris explains, "I find that the real value of the formula is in its construction, as it reveals the four factors that companies can impact to grow sales productivity (i.e., increase their sales velocity)." These are the four factors, according to Chris:

- Increase number of new opportunities
- Increase average selling price
- Increase win rate
- Decrease sales cycle length

Of these, Chris says that increasing win rate—or the conversion rate across the funnel—has the greatest impact since it's the variable we have the most control over.

"Increasing conversion rates starts with making sure we are engaging with the best possible set of targets (ICP, buyer personas) and then involves applying skills and processes in an effective and efficient manner. These are all factors that a company can control," Chris explains. "The impact of increased conversion rates at the top of the funnel has a multiplier impact downstream that is very meaningful."

For Tara Corey, vice president of marketing operations at Qlik, inspecting win rates was key to finding the red—and thus improving their overall success. She and her team determined that 35 percent of the company's leads converted less than 1 percent of the time. But when they applied predictive models, they went from MQLs to 6QAs. The 6QAs converted at two to three times the average rate. By prioritizing qualified accounts using predictive scores, the Qlik team was able to stop spinning its wheels chasing leads that were unlikely to convert, and that freed them up to spend more time on outbound prospecting. In fact, with AI-driven insights, Qlik was able to reduce the time the team spent sorting through and following up on leads by between 30 and 40 percent.

Chris says something about conversions that's a little esoteric, but it really resonates with me. He points out there are two definitions for the verb *convert*. When we're talking about conversion rates, we usually focus on the first definition: "to cause a change in form, character, or function." But Chris proposes that we might be better served if instead we focused on the second definition: "to change one's religious faith or other beliefs."

I love this! What we really want when we're seeking conversions is for buyers to become believers in us, our organization, and our solutions. We want them to *want* to take the next step in the journey with us. And it's a really good way for sellers and marketers to give themselves a customer-first gut check: If you were in your customer's shoes, would the experience you're giving them change their beliefs at this step in the journey? What about at the next step? And the next?

If the answer is no to any of those, then you've found your red. By fixing it, you'll increase your conversion rates while also vastly improving your customer experience.

I know this is a little evangelical for a business book—but I'm passionate because I've seen it work! And while I don't want to come across as cultish, it's important to say this: If you don't believe that this level of focus is the right move for your organization, and if it's not something you're ready to religiously apply to everything you do, it's okay to stop reading now. If you prefer to keep your focus on scoring leads and attributing every MQL to the appropriate ebook download, this approach is not for you. And that's okay. But if you are willing to put in the work, to re-examine every step in your process, find the red, and improve it, you *will* see results time and time again.

Step 3: Design your go-to-market plan

If you're still with me, I'll take it to mean you're all in! You've aligned on your revenue operating model, which means you have your quotas spelled out for pipeline, bookings, upsells, renewals, etc. It also means you've come up with your sales headcount plan, you've found your red, and you know the key spots in your process that you're going to improve.

Now it's time to create your go-to-market (GTM) plan. Your GTM plan spells out the specific campaigns you're going to run in order to achieve the revenue operating model you've established. Consider it your capacity plan—it ensures you have the coverage needed to meet your goals.

Which brings me to my next point. No team, no matter how well-resourced, has unlimited capacity. Your capacity will vary based on the size, skills, and resources of your team as well as your deal cycle time. But whatever your capacity is, you need your GTM plan to spell out how many campaigns you can implement and how complex those campaigns can be. In order to scale campaigns based on complexity, length, and resource needs, it's helpful to break them into tiers, with the first tier being the most resource-intensive, the second tier being less so, and the third tier, once it's up and running, more or less operating in the background. I'm going to tell you about the three tiers we use at 6sense, but if you have a smaller team you may only be able to manage two tiers. You'll figure that out when you start mapping out your capacity.

Tier 1 campaigns

Tier 1 campaigns are the types of campaigns we marketers live for. These are what I call "mind-blowing moments." Others call them "lightning strikes." Whatever you call them, the idea is the same: Tier 1 campaigns are designed to knock people's socks off. Ideally, these will create a ton of pipeline and revenue, but they'll do more than that: They'll drive market awareness and drive your category plan forward. If you want to create or lead a category, Tier 1 campaigns are key.

So what falls under the category of a Tier 1 campaign? Think the big stuff—significant product launches, acquisitions, funding, important industry trade shows, your own conference, and so forth. These are the campaigns that are so high-impact that people talk about them for years to come. They're so big that most teams will only be able to pull off one or two per year (if that).

What to know about Tier 1 campaigns

- They require significant coordination across the entire organization.
- They should have their own branding, social campaigns, and company enablement.
- They're about more than just a pipeline goal—they are designed to further your big ideas and your company leadership.
- An advanced team can pull off one per quarter, max.

Tier 2 campaigns

Tier 2 campaigns are more bite-sized. Tier 2s are point-in-time projects that are geared toward increasing pipeline or engagement in a focused account segment.

Some examples of Tier 2 campaigns are running a competitive takeout, amplifying an event, launching a webinar series, or doing a co-sell with a partner.

What to know about Tier 2 campaigns

- They're time-bound based on season, a show, market news, etc.
- They are focused—maybe on a persona, install base, geo, etc.
- They tie to a micro-segment or a subsegment; they're not run against your entire ICP, but rather a subset of select accounts.
- They support larger themes and branding.
- They typically tie to an account engagement and pipeline goal.

NO FORMS. NO SPAM. NO COLD CALLS.

Tier 3 campaigns

Tier 3s are your bread-and-butter campaigns. They're the ones you run to programmatically build and accelerate pipeline. They're initiatives that are always running without requiring a huge effort.

Your persistent digital presence is an example of a Tier 3. Sometimes the initiatives you try as a Tier 1 or Tier 2 that end up being wildly successful graduate to become Tier 3s. Assuming you have an account orchestration platform and the ability to set up dynamic segments, Tier 3s basically just work on their own. All they require from your team is a periodic refresh. For instance, every quarter you might look at your Tier 3s and see if they need fresh creative, new content, etc.

What to know about Tier 3 campaigns

- They are ongoing for six months or more, but they're refreshed quarterly.

- They provide programmatic, "always on" air cover.

- They tie to master segments (e.g., ICP, customer, open opportunities), unlike Tier 2s, which tie to subsets of accounts.

What every campaign has to have

It would be easy to look at this tiering system and start filling your GTM plan with a few campaigns from each level and call it a day. But we're more strategic than that, right?

We know that every campaign must have a business objective. Every single thing we do needs to tie back to a specific business goal. Typically these campaigns are about generating pipeline (though Tier 1s need to do more). Specific goals might be to increase win rate by X percent, to increase deal velocity by Y days, or to meet a certain customer adoption objective.

In addition, every campaign should tie back to an account segment. Depending on segment and objective, the number of accounts you're targeting will vary. I'll get into that in greater detail in the next section when we dive into execution.

If you're not explicitly stating the business objective and account segment you're targeting with each campaign, it's really easy to just start dropping things into the plan without giving them the thought they deserve. Force yourself and your team to define the business objective and examine the data for each campaign before committing to it. We have a saying around here: No segment, no creative.

A solid GTM plan eliminates "random acts of marketing"

Creating a solid GTM plan with a tiered system is a great way to hyper-prioritize what's really important to your overall goals and strategy. When you understand your capacity, down to the exact number of campaigns per tier your team (and budget) can manage, you're able to ensure you're only saying yes to the absolute best campaigns that will help you meet your objectives. Here are some of the reasons this approach is so effective:

1. We all know how "random acts of marketing" can take over if you don't have guideposts in place. Looking at your capacity through a tiering lens ensures you don't spend all your time on a bunch of little dippy things that don't add up to much—a webinar here, an ebook there. When you create your GTM plan, everything needs to be grouped under a theme or business objective. Your plan gives you an immediate visual of how each thing you do reinforces and amplifies everything else.

2. You keep customer experience front and center. With your GTM plan in front of you, you can zoom out and ask yourself, "Is this a plan that creates value for my audience? Are these campaigns adding value to my customers and future customers?" If the answer is yes, *onward.* If not? Time to get back to work.

3. It's motivational for your team. No one gets jazzed about getting another pile of Asana tasks dropped on them every day—but everyone wants to be part of doing cool stuff. A well-designed GTM plan outlines all the cool stuff and gives context for why we're doing it. Suddenly all those tasks make sense and take on a higher purpose, since they all fit into an overall plan.

4. This GTM framework allows marketing, sales, and customer success to confidently see if there are enough campaigns hitting the market to meet our revenue plan. And just as importantly, it lets them see why their ideas or requests that are outside the plan are not getting done. I've said it before; if people can't see what's happening in marketing, they'll happily fill the void with their own ideas for things you should do!

5. The tiering system provides shorthand for the team to use. When my team hears that a campaign is a Tier 3, they know it means they do X, Y, and Z. We're not starting from scratch. That sort of baked-in understanding makes it easier to manage workload and expectations.

GTM STRAWMAN

	MAY		JUNE		JULY	

TIER 1

- Big New Product Launch

TIER 2

- Industry Event
- Customer Webinar Series
- New Partner Launch
- Competitive Takeout
- Persona-Focused Dinner Series
- High Touch Tier 1
- High Touch Tier 1
- External Sponsored Webinars

TIER 3

- Executive Meetups: Weekly Virtual Coffee Talk & Happy Hour
- Quarterly Direct Mail Drop
- Monthly Customer User Group
- TOP Keywords (*Intent Keywords) Predictive Analytics // Sales Productivity // Website Personalization // Lead Generation

Step 4: Execute using the five-step account-based formula

You've aligned, you've strategized, you've planned, and you've planned some more. Now it's time to turn all that hard work into *fun*—let's execute some campaigns!

When it's time to execute campaigns, naturally we're still thinking in terms of ABM. So every campaign is account-based, not lead-based. That means we'll use that five-step ABM flow that I introduced in Chapter 3:

Now, if you have the tech that I outlined in Chapter 3, you can lean on it for a large chunk of the process. The right tech does a lot of the heavy lifting, but of course, it won't do everything. You and your team need to define the key elements of any campaign:

- Your business objective

- Your budget

- Your content and creative

- Your prospect experience (meaning activation channels like direct mail, email, BDR outreach, events, and special programs)

Let's take a look at the five ABM steps and drill down to see which parts will require humans and which can be left to the tech stack:

STEP 1 SELECT THE BEST ACCOUNTS

Start by defining the business objective. Do you want to enter a new geo or industry? Do a competitive takeout? Introduce a new product or feature? You and your team need to decide on this.

Once you've done that, your tech stack will use real buyer intent and activity data that buyers are leaving behind as a digital footprint on the web to identify the best accounts for your business goal. Your AI-based platform will score activity against your current ICP, but it also continually learns what behaviors are leading to new opportunities. It should adapt and continue to surface the best accounts for you to target. It should also deliver insights into the account's buying stage, who is on the buying team, and what they care about. All those predictive capabilities come together at this stage to ensure the accounts you're targeting are the right ones for you.

STEP 2 KNOW ABOUT THEM

Your technology will provide rich insights about the accounts. It'll capture prospect buying signals from the CRM and marketing automation systems as well as digital footprints from across the B2B web. This includes search data and research activity across trade publications, blogs, forums, etc. This is where that embedded CDP comes in handy!

STEP 3 ENGAGE THE RIGHT WAY

With this data and the insights provided by the platform, you can now determine the content, creative, budget, and prospect experience. Your technology will orchestrate these insights using AI to ensure the right message is delivered to the right person at the right time on the right channel. That means no more hoping your message hits at the appropriate buying stage or to the relevant personas.

STEP 4 COLLABORATE WITH SALES

I can't overstate the importance of a well-designed tech stack here. It literally makes or breaks the relationship between sales and marketing. With the right technology, both sales and marketing are on the same page knowing which accounts are showing meaningful activity, where they are in their buying journey, and what efforts are working to get them moving through the funnel. Without technology, we're using subjective measures to rate accounts (like my nemesis the MQL). An account engagement platform integrates seamlessly with your CRM, marketing automation platform, and web personalization tools to ensure you have a single source of truth across the entire revenue team. *Bonus: No more "stuck leads" report!*

STEP 5 TRACK REAL STUFF

Your technology should provide real-time tracking of budget, ROI, accounts reached, personas engaged, and pipeline created/influenced. This is another way that technology helps sales and marketing collaborate, since tracking and reporting on a common set of metrics eliminates finger-pointing and unites everyone as one revenue team. An AI-based platform allows you to track new accounts that are in-market, as well as meaningful metrics like engagement levels, to understand which tactics are actually working to reach your targeted accounts.

So that's it. That's how campaigns get executed in an ABM world. If you've ever wondered how ABM can be implemented at scale, here's your answer—it's with these five steps, plus a tech stack that does the heavy lifting for you.

To illustrate how it plays out in the real world, I will walk you through three actual campaigns we've run—one in each tier—to show you exactly what happens at each step, and how we're able to achieve next-level results without spinning our wheels or burning ourselves out.

Tier 1: The mind-blowing moment

As I said, Tier 1 campaigns are the stuff marketers live for. Tier 1 campaigns are your chance to have a massive impact, and not just on your organization and market. They are an unbeatable opportunity to stretch your creativity and big-thinking muscles.

In other words, I love Tier 1s. And of all the Tier 1s I've ever done, the one that I'm most proud of was our play at the SiriusDecisions Summit, which is a *huge* industry event for us. And to be honest, it's one we almost didn't do. When I pitched it, not everyone on the team was on board. They argued that we were already diamond-level sponsors and doing more would be overkill.

SD SUMMIT

WEST AE OR ISR NAME:	REP NAME

SD SUMMIT 2019 GAME PLAN OVERVIEW

What is your overall plan for you week at SD Summit? How will you engage prospects at the 6sense Club, Party, or anything else? How will you spread your time across days? What are your goals for the week? Will you focus on customer, partners, etc.? How are you leveraging our executive team? What customers are you going to connect with for references?

ACCOUNTS ATTENDING SIRIUSDECISION SUMMIT

ACCOUNT NAME	CONTACT NAME & TITLE	OPEN OPPTY'S	OUR OBJECTIVES?	PLANNED ACTIVITY / TIMING
ABC Company	John Q Customer	List any open opportunities and customer contact for each.	What is your objective for this account at SDS19?	What event, meetings, activities, etc., do you have planned for this account?

BLACK CARD LIST

NAME	ACCOUNT	TITLE
1		
2		
3		
4		
5		

About

Are you signed up to learn about the top trends and opportunities in the B2B space from leading analysts? 6sense will be there to let you in on what it takes for your business to synchronize your strategy, processes, content, technology, and analytics so that your company delivers the right message at the right time to the right person at every stage of the buying process.

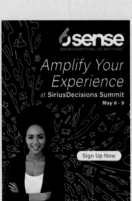

But here's what I know about these types of events: Being just one more company on the trade show floor—regardless of your sponsorship level—is not going to make you stand out. And I *knew* we could stand out and make a huge splash. So I took my own advice and played offense. I trusted my instincts and decided we were going all in on this event. And I'm so glad we did. It was *amazeballs*—a shining moment for 6sense and for our entire team.

Let me walk you through how we pulled it off, within the context of our five-step ABM approach:

1. Select the best accounts. To start, we needed to define our business objectives. Remember, with Tier 1s you're doing more than just generating pipeline. Yes, we knew we'd walk out of this with an F-load of new pipeline, but that wasn't our only objective. Our main purpose was to create a mind-blowing experience for our customers, our future customers, and our team. Remember in Chapter 1 when we talked about the magic that happens when employee experience and customer experience meet? Well this Tier 1 play was designed to get our team completely revved up so they'd be amped to show off 6sense and put our absolute best face forward.

   From the customer experience perspective, we wanted to show current and future customers *mad love*. We wanted them to be clamoring to meet with us. We wanted to get in front of as many of our best prospects as possible so we could create meaningful experiences and get them crazy excited about collaborating with us.

   We used our platform to build a segment with the best in-market accounts that were an ICP fit and were going to be at the event. This was the list of accounts we'd work on scheduling meetings with at the event. And we asked the sales team to nominate their super-high-value accounts for another play we had up our sleeve, which I'll tell you about in a minute.

2. Know about them. Once we had our segment built, our technology gave us rich insights into everyone in it. We knew their industry, their top searched keywords, where they were in their buying journey, and other key information. We ran a data enrichment plan to buy contact details so we had everything we needed to get meetings booked in advance.

3. Engage the right way. Now that we had selected the best accounts and knew everything we needed to know about them, we were able to start engaging with them the right way. Before the event, this included tailored outreach that spoke to their interest, industry, and buying stage—insights that make our AEs much more likely to get a positive response than the generic, "I see you'll be at the event! Can we set up a time to talk?"

We also created a microsite specifically for 6sense at SiriusDecisions, where we listed all our activity, speaking sessions, events, parties, etc. It also included a link to request a meeting with us. We ran ads that matched the microsite, so that our prospects were surrounded by consistent messaging from us.

At the event itself, we knew we wanted to turn heads and get people talking. We also knew we wanted to provide massive value to our customers and future customers. So we took over a nearby restaurant and set up a private, high-end lounge, which we called Club6. It was as high-end as you can imagine, and it was a place I still want to hang out. It had a concierge, a latte bar, whiskey tastings, shoeshine … you name it, we had it. But here's the catch: To get in, you either had to be in a meeting with one of our AEs, or you had to have one of our exclusive Black Cards—and we only offered those to the high-value accounts I mentioned above. And, of course, everyone who saw or heard about Club6 wanted in. Talk about FOMO.

But it wasn't all about glitz and pampering. We were laser-focused on our business objectives, including completing tons of meetings with the right accounts and moving them through the buying process. We set up a command center that could instantly help us make sure we were getting meetings, then second meetings, and pulling in whatever partners and subject matter experts we needed to help deals progress. Because after all, everything we needed was right there, so why wait? Rather than have just one meeting, we wanted to be able to cover five or six deal steps in four days.

And finally, we walked into the event with a buttoned-up post-engagement plan to make sure it would live on long after we all got back home. It included case studies, which we featured in a follow-up webinar series called "Meet the Senseis." That became a nurture track that created value for connections we made at the show.

4. Collaborate with sales. We collaborated closely with sales at every single step of this play. Starting very early, reps used the insights afforded by our technology to set meetings and design personalized gameplans for each key account with the goal of delivering a world-class experience. We worked with the head of sales to create expectations and set a meeting goal. And, of course, we asked them to tier their accounts and tell us who was worthy of the coveted black card. We had meetings with the sales team with increasing frequency as the show date grew closer, so that by the end we were entirely aligned on processes and expectations. Then we had everyone come to the event a day early for onsite training, which is critical when it comes to getting everyone on the same page.

During the event, all AEs had dashboards of their accounts where they could look at engagement on a daily basis and try to schedule demos or follow-up at Club6. And when meetings did happen, they could take next steps right away. Because they have 6sense, the AEs also got Slack alerts on accounts that were increasing or decreasing engagement. One AE saw a spike on an account he hadn't been able to schedule a meeting with in advance, so he reached out during the event and ended up scheduling several meetings—and ultimately closing the deal.

5. **Track real stuff.** We went into this event saying we wanted to generate an F-load of net new pipeline, and we did. We tracked meetings scheduled and meetings completed and blew both goals out of the water. We tracked how many of the Black Cards got picked up—around 80 percent.

   And in terms of making a splash and creating a buzz? That couldn't have gone better. It showed in our website traffic from ICP accounts, which went through the roof. But it also showed in this feedback from industry leaders:

   > "Stole the show at SD. Most talked about. Most attended. One to watch." — Industry analyst

   > "No idea how you pulled SD off. You look like a company 10x your size." — Partner CMO

   > "I'm jealous of your marketing." — Competitor CEO

That's an example of what you can accomplish with a successful Tier 1. As you can see, it takes a ton of work to plan, execute, and measure your success—which is why most teams can only handle one a quarter, if that. Now let's take a look at an example of a much lighter lift—a Tier 2—and the steps involved in that.

Tier 2: The competitive takeout

A Tier 2 campaign isn't nearly as complex as a Tier 1. It's a relatively low lift, though of course it does still require time and effort. So when our team wanted me to launch a competitive takeout campaign after one of our competitors fumbled a product release, my first instinct was to say, "No, we've got a ton on our plate, and by the time we get the entire thing mapped out this will be yesterday's news." Plus, I'm not a huge fan of competitive takeouts, which are campaigns that are designed to divert interest from a competitor and toward us. But sales was super into the idea, so I got on board. And in the end, it turned out to be a pretty successful campaign—and we pulled it all off in *two days!*

Here's how it went down, following the five-step ABM process:

1. **Select the best accounts.** Our objective was to take business from this competitor. Our platform identified around 200 accounts that were currently using the competitor's technology solution or actively researching the competitor's solution based on keyword search analysis.

2. **Know about them.** Our platform also identified the key personas on the account, along with additional keywords they were researching, to provide us with more detail on what they cared about. We used those insights to determine the budget,

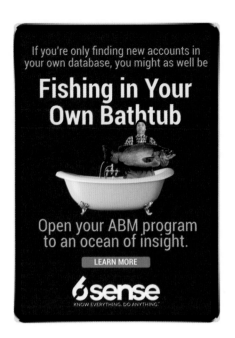
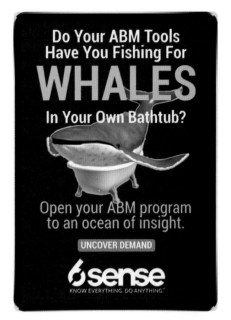

creative, and content. Based on the Dark Funnel™ intelligence uncovered by the platform, we huddled and came up with our creative. We ran a set of ads through an A/B test in 6sense and quickly got feedback on which message was resonating. And it was pretty funny, if I do say so myself.

3. Engage the right way. We ran display ads to the 200 accounts based on the insights we had gleaned in Step 2. The message was tailored to people who weren't satisfied with their current solution—but it was classy and kept things light. The call to action was to put us to a real, live test so we could prove we could perform better than our competitor.

   Our platform orchestrated the campaigns, making sure the ads got in front of key personas in the target accounts. It automatically triggered BDR outreach when accounts reached decision stage.

4. Collaborate with sales. Our platform kept marketing and sales on the same page throughout the campaign. It automatically updated the opportunity record directly in our CRM, allowing our AEs to easily see which accounts were viewing the ads, which accounts visited our website, and which accounts had responded to BDR outreach. In addition to that activity data, our sales team could also see which personas were engaging and what topics they cared about. And finally, account owners received an alert when an account moved into the purchase stage, letting them know it was time to act.

5. Track real stuff. Our technology tracked how much we spent, how we increased engagement, what open opportunities we influenced, and ultimately, the new opportunities we created.

So, how did it all turn out? Amazingly well. This was another a-ha moment for me—we were able to net incredible results with only two days of effort and a total spend of $237! We increased engagement, identified (or moved) accounts as "in-market," influenced existing opportunities, and even created one new opportunity. We responded in a timely and agile way to changing market conditions and built all of our creative based on what we knew our audience was interested in. And because we didn't have to spend any resources arguing over which accounts to include or what our messaging should be, it allowed us to stay entirely focused on our business objective.

PROGRAMMATIC APPROACH

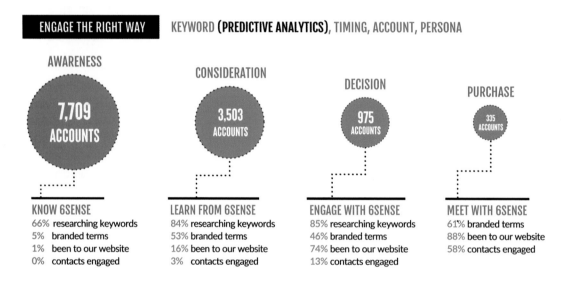

This is what I'm talking about when I say that with the right tech stack, agile, transformative marketing is possible. It allows you to put marketing back where it belongs—as close to the customer as possible.

Tier 3: A programmatic approach to printing pipeline

An integral part of our business is consistent pipeline generation. For this example, I'll walk you through a programmatic campaign—one of those always-on initiatives that works in the background, dynamically adjusting to target the right accounts and deliver personalized experiences. This is what keeps our business humming.

Because of our insights, we can deliver new dimensions of personalization. As you'll see in this example, we personalize everything for the account's buying stage and what they care about—dynamically and with a high degree of accuracy.

1. **Select the best accounts.** Our business objective is to deliver an engaging experience to target enterprise accounts. Our platform surfaced only our in-market ideal customers (the IICPs I keep telling you about), which whittled down our ICP list of 37,000 accounts to a much more manageable 2,000 accounts that were showing buying intent. And as this campaign runs, our list of accounts is constantly updated based on the signals our tech is picking up on.

2. **Know about them.** Our technology gives us insight into the criteria used to make up our IICP. For example, we can see that the best accounts are primarily U.S.-based, have a marketing automation platform installed (e.g., Pardot, Salesforce Marketing Cloud, Marketo, Hubspot), have more than 100 employees, and are in certain industries. It also tells us their buying stage so we know when those accounts are in-market and when they move to 6QA status—that window of opportunity when accounts go from researching to ready to take a meeting.

Using these insights, we're able to create messaging and outreach that's not just based on demographic, firmographic, and technographic data, but also timed to exactly where each account is in their buying journey *and* tailored to the keywords they're researching.

The timing is especially important in this campaign since the goal is to take accounts from wherever they are in the buying journey and turn them into pipeline. Stage-based content is nothing new—we've always mapped out our messaging to buying stage. The difference now is that we don't just put the content out there and hope the prospect will find it at the right moment. Now our insights allow us to confidently deliver the right content for each buying stage at exactly the right time, across channels.

Also incredibly important are the keyword insights we have. Thanks to our technology, we have completely revolutionized the way we create and deliver content. We are no longer guessing about what accounts care about. Our intent data give us supercharged intelligence to tailor our creative and content to align with the exact topics our ideal, in-market customers are actively researching. In this case, the keyword we're focused on is "predictive analytics," and we create the information based on that. Remember, our goal in this no-forms, no-spam, no-cold-calls reality is to understand our customers better so we can be their preferred source of learning at every step in the journey.

Armed with these critical insights, we set our budget and map our content, ads, value cards, and cadences to buying stage and keyword. Here's what that looks like.

3. **Engage the right way.** The right insights and orchestration capabilities allow us to engage the right way. For this campaign, we engaged using a mix of tactics. The first is display ads, which provided aircover based on buying stage and keyword.

We then used the same IICP accounts in our Google retargeting and LinkedIn strategies, focusing on "predictive analytics" across buying stages. Google retargeting and LinkedIn amplification are basic tactics, but because we're able to overlay our IICP accounts into each of these platforms, the bid engines are able to automatically increase spend on high-value audiences, while lowering bids for lower-value audiences. Not only does this ensure better targeting and click-throughs (which matter with these platforms/ strategies), it's key with limited resources to make a bottom-line impact and ensure a consistent experience across channels.

A big part of engaging the right way entails creating a seamless, integrated, and consistent digital experience. So when the ads do their job and these target accounts visit our website, we want to make sure that what they see aligns with their expectations—whether or not they got to us by clicking through the ad. That's possible thanks to our technology, which lets us match anonymous visitors with accounts (and accounts with buying stage and intent), regardless of traffic source.

There are two key ways we provide a personalized content experience to our website visitors, and both are based on buying stage and intent. The first is with our chatbot, which recognizes the accounts that are visiting our site and pops in with friendly and tailored recommendations. So for instance, an early-stage visitor who's interested in predictive analytics may get a recommendation to check out our TalkingSense video on predictive analytics (learn more about our video strategy in the sidebar on page 128).

The second way we provide a customer-first (and more effective) digital experience is with a personalized content hub. The content that an early-stage visitor interested in predictive analytics sees on our site will be vastly different than what a decision-stage visitor researching predictive analytics will see, for example. And the hub is dynamic, so as an account changes buying stage or areas of interest, the content will change to match it and usher them through the funnel toward pipeline.

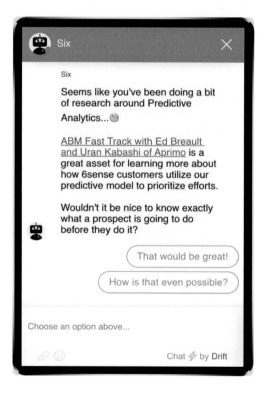

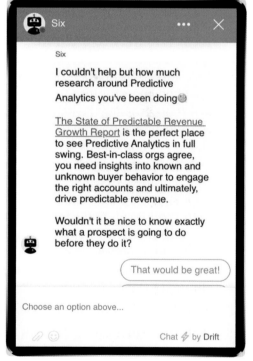

And it works amazingly well—which we know because we can watch accounts as they progress through the funnel, we can see when and how they engage, and we know specifically which marketing efforts are influencing them. But every so often we get an account close to the finish line—then things stall. In those cases, we need to show a little extra love, and we do that with a highly personalized take on direct mail. For our high-value, qualified opportunities that have shown interest but (for whatever reason) aren't progressing the way we expect them to, we use a service called Alyce to send a personalized gift designed to grab their attention and re-engage them. I'm not talking lame squishy balls or a 6sense mug—Alyce cross-references the person's online presence to determine their interests and then curates gifts that are sure to make a personal connection. It then populates a personalized e-store with gift options most likely to resonate with the person and that the person can select or choose to donate the value to charity instead. What I love about Alyce is that we're not sending people junk, and we're not wasting money on random swag. We're sending timely, personalized gifts with a specific business goal: to move an account through the buying journey.

This may seem like a lot of avenues of engagement for one campaign, but with the right technology, it's seamless. While it requires watching the top keywords that are bubbling up to ensure we are adapting to what our market cares about, systems are in place so our orchestration platform can handle the bulk of the work for us.

4. **Collaborate with sales.** As I've said, we don't focus on inbound; we focus on in-market. We know when in-market accounts "6QA", it's time for our BDRs to start engaging. At that point, we enrich our account data to make BDRs' outreach as efficient and effective as possible—without wasting their time tracking down company information and reading a thousand press releases and articles to get to know the account. Instead, our platform gives us the ability to trigger what we call a SmartPlay. When accounts move from awareness to consideration, marketing immediately begins building and enriching a dossier on that account, including information about the entire buying team. The moment an account crosses over to decision/purchase (6QA), the BDR team is equipped with all of the information it needs to immediately start engaging with the account. They also have information about everything that happened along the buying journey to cause that account to 6QA, and they can see all of the personas on the buying team and how they have engaged across all of the buying stages. Again, this helps them personalize their outreach.

    Sales is also in the loop, working in tandem with the BDRs to ensure they understand the entire buying team—including the content they have consumed and even competitive threats. That means sales goes into first meetings prepped and ready to talk about what they know the future customer cares about.

5. **Track real stuff.** This is an always-on campaign designed to generate engagement and drive the pipeline needed based on our operating model. We measure success by tracking how accounts convert at each stage of the funnel and into the sales process. We also drill down into engagement statistics across the journey to find places we need to optimize.

    Here's what we've seen as a result of our Tier 3 campaign approach:

    - Based on our view-through rate (VTR), we can see we're consistently getting the right accounts to our website.

    - Just *one day* after launching new chatbots that recognize accounts and personalize conversations mirroring our journey-based ads, we booked a meeting.

    - With dynamically personalized content hubs, our time on site is two to three times better than the industry average.

    - Personalized gifting has been wildly successful, netting a 70 percent better response rate than the industry average—because it's based on real in-market insights!

    - We're consistently hitting our goals for the number of accounts we want to move to 6QA as well as our opportunity stage 0, 1, and 2 goals.

- BDRs are generating pipeline that's more than double the industry average, supporting our growing sales team and targets.

- We've done all of this while maintaining an industry-leading CAC!

STAGE 0s , 1s , 2s

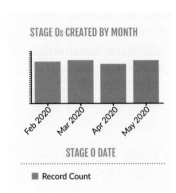

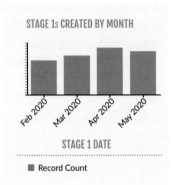

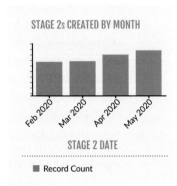

The plan in action: No forms, no spam, no cold calls

Did you notice what was conspicuously absent from each of these campaigns? That's right—the three verboten tactics: forms, spam, and cold calls. And does it look like our results suffered from their absence? *Hell no.* In fact, the whole reason we were as successful with each of these campaigns as we were is that we didn't piss off our customers by throwing up roadblocks to their learning, annoying them with irrelevant content, or harassing them when they weren't ready to hear from us. Instead, we followed our proven steps and made decisions based on real, data-based insights. When you do that, it's almost impossible to provide a bad customer experience. Process and insights are the secret sauce when it comes to real engagement with your future customers.

Following the five-step ABM process is essential if we want to bridge the divide between how B2B buyers want to buy and how sellers and marketers have traditionally operated. The result is a profoundly improved customer experience—and a straightforward path to meeting and exceeding your business objectives.

Now, how will you execute?

I hope these examples get your creative juices flowing on all the ways you can create amazing experiences. I could go on all day, writing up scenarios we have run and ideas for new ones. Remember, it all goes back to your business objective, budget, content creative, and the tactics at your disposal. The platform orchestrates the rest. Here are some plays to try:

Tier 1

- New Product Introduction
- Funding Announcement
- New Research Report

Tier 2

- Territory Warm Up
- Deal Blitz
- Increase ROI from an Event Series
- Door Opener

Tier 3

- New Customer Welcome Program
- Deal Acceleration Program
- Content Syndication

You've executed your campaign, but there's no time to rest on your laurels. There's always room for improvement, which we'll uncover in the next step.

Why We Have a Video-First Content Strategy

Our content strategy is all about providing a useful, relevant, and friction-free user experience—one that gives our future customers the information they need, when they need it, without making them jump through annoying hoops or hand over personal information. One of the key ways we do that is by personalizing content for intent and stage in the buying journey so we can engage in the right way, at the right time (which we described in our Tier 3 example).

Another way we make the user experience as easy and useful as possible is with our video-first content strategy. That's because video is increasingly becoming customers' first choice in how they consume educational content, and the trend is set to continue. "The amount of video content people consume online just keeps increasing," says Justin Gutwein, 6sense's content marketing manager and video master. "It's just the most engaging, clear way to communicate."

According to Forrester Research, "The human brain processes video 60,000 times faster than text ... B2B buyers are wired to deal with visual information and to remember stories. Reading large blocks of text is the type of heavy lifting our visually oriented brains are wired to avoid, which makes video the perfect medium to deliver information that business buyers will pay attention to."[1]

So what does a video-first strategy crossed with an intent + stage-based approach look like? Well here's how we do it:

- **Target.** You can't watch videos from under a rock, so once again, we spend no time on accounts in the target stage.

- **Awareness.** This is when accounts know they have a problem, and they're just starting to look for solutions. This is a prime time to get in front of them with useful content since we want to earn their trust early so we can continue to educate them throughout their buying journey. For accounts in the consideration stage, we have our TalkingSense video series—a thought leadership series designed to establish the 6sense team as the people to learn from. In it, we feature 20- to 30-minute interviews with industry thought leaders about the topics we know our prospects are interested in learning about, thanks to our intent insights. So for instance, for the keyword "ABM", we have a TalkingSense episode called "ABM Trends," in which I interview Gary Survis of Insight Partners about the latest and greatest trends in account-based marketing.

---

1   https://go.forrester.com/blogs/create-more-video-to-engage-your-b2b-buyers/

Consideration. In this stage, accounts have some understanding of their problem and the fact that solutions exist to address it. At this stage, we want to get our message in front of them and make it as easy as possible to learn from us. So for accounts in consideration stage, we have our MakingSense series, in which we do deeper dives into the topics our prospects are researching. Again using ABM as an example, we have an episode called "MakingSense of ABM (Account-based Marketing)," in which we help our prospects understand ABM in a way that aligns with both their buying stage and our business goals.

Decision. In the decision stage, accounts are weighing their options and deciding which one to go with. This is a great time to engage with buyers and provide proof points and validation. We know that when they're making tech buying decisions, 68 percent of decision-makers consider case studies to be the most valuable format.[2] So for this stage, we have videos with customer stories that help our prospects see firsthand how our solutions help others like them reach their goals. An example is a series of short videos with Saima Rashid of PTC, whom you met in Chapter 3, in which she talks about specific problems 6sense helps her solve—like identifying anonymous accounts.

Purchase. In this stage, our potential customers are comparing solutions, scheduling meetings, and deciding which solution is the best fit for them. We want to paint a picture of what it's really like to use 6sense, and we do that with our 6 for 6 series, in which we show how different roles within our organization use 6sense in their daily lives. For instance, we have a video called "How Our BDRs Use 6sense to Personalize Outreach Cadences" in which one of our BDRs gives a walk-through of how she uses 6sense to make her prospecting more intelligent and to drive more pipeline.

of being video-first is that we can use the videos we create to spin off even more ustin explains, "We are able to take that piece of pillar content and break it down dcast, shorter videos, blogs, infographics, etc. That way, we can take one big-nt, thought leadership piece of production and get lots of extra content out of it." e seeing impressive results from this strategy: Our average session duration is t longer than industry average. In other words, once people come to our website, icking around for a long time and learning from us instead of our competitors— e intended.

ps://www.forrester.com/report/Now+Tech+Online+Video+Platforms+For+B2B+Marketin

IT'S A SIMPLE QUESTION. WAS OUR MARKETING CAMPAIGN PROFITABLE OR NOT?

© marketoonist.com

Step 5: Inspect what you expect

Our CEO, Jason Zintak, is a brilliant CEO and GTM legend (and let's hope he never reads this, because he hates when we brag). One thing he taught me is to always "inspect what you expect." What does that mean in this context? Well it's not about attribution, and it's not about measuring for the sake of measuring. Instead, it's about inspecting each campaign against the goals we set up, seeing where it performed and where it didn't, and adjusting accordingly.

What I love about our segment-focused, account-based approach is that we can measure our campaigns at a granular level. We have the means to do it, and we need to—because that's the only way we can improve our campaigns and make sure that our precious budget dollars are engaging accounts in a meaningful way and driving predictable, measurable results.

So for every campaign, we need to measure cost versus increasing or decreasing account engagement, 6QA created, open opportunities, pipeline, and bookings. This allows us to see when certain elements of a campaign are underperforming, to benchmark our overall performance over time, to evaluate (and double down on) our top programs, and to cut what's not driving revenue.

So how exactly should you go about "inspecting what you expect"? I think of it like a tube of toothpaste. You want to start at the bottom and tightly roll up to get the every last drop of toothpaste in the tube. If you just go squeezing here and there, you're going to leave a lot of toothpaste in the tube. We want to do the same thing with every campaign we run.

For a Tier 2 campaign, here's what the roll-the-toothpaste inspection looks like:

- **Accounts reached.** Did you hit a critical mass of accounts you were targeting? If not, check your segment and bidding and make improvements.

- **View-through rate.** Was the ad interesting enough to get people to your website? If not, reevaluate the creative.

- **Account engagement.** Did you move the account forward in the buying journey? If not, look at the digital experience. What was on the page? Was it personalized for what your accounts care about? How long did they spend on the page? What content was consumed?

- **Meetings booked.** Did you have a compelling enough call-to-action? Did you hamper the meeting request with a cumbersome form? Walk through the process your future customers went through and see how you can make it easier and more attractive for them to book a meeting.

- **Pipeline created.** How was your BDR outreach? Was it timely? Did it use multiple channels? Did it address multiple personas? How personalized was it? Make improvements where necessary.

What you'll learn: No one is perfect

We've had some major successes using the process I've outlined in this chapter. But we've also found lots of room for improvement, thanks to inspecting what we expect.

For example, a few months ago we ran a campaign called "Do the Match." We had super-high hopes for it because it was grounded in one of our strongest differentiators: Our ability to match intent signals to accounts.

We set about creating the campaign and defined our business objective: To grab market share based on this differentiator. We set our creative, content, and budget and got to work creating some ads, a landing page, and a CTA that allowed prospects to put us to the test. We built our segment and the insights looked great, so we pressed play.

Well, we didn't get the results we expected. We reached a lot of accounts, but when we squeezed the toothpaste tube we realized our view-through rates weren't great and our engagement and conversions were worse. The culprit? Our creative. It was just kind of blah, and it wasn't engaging people the way we needed it to. So the whole campaign suffered.

At this point we could have scrapped it, but because we took a systematic look at what went wrong, we saw that we could make some tweaks and breathe new life into it. And we believed that if we fixed the problems, the campaign would provide real value to future customers. We tried again—this time with killer creative revolving around Valentine's Day. People loved it. It had amazing results both in terms of engaging ideal customers and creating new pipeline.

Lesson learned: Creativity still matters, and don't throw out the baby with the bathwater! Sometimes a campaign just needs some small adjustments to yield the results you knew it could have.

Another example I think about when I consider the value of JZ's advice to inspect what you expect was around Dreamforce week. The Dreamforce conference is like the Mardi Gras of the tech industry. It's a great opportunity to get in front of pretty much everyone you'd ever want to meet with, but it's also absolutely massive—meaning it can be really challenging to stand out.

Well, if there's one thing I love to do, it's to stand out. So we went all in on our Dreamforce presence. We created and refined a segment with our ideal potential customers who we knew would be there. We ran targeted, effective display ads. We created an amazing microsite to help people navigate their Dreamforce experience. We ran a fun and informative social campaign about the event. We offered white-glove concierge service for our customers at our office. I presented some wildly popular sessions at various ancillary events. And, of course, we threw some kickass (and strategic) parties.

In other words, we engaged the right accounts in the right way and provided a *ton* of value.

During the week, we were pumped. It was going *so damn well*. Everything went off without a hitch. We were getting incredible feedback and praise. And we were meeting with all the right accounts. We fell asleep dreaming of the buckets and buckets of pipeline we'd be filling when it was all over.

And then ... we got home, exhausted and hungover like everyone else, and things fizzled. Instead of gushes in our buckets, we were seeing drips. This did not line up with the signals we were getting at the event.

We quickly started to "inspect what we expect." Looking at our predefined goals and our processes, we could see where our expectations and our reality were misaligned. It turned out that our follow-up was suffering in part due to timing: Dreamforce happens right before Thanksgiving, and when people get back home, it's difficult to get them on the phone. So we adjusted our post-event engagement to accommodate the new reality. We created new content experiences to allow prospects to continue to learn from us. We re-examined our cadences and added those personalized Alyce gifts for high-value prospects. And we re-engaged in the new year, once the holidays had passed and people were ready to take on new projects again.

After making those adjustments, we were back on track—and Dreamforce week ended up being one of our higher-performing programs for 2019.

Another possibility, of course, is that you'll inspect your campaigns and determine that they're not worth saving. In that case, you can rely on your data, calculate your costs versus your results, and feel confident pulling the plug if it's not performing and isn't likely to perform even with adjustments.

Step 6: Communicate and repeat

If you haven't noticed by now, I'm an open book. Not just because it's who I am as a person, but because I know transparency is essential for building trust. And trust within an organization is essential for success. It's one of the reasons I'm such a fan of the V2MOM structure—full transparency means that we're all aware of what everyone is doing across the organization, where we're smashing expectations, and where we're struggling. I can't overstate how important it is to communicate openly and honestly in order for an organization to function together as a team instead of in competition with one another.

This culture of transparency and trust is essential with everything we've covered in this chapter as well—your revenue plan, your "red," your go-to-market-plan, your execution, and your results.

Communication is key here, but so is the right technology. At 6sense, our sales leader, our customer success leader, and I are all looking at the exact same dashboard. We're working off the same data—and we all trust the data—so we all know what's working and what isn't. We have a rare sort of alignment across the revenue side of the organization, and I credit a lot of that to our transparency, good reporting, and quality data.

There you have it. You've gone through the entire process for putting this new approach to sales and marketing in practice. But you're not done—you need to keep repeating this process, refining it, and sharing your amazing results. And if you need some inspiration, just look to the Impartner case study on page 134. When I need to be reminded of how all this hard work pays off, I remind myself of their story. They've fully embraced orchestrated account engagement and are crushing the prospect experience in ways that get me so fired up. I bet they'll light a fire under you too.

How Impartner uses insights to win with Personalization

Impartner is an industry leading partner relationship management (PRM) company and one of our 6senseis. They've totally transformed their sales and marketing approach—as well as their customer experience—by running their campaigns through the ABM process outlined here. As a result, they've been delivering personalized experiences at such an inspiring level.

Jordan Linford, Impartner's director of demand generation, spoke about a few of their most successful campaigns at our Breakthrough event in Napa late last year, and I was seriously blown away. Here's an example of their two best-performing campaigns, both made possible thanks to trustworthy intent data, predictive modeling, account-based orchestration ... and, of course, a super talented team.

The "New Channel Chief" campaign

The marketing team at Impartner noticed a sweet spot in their buying journey. When accounts had a high intent score plus a new channel hire in a decision-making capacity, conversion rates were really high. So they decided to capitalize on that with a super-personalized campaign.

Here's how it works: Impartner uses 6sense to identify accounts that fit their firmographic profile, who have high intent scores, and who have hired a new channel chief in the past six months. They then take a brand-new iPad and load it up with a personalized Impartner user portal, a demo video, and an ebook for channel chiefs. A BDR reaches out to the new hire to ask if they're interested in receiving this new iPad. (And who would say no to that?)

They then send off the iPad with a note that says something along the lines of, "Welcome to your new role! I know you're eager to make a real difference in the company you just joined. Our research shows that one of the best ways to make a difference is [fill in the blank]. And here's a personalized portal I've loaded for you

When the prospect opens the portal, Impartner gets alerted, and the salesperson reaches out to offer a demo on the spot. Talk about engaging the right way!

It's a pretty radical way to get a prospect's attention, but it's super-tailored and timed exactly right—and it's been incredibly successful. "When people hear we're sending out iPads they think, 'Wow, that's expensive,'" Jordan says. "But when you see that we can convert around 40 to 44 percent, it just makes sense financially." Plus, Impartner has been able to decrease overall marketing spend elsewhere by cutting all the campaigns that weren't yielding results, which freed up money to spend a bit more on the accounts that are most likely to close.

The "Red Carpet" campaign

Another hugely successful campaign they run is called their "Red Carpet" campaign. As the name would suggest, this is a real VIP-level campaign aimed at high-value accounts. To select their best accounts, Impartner sets up a segment in 6sense for enterprise accounts that fit their ICP. Then they start to watch for activity. As soon as they see a spike in engagement, Impartner gets to work creating a dynamic landing page specifically for that company. The landing page displays content they know the company is researching and speaks to their specific pain points. They target them with coordinating ads that specifically mention the company by name.

When the account starts showing the right engagement signals, a BDR will reach out and start a discussion, again driving them to the customized landing page. The outreach is so targeted and specific to what the prospect's challenges are that it's almost impossible for them to say no. Red carpet campaigns boast a response rate of 64 percent, and 42 percent convert to an active sales opportunity!

Even with these highly personalized, sometimes pricey campaigns, Impartner is seeing incredible results from implementing the right technology to power their ABM strategy. Their customer acquisition costs are way down, they have more ways to reach customers, and they've opened up into two more verticals that they never knew were available to them. Deal sizes are larger, and overall marketing spend is down, despite the fact that the organization has grown exponentially.

CHAPTER 5

THE MODERN SALES ORGANIZATION

I decided to write No Forms. No Spam. No Cold Calls. *because I saw many of my marketing and sales colleagues struggling to connect with customers and future customers in a meaningful way. I knew that it was time to shake up how we do things—and so I put down on paper everything I've learned about modern revenue operations through data, tech, and true account-based engagement.*

The response has been ... wow! I've heard from so many of you that the book provided the roadmap you needed to change the direction of your companies. That you've been able to ditch the old, tired tactics that were pushing customers away instead of drawing them closer. And that the book has helped your teams get aligned on a modern, strategic approach to sales and marketing.

I've also heard from several readers that you wanted to learn more—specifically from the sales perspective. Because after all, though I work closely with sales and was a seller in the past, I'm not in the trenches day to day. So for this, the newest chapter of No Forms. No Spam. No Cold Calls., I'm handing over the mic to my friend and colleague Mark Ebert, chief revenue officer (CRO) at 6sense. He's one of the best at understanding modern selling principles—and putting them into practice to lead one of the most effective, productive, and happy sales teams I've ever worked with.

The CRO Perspective: A New Era of Selling

Selling has transformed dramatically since I got my start 17 years ago. Back then, the sellers I knew (myself included) took pride in the grind mentality. Working 14- or 15-hour days, seven days a week wasn't just the norm, it was a badge of honor. I felt like a hero when I would single-handedly prospect, work, and close a deal the hard way. Taking a deal from beginning to end all on my own felt like the greatest accomplishment of all. The harder I worked to get the sale, the sweeter the success.

I'd bet a lot of us who are now CROs or CSOs grew up in the same culture. We learned to value the first-to-the-office, last-to-leave, limit-pushing mentality. But selling has come a long way since the *Glengarry Glen Ross* days, and the teams we're now leading are not interested in that type of grind.

The shift has been underway for years now, but Covid accelerated it. After two-plus years of being grounded, working from home, and unable to visit customers, sellers are reassessing their values and priorities, and they're getting serious about work-life balance. That means they want to work smarter, not harder. They want to hit their numbers without killing themselves to do it. There's a bigger focus on mental health and balance, as well as a recognition from sales leaders that productivity *only* comes from sellers who are mentally fit and ready to perform.

Some things haven't changed, of course. Sales is still a really hard job. Success still depends on talent, dedication, and really hard work. But we now have tools, strategies, and data available to us today that can make that work pay off.

I'm not suggesting we ease up on our goals or expectations. The opposite, actually. Sellers still need to hit their numbers, and as sales leaders, we still need to hold them to the same high standards we've always expected. I'm arguing that the path to running a high-performing team is vastly different than it used to be. We now have data and tech at our disposal that can increase efficiency and attainment in ways that would have seemed like science fiction even 10 years ago. And as sales leaders, it's our responsibility to provide the toolset to enable sellers to work as efficiently as humanly possible.

In this chapter, I share my vision of modern sales leadership. I believe that with the right data, tools, leadership tactics, and strategy, CROs can set up their teams—and their companies—for growth and a more predictable path to building pipeline.

Lighting Up the Dark Funnel™

A big difference in how we successfully sell today gets to the core of how modern B2B buying happens. Buyers now conduct most of their research online (nearly 70 percent, according to Forrester), and they do so anonymously. They also do their research so thoroughly that many have come to some kind of buying decision before ever explicitly engaging with us.

Buyers visit dozens—or even hundreds—of online resources across the Internet, mining information from industry publications, blogs, social networks, influence outlets, and review sites like G2 and TrustRadius.

In addition to this external research, buyers are also anonymously exploring your website. Since this traffic has historically been hard to de-anonymize, most revenue teams have simply ignored it and relied instead on website forms to cajole visitors into handing over their contact information.

But as Latané has explained, buyers are increasingly hesitant to identify themselves to us just for a free ebook. In fact, only 2–5 percent of all B2B website visits result in a form fill. We know that there are far more legitimately interested buyers surfing your site than that—after all, they're visiting for a reason.

Unless you know what buying teams are doing—both on your website and off—you're never quite sure which stage they might be at in the buying process, or how that might align with your sales funnel. That's even true for those elusive form fillers. They might have just filled out a form on your website for the first time, but do you really know where they were before that, or what they know already?

The good news is that as buyers do their research, they leave behind a goldmine of digital breadcrumbs that can help us better serve them—but only if we have the ability to pick up and examine those crumbs.

This breadcrumb trail exists in what we call the Dark Funnel™, a data realm full of signals about buyers' interests and intent—the kind of data that can help us move accounts through the sales funnel. These signals are brimming with incredibly useful and actionable intent data that sellers can use to provide more relevant value and sell more effectively.

The great potential of the Dark Funnel™ lies in combining those countless, disparate intent signals spread across the Internet into a cohesive picture. This picture can empower your revenue team to navigate prospects through the sales funnel with confidence and answer important questions:

- How many companies are in market for what you offer?
- Where should your sales and sales development teams invest their energies?
- What stage of the buying journey are buyers in?

When you can't see into the Dark Funnel™, you run the risk of missing deals you could have won or coming in so late to deals that your sellers can't effectively compete. You can even alienate buyers by totally misunderstanding them.

Some of the insights that exist in the Dark Funnel™ include the following:

- The duration of an organization's buyer journey
- The size of the buying team
- The sources where those team members get their information
- The financial situation their company might be in, which informs their ability or need to purchase new solutions
- The technological condition they're in, which tells you if their tech stack is compatible with your solution

In addition to information about where the buyer is right now, the Dark Funnel™ also holds insights about where they're going next, so you can predict and prepare for an upcoming need.

For instance, did a potential customer just make a purchase that's in the same ecosystem your product is in? If so, now is probably a good time to engage. On the other hand, if they just signed a two-year contract with your competitor, it would be valuable for your team to know, so they can work the account from other angles and perhaps prioritize elsewhere in the short term. In strategic sales, buyers may decide to switch 12+ months before the renewal is up, which means that's go-time to start turning the ship around.

Another important indicator is hiring trends. A change in leadership often signals a good time to reach out—especially leadership that's related to the product you sell. If you sell benefits software, it's valuable to know when a new CHRO comes on board. But any hiring activity can be significant, depending on your focus. For 6sense, seeing that a company is hiring a lot of BDRs is a great sign that they could soon be in the market for our solution.

Market updates can also signal that it's a good time to act. One of our customers sells data rooms. They know that companies that are engaging in merger and acquisition activity will have increased needs for secure data rooms. Being alerted to that kind of market change allows this customer to get into deals faster than the competition by predicting an upcoming need.

As modern sales leaders, it's our responsibility to provide the infrastructure that allow our sellers to do their jobs effectively and efficiently. By lighting up the Dark Funnel™ with the right revenue technology solutions, you can accurately connect those bread-crumbs back to the companies leaving them.

Being able to stay on top of all these difficult-to-track signals, and then having them seamlessly aggregated and served up to your team, gives you a competitive edge. It takes what was previously in the dark and turns it into a revenue moment.

Here are some of the types of information we find in the Dark Funnel™:

	BEHAVIOR	READINESS	PSYCHOGRAPHICS
EXTERNAL DARK FUNNEL™	1 Accounts researching solutions like yours 2 Accounts comparing competitor solutions to yours 3 Accounts purchasing tangential solutions 4 Accounts researching keywords relevant to your category or solution	1 Accounts with expiring competitive solutions 2 Accounts with the financial ability to buy your solution 3 Accounts with an unmet need or problem they want to solve	1 Insights into how to approach key buying committee members
INTERNAL DARK FUNNEL™	1 Accounts that are showing intense interest on your website 2 Buying committee members that are engaging but not yet MQLs 3 Sales rep interactions (not normally entered into CRM) 4 Sales contacts (not normally entered into CRM)	1 Product usage for positioning upsell opportunities 2 Second and subsequent leads from companies with open opportunities	1 Account health scores for upsell and cross-sell 2 Customer support case content

Putting Reps in a Position to Win

Uncovering the insights hiding in the Dark Funnel™ is a big part of how modern sales leaders structure their strategy and put their teams in a position to win.

CROs all have a revenue goal we need to meet, and we work backward from that number to develop our strategy. We determine our capacity plan to make sure we have enough reps to hit our target and then calculate quota based on conversion rates and historical attainment. Then we make sure we optimize territories, accounts, etc. to the field.

Traditionally, we have three main buckets to pull pipeline from when it comes to net-new business:

- **Inbound.** These are the hand-raisers, plus the list marketing drums up for us.
- **Outbound.** These are the opportunities the sales team creates for themselves through prospecting.
- **Partners.** These are opportunities created within our partner ecosystem.

This arrangement doesn't give CROs as much control over the plan as we wish we had, and traditional lead-based marketing has left a lot to be desired. Thankfully, that's changing as more and more CMOs adopt modern account-based engagement practices. But still, inbound is a bucket that's not in sales' control. So we've relied very heavily on prospecting to build pipeline.

And if we're being honest, our outbound efforts aren't always reliable, either. We often decide which accounts to target based on logos and hunches. Our reps will pour hours, days, months into pursuing a big-name prospect only to hit dead end after dead end. And for modern sellers who expect to have the tools they need to make their hard work pay off, this can be more than demoralizing—it can be the path to the exit.

But for sales leaders who can see into the Dark Funnel™, they have the ability to be more data-driven and efficient with how they predictably build pipeline.

Of all the companies we could sell to, there are some that are absolutely not in-market for what we're selling, and maybe won't ever be. Others are just beginning their research. Yet others are in the middle of evaluating options. Big data and machine learning make it possible to understand where every account is in their own buyer's journey specifically for the product category that you sell. This then allows us to translate that into a score that changes over time.

These scores are a tool we can use to determine when to trigger certain sales and marketing behavior for outbound prospecting. At 6sense, we call accounts that are showing readiness to buy *6QAs (6sense Qualified Accounts)*.

The 6QA brings process and artificial intelligence to lead and account scoring, which to date has been largely a rules-based exercise informed by subjective human judgment.

To accurately identify accounts that are most likely to convert to opportunities, we use predictive models based on historical opportunity data, and the AI continuously learns from ongoing opportunities, intent signals, and engagement activity across channels. This is based on real data from the CRM, marketing automation platform, and 6sense's proprietary intent network that is all processed by AI and machine learning models.

These models work to actively predict what accounts are an ideal fit, when they may be ready to buy (6QA), and how well the prospecting team is doing at reaching them.

- *Account Profile Fit Score.* A measure of how similar a company is to your ideal customer profile (ICP), using firmographic and technographic factors. Accounts are given both a numeric score (1–100) and a classification (strong, moderate, or weak fit).

- *Account Buying Stage.* Where an account is in the buying journey (target, awareness, consideration, decision, or purchase). Accounts in the decision and purchase stage are considered to be a 6QA and ready for immediate sales outreach. In addition to the buyer journey stage, every account is given a correlated numerical account intent score. The higher the intent score, the further an account is in its buying journey and the more likely it is to open or progress an opportunity.

- *Account Reach Score.* A measure of the quality, quantity, recency, and diversity of outreach activities across personas and channels on a given account compared to those of previously won opportunities. It evaluates a prospecting team's effort so they can prioritize further engagement activities. Accounts are given a reach classification (high, low, or no reach).

6SENSE SCORES

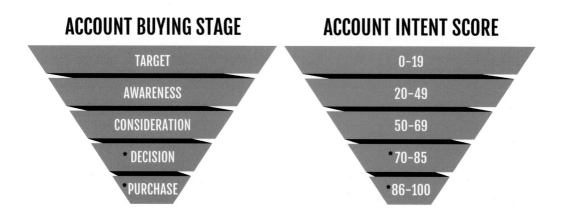

ACCOUNT BUYING STAGE

- TARGET
- AWARENESS
- CONSIDERATION
- *DECISION
- *PURCHASE

ACCOUNT INTENT SCORE

- 0-19
- 20-49
- 50-69
- *70-85
- *86-100

Indicates the likelihood of an opportunity opening/progressing in the next 90 days (*higher likelihood)

ACCOUNT PROFILE FIT

STRONG | MODERATE | WEAK

Reflects how closely the company's firmographic profile resembles accounts with past and current opportunities (Example: industry, revenue, range, etc.)

There's no arbitrary point system here. The scores are driven by big data—including all that Dark Funnel™ data—and AI predictions. Subjectivity is out of the equation, meaning there's no more, "I think an ebook download is worth 2 points, and marketing thinks it's worth 3 points."

Right from within our system, we can run backtests to prove out our assumptions about which accounts are the best to work. We can actually report back how much higher these accounts convert to open opportunities because we are reading direct from our own data in CRM.

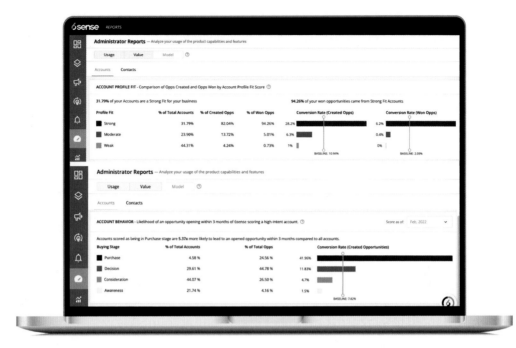

For instance, here we can see that our conversion rates are vastly higher for strong-fit accounts and accounts that are in the purchase stage of the buying journey. So it's clear that these are the accounts we should be working—no guesswork or opinions involved. And that does wonders for sales and marketing alignment. We can agree that working more accounts is not the answer; it's all about working the right accounts.

One More Dial to Turn

With 6QAs, I can apply a formula to our entire sales motion. Based on our company's historical attainment data, I ask the following:

- How many accounts do my reps need to have in their names?

- What's our conversion rate for 6QAs?

- How many 6QAs do I need to distribute to everyone?

And I have some control over the results: I can adjust criteria for the 6QA to ensure we are working enough accounts to predictably build enough pipeline. In addition to qualifying accounts based on buying stage, intent, and fit, we can also layer on other considerations:

- Region
- Vertical
- Industry
- Solution
- Segment

So for instance, if we need more 6QAs to feed to reps in a particular segment, we can customize the criteria used to define a 6QA to include more accounts by lowering the score threshold.

We recently wanted to increase the number of tier-one accounts we were targeting, but we still wanted to engage them at the moment (and in the way) that was most likely to result in a conversion. We adjusted our qualification criteria so that tier-one accounts that were in consideration stage and were also researching us or our competitors on G2 would be identified as 6QAs, since we know that G2 research is a good indicator of readiness.

Another example: A network security company may know that if an account increases its spending on network security in general, that's a prime time to reach out. So they could specify that whenever an account crosses the $500k per year threshold of spending on network security, the account 6QAs regardless of their other criteria.

Conversely, if we have too many accounts in a particular segment, we can dial back on the accounts we prioritize by narrowing the qualification criteria. With the high volume of accounts we have in the commercial segment, for instance, we can decide we only want sales reps to prioritize companies that are in the purchase stage. Then marketing can work the earlier stage accounts with automated plays so that the criteria for being handed over to sales is steeper. And again, we can backtest to see whether our assumptions prove to be good ones, which keeps sales and marketing on the same page at every point in the process.

This approach allows us to work with our partners in marketing to manage our sellers' capacity and make sure they're working the absolute best accounts that they can. We've seen a 50 percent increase in our win rates with this approach—again because we're putting sellers in a position to win.

Having this list of objectively good accounts to work gives us sales leaders more control over the entire demand funnel. We now have another lever to keep our sellers fed—without having to cross our fingers and hope for good inbound leads. That's because the 6QA is a proven demand signal, based on buyers' propensity to buy. It's not based on marketing arbitrarily scoring activities like form fills, as is the case in traditional lead-based marketing and selling.

The 6QA can make a big difference in creating a successful revenue operating model. It signals the ideal time for the handoff between marketing and sales. Before an account becomes a 6QA, marketing is examining earlier demand signals and warming the account. When the account becomes a 6QA, we know it's the optimal time for sales to reach out and get the best results. It helps optimize time across the entire revenue team.

To be clear, the 6QA is not revenue served up on a silver platter. Your sales team still needs to work it, and of course, they still need to work the entire account from the start, not just one lead (contact). And depending on your specific situation, the level of sales involvement with earlier-stage accounts will vary.

The 6QA is not a magic bullet, but it gives our reps a simple and trustworthy way to prioritize their time. Every morning they can log into their dashboards and see which accounts are most likely to be receptive to their outreach today, and they can plan their days around that.

What about those early-stage accounts?

Sometimes when I talk to CROs about this "new school" approach to account prioritization, their hackles go up. The idea of abandoning accounts in the awareness and consideration stages in favor of those in the decision and purchase stages just doesn't sit right. Aren't we too late at purchase and decision? Shouldn't we be working those beginning stage accounts so we get into deals earlier than our competition?

There are certainly times when sales needs to work accounts before they get into purchase and decision—for instance, in companies with a narrow ICP, or in specific segments. But the 6QA can be an important tool in your belt for determining the best time to work accounts.

I'm not advocating for abandoning early-stage accounts. I'm arguing that devoting sales resources before an account is ready isn't the best use of time, nor the best way to provide a positive customer experience. For most of our accounts, it makes the most sense for our marketing department to keep working on engaging and educating not-yet-ready accounts through advertising, content syndication, direct mail, events, email, and more.

Conversely, if your sales targets are so high that sales needs to work earlier-stage accounts, then that's what you'll do. It's helpful in either situation to at least know where these accounts are in their readiness and have assumptions for how long and how hard we may have to fight to convert them.

Our tech then keeps an eye on each account's level of engagement. We make sure we continue to earn their trust and stay at the top of their minds so that when they do make that shift to decision or purchase, they're eager to hear from us. All those touches from marketing are recorded and visible to the entire team, creating full transparency and alignment. AEs are able to see when and how marketing is nurturing accounts, and it raises the red flag if any accounts are getting left behind.

So no, we're not ignoring early-stage accounts. Our process makes it clear who's responsible for what, and when so we can progress accounts through the journey using the most ideal method at each stage.

REVENUE OPERATING MODEL

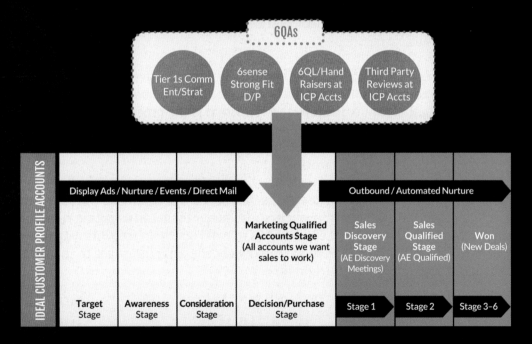

Accounts > Leads

We know that modern buying teams for big B2B purchases include six to 10 individuals.[1] That's a big reason that the old lead-based marketing and sales strategies just don't work anymore—getting one individual on board does little for us if we need the buy-in of an entire buying team in order to close a deal.

As I explained, the 6QA is a very important signal of intent. And when we see that signal, our BDRs and AEs need to kick into gear working the entire account. In earlier chapters, we cited research that shows a single person showing activity converts less than 1 percent of the time. But when a second or third person is engaged, the activity is far more meaningful—and likelier to become an opportunity.

That's why everyone across the revenue team—marketers and sellers alike—needs to be dedicated to multithreading accounts or connecting with multiple personas across the buying team right from the start. The longer the opportunity goes on, the harder it is to engage and set meetings with multiple contacts. That's why using leads rather than accounts is so ineffective; MQLs are inherently single-threaded. I want to ensure that Latané and her team are helping us throughout the journey to get as many key buyers engaged as possible.

When marketing teams are measured or comped on how many MQLs they create, we're set up for single-threading (and sales-marketing misalignment) from the beginning. Same is true when BDRs are comped on only booking a single meeting. A more modern approach—one that ensures multithreading at every stage of the process—is to comp based on engaging multiple personas.

The idea of multithreading, of course, is not new. Sales leaders have been preaching it for years. But even though we all know how important it is, it can be pretty hard to get our teams to really buy in. I think the big reason for that is the process today is clunky and cumbersome. If we tell our sellers to engage multiple contacts but don't give them a fast and easy way to find those contacts, purchase their contact info if needed, and know about those contacts, we're making it too hard.

Here's a place where modern tech makes all the difference. We now have the ability to match specific activity with different buyer personas so our team can engage in relevant and meaningful ways. It also makes it easy for AEs to build out their accounts with quality contact data for multiple contacts so we can deliver the right messages to the right people within the buying team, at the right time.

---

1   https://www.gartner.com/en/sales/insights/b2b-buying-journey

The idea is to use tech that makes it so easy to multithread that reps almost can't *not* do it. Because as we know, we can preach the values of engaging multiple personas all day, but if we put up barriers to doing it, it's just not going to happen. On the other hand, if we serve it up for them, there's no excuse not to do it. They can see, "This is your next best action. This is the next persona you need to engage. Click here to instantly acquire their contact data. Click here to add them to a cadence …" In a matter of three clicks, they can easily do what we've been telling them to do forever: make multithreading a reality.

Then, as leaders, we can feel good about having given our team every tool necessary—and then holding them accountable. We can easily see which personas are being worked as well as how and by whom. When there are gaps, we can make sure they get filled.

This level of visibility is very helpful for our forecasting. Since accounts with multiple engaged personas are much more likely to close, I train my managers to track this in forecast calls. We look at a persona map that tells us at a glance—red, yellow, or green—where we're hitting our multithreading goals and where we're missing.

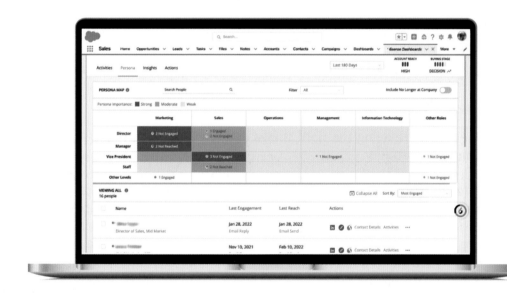

Using principles similar to the ones we use for our account predictive models, we can gauge whether a persona is likely an ideal buying team member and then measure how well we're engaging them. By merging historical opportunity and contact data with continuously updated engagement activity, intent signals, and enriched contact data, we can create an incredibly accurate picture of the buying team.

These models work to actively predict what personas are most important for buying decisions and how well your team is engaging with each member of the buying team.

- *Contact Fit Grade.* A measure of how important a persona is for closing deals and whether contacts that align to these personas exist in CRM or MAP. Uncover gaps in the buying team and acquire them when needed to accelerate deals. Contact personas are given a grade of strong, moderate, or weak profile fit.

- *Contact Engagement Grade.* A measure of how engaged a contact is with your brand based on a comparison to previously won opportunities. This model goes beyond arbitrary lead scoring and uses big data to understand the level of engagement or your contacts to predict success. Each known contact is given an engagement grade of A, B, C, or D.

Prioritization in Action

As we've learned, modern tech and AI can tell us two very important things:

1. The best accounts to work
2. Whether we're doing the right things and engaging with the right people to open an opportunity

With that information, we can help our sellers transform how they prioritize their time. In sales, time is our greatest resource (some would argue our *only* resource). As sales leaders, it's our responsibility to give our people the tools they need to prioritize and structure their days to ensure the most success in the least amount of time.

By keeping your BDRs and AEs laser-focused on right-fit, in-market accounts—and by making it easy for your reps to engage multiple personas on those accounts—you can make sure they're making the best use of every single day. So instead of low-impact activities seemingly done at random, we can serve up the activities that are likely to lead to the outcomes we need.

Instead of working lots of accounts a little bit, reps can work a few accounts a lot—surrounding the accounts with the types of outreach that are proven to work.

For instance, if an account was researching your competitor yesterday, or if they anonymously visited your website, or if they were checking out your reviews on G2 or TrustRadius, that's pretty valuable information and a good indicator that they might be in market to buy. With tech that can peek into the Dark Funnel™ and see these activities, weigh their significance based on persona, recency, and frequency, and send the signal when it's time to prioritize outreach on that account, our reps can spend their time in the places with the highest likelihood of opening an opportunity.

In addition to helping your reps decide which accounts to prioritize, revenue technology also makes it incredibly easy for them to reach out to the right contacts at those accounts. It arms them with contact data as well as rich insights about what these potential customers are researching right now. That means reps can contact these accounts easily and deliver a message that is hyper-relevant and likely to resonate. They'll know what complementary and competing tech the prospect has, so they can talk about how their solution compares to (or works with) what's already in their stack.

Let's take an example from Derek Levine, who was recently promoted from AE to director of enterprise sales for 6sense:

> When I see an account is in market and is researching "predictive models," that's flashing lights because that's a huge differentiator for us. This informs me of the pain the account is researching and what I should be leading with in my LinkedIn messenger, my Drift videos, my LinkedIn voicemails, my cadences. And since I have contact information for multiple personas on the account, I can tweak these messages a bit for each contact and multithread the account from the beginning.

Note that Derek isn't doing just one thing. He's not just leaving a voicemail, checking the box, and moving on to the next account. He's coming at it from a plethora of angles. That's what I'm talking about when I say that this isn't a magic bullet—it still takes skill, effort, strategy, and tenacity on the part of our sellers.

One of the reasons he can bring his A-game to every customer outreach is that he's not trying to work a list of 500 accounts. He has a select list of the accounts most likely to convert to an opportunity, so he can take the time to get to know them and work them with highly personalized, multichannel, multi-persona outreach.

We've seen this prioritization approach work time and again for our own team and for our customers. In fact, we did an analysis[2] and found that within just two quarters of using this approach, customers were putting 56 percent of their effort toward in-market accounts, and those accounts were driving 79 percent of their revenue. That's a 1.4x efficiency multiplier over working accounts not identified as in-market, meaning the same revenue can be generated with 40 percent less effort (or 40 percent fewer leads!) when the revenue team focuses 100 percent of their efforts on 6sense accounts.

We saw other big benefits as well. Within the first four quarters of our customers prioritizing in-market accounts (we update this data on an ongoing basis):

- Average deal value was 2x higher.

- Win rates improved 10 percent.

- Average days to close was down 25 percent.

The improvements in both revenue maximization and revenue effectiveness make a big difference in hitting your revenue targets as efficiently as possible. For example: If deals from 100 non-6QA accounts deliver $100K in revenue, our analysis indicates deals from 100 6QA accounts will deliver $220K.

Those numbers are pretty impressive. And they're only possible because of the modern tech we have available to us. Whereas we used to prioritize based on general data like company size, revenue, and industry, we now have the ability to hone in on more relevant data—the kind that shows us an account's propensity to buy at any given point in time. These accounts are the ones with the highest conversion rates, so less effort will net greater results. It's the key to helping your reps hyperfocus their time and have the most success in a modern selling environment.

At the same time that we're staying focused on these in-market accounts and working them voraciously, we're also keeping our eye on ways to build demand throughout the funnel. Sometimes that means working accounts in earlier stages to help them to understand that they have a problem, and that we can solve it. And in strategic accounts, sellers may need work every account every day no matter what stage they're in. But understanding the urgency of the 6QA can be very helpful for helping sellers prioritize their time and energy.

---

2   https://6sense.com/resources/home/business-impact-framework?x=SdZuOZ

WHY FOCUS ON 6SENSE QUALIFIED ACCOUNTS (6QAs)?

A 6QA is an account within your Ideal Customer Profile (ICP) that has reached the Decision or Purchase stage (intent > 70) and has no open opportunities. An account stays in 6QA for 60 days or until an opportunity opens.

80%
Opportunities
Came From
6QAs

70%
New Business
Revenue From
6QAs

33%
Higher New Biz
Win Rate From
6QAs

ASSIGNING AND WORKING 6QAs DIRECTLY TRANSLATES INTO OPPORTUNITIES AND REVENUE.

In-Market Accounts Drive the Revenue Team

"77 percent of opportunities created are ones that 6sense identified as being in decision and purchase stages. The concept of "in-market" accounts has permeated not only the sales team, but the entire revenue operations team."

~ Casey Carey, *CMO*, Kazoo

Old-school vs. new-school territory design

Territory design is another important aspect of sales strategy that is being transformed by modern approaches. Traditionally, territories have been static lists of accounts that salespeople work all year long—regardless of whether or not those accounts are showing intent.

In strategic sales, that list might be pretty short and made up of only big-ticket accounts. But further downmarket, reps can have hundreds, maybe even a thousand accounts in their name. And they're supposed to be working them all. Of course, that's impossible, so they instead set their eyes on the biggest logos, hoping for a big payoff. And whether those accounts are in market or not, they work them—often pouring months into accounts that will never become opportunities.

Just as big data and AI have changed how we can help reps prioritize their outreach, they've also changed the way we design territories to begin with. We're now able to bring dynamic territories into play, periodically shedding the accounts that are showing no engagement and replacing them with fresh accounts that are interested right now.

This dynamic, data-driven approach does two things: First, it allows us to narrow down the number of accounts a rep is expected to work, so they can dedicate their full attention to the ones that are likely to convert.

Second, it boosts confidence, big time. When they're only working accounts that are proven to be in-market, reps' attainment skyrockets. And knowing that they'll be able to refresh their list with new, interested accounts every few weeks or months keeps them optimistic about future wins.

Before we had the revenue technology tools currently available to us, this dynamic approach to territory design would have been too labor-intensive to be feasible. But now, with a constantly updated view into what our prospects are doing and the AI to turn that into action, the process is pretty effortless. It's also infinitely flexible—allowing sales leaders to tailor it to their company's specific situation and to refine it in a way that makes sense for each segment.

This is another place where we need to rethink our glorification of the grind. Some sellers have a hero mentality—they think they earn a badge of honor by creating an opportunity from something ice cold. But a lot of times, that's not the fastest or easiest path to revenue. So when possible, depending on the number of accounts in your TAM and other considerations specific to your industry, focusing on fewer in-market accounts is something to consider.

Depending on your TAM and how many AEs you need to hit your revenue targets, simply knowing what you have to work with is helpful. If you have to distribute mostly cold accounts to your team because of your particular situation, that's fine. But getting clear on that can help you understand the profile of the sellers you want to hire, or how you train them to challenge the status quo.

Simply having objective data about what you have to work with is invaluable—both for CROs and our counterparts in marketing.

When Less Is More

Some reps, and even some sales leaders, balk at the idea of smaller territories. They think that a mile-long list of accounts correlates with greater opportunity. But in fact, it doesn't. Having a honed list of the right accounts is far more efficient and sets reps up for greater, more efficient success.

Derek Levine shared his thoughts on what it was like for him to shift from previous roles with massive lists of accounts to 6sense, where he had relatively few:

At previous companies, I had 750 accounts in my name. Some companies have 1,000. How do you even work that many accounts? Usually what happens is reps and marketing will focus on the biggest, sexiest logos.

The problem is those accounts may not be interested in what you have to sell. Or they may have just signed a contract a month ago, or they might not have budget.

At 6sense, the big shift (and how I've been so successful) is that I focus on the accounts that are going to turn into pipeline. So at the beginning of every quarter, I start with 60 accounts. That's it. When I first saw that, I freaked out, thinking, "How am I going to hit my number with 60 accounts?" But then I realized 40 of these 60 are in decision and purchase stage, and if I reach out to them with the right messaging at the right time, the likelihood that they'll convert into an opportunity is far greater than if I spend countless hours at the wrong time with companies that aren't in-market.

Old-school marketing and sales get together and make a list of accounts based on TAM fit and revenue. And that's how reps start their quarter or year.

At 6sense I re-tier my accounts every quarter. I keep 20 as tier ones and the others are kept in my name based on where they are in their buyer's journey or the intent they're showing. I keep the low-hanging fruit that I haven't opened up opportunities for yet, and we dynamically change unassigned accounts once they 6QA. So we start the quarter with 60 accounts but may end the quarter with 120, when we do the same exercise again.

DYNAMIC TERRITORIES

THE OLD SCHOOL ANNUAL PROCESS

DYNAMIC TERRITORIES

Every December, SalesOps creates the initial list

Manager revises it

Mgr and Reps iterated through changes

Ops updates CRM in February

Reps are spending time on accounts that are not in-market and missing out on good opportunities

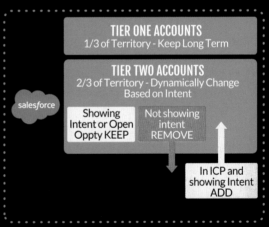

TIER ONE ACCOUNTS
1/3 of Territory - Keep Long Term

TIER TWO ACCOUNTS
2/3 of Territory - Dynamically Change Based on Intent

Showing Intent or Open Oppty KEEP

Not showing intent REMOVE

salesforce

In ICP and showing Intent ADD

Reps keep their tier ones and are dynamically assigned good in-market accounts. They are working the right accounts!

Getting into New Markets + Verticals

In any growing company, there will come a time when you need to find new accounts to sell to, and you'll need to find the best ways to start addressing more and more of your TAM. As always, prioritization is key here. As we've learned, being laser-focused on where you place your bets yields much greater rewards than trying to reach every possible account.

This comes into play when we're thinking about geo or vertical expansions—both expensive propositions. These endeavors are high risk, high reward, so it's essential to choose wisely. The same insights that inform our territories also take the mystery and guesswork out of deciding whether to break into new markets or verticals. With data and AI showing us which companies are in-market at any given time, we can build out segments related to industry, company size, location, etc., and learn precisely how much potential opportunity exists.

Here again it's essential to work shoulder-to-shoulder with your CMO—and it's really important that that person be someone who understands how to use data and insights strategically. I'm lucky to have that partner in Latané, who is always careful to make sure I don't just hire AEs or spin up territories without her. Just like I'm always cognizant of having enough accounts for all my sellers, so is she. Together, we need to evaluate any new market to ensure that we'll have enough accounts to support our sellers—as well as a winning strategy to help them succeed.

In the past, without modern tech to support expansions, we'd end up in one of two scenarios. The first was analysis paralysis, leading to decisions made with the proverbial dart thrown at the wall. I've seen this type of scenario play out time and again. Go-to-market planning meetings and market modeling are happening in philosophical discussions instead of data-driven, strategic ones. A company hears that their competitors are opening a Hong Kong office, and all of a sudden they're convinced they need to break into APAC. But is there actually any data supporting that move? Or is it just a gut-level fear of missing out on what your competitors are doing?

In the second scenario, teams would pour hundreds of thousands of dollars, and many months, into an involved expansion-planning process. That's the situation Jessica Klek, vice president of strategic sales at 6sense, found herself in at a previous company when she was working to build out a new vertical—without the help of technology to identify in-market accounts.

"We hired a consultant, we did a full analysis, we did our due diligence ... and we spent six figures. But at the end of the day, it didn't provide the data that we needed to ramp quickly," she says. "The accounts we identified weren't even in-market, and a lot of in-market accounts were left on the table."

The difference was crystalized for her when she met with a 6sense rep who helped her set up audiences and segments for the new vertical she was trying to build out. Almost instantly, she had a clear picture of how many accounts were in-market in her new vertical, and the information was data-based, current, and wildly accurate—a sharp contrast to the experience she had just had working with an expensive consultant.

That type of agility is a huge advantage for fast-growth companies. The revenue teams that win consistently are the ones that keep their finger on the pulse of all the opportunities and carefully choose the best ones to pursue—quickly, not after months and months of working with consultants and poring over spreadsheets.

With an AI platform that helps us make these big decisions based on the best data and insights, we're not only more agile, we're also more confident. Because the truth is no matter how impressive that consultant's deck is, none of the recommendations they make are tested. With our modern approach, on the other hand, we can start testing our predictions before we ever hire our first AE. Marketing starts warming the new vertical or geo with display ads and social ads to test our messaging and see how it resonates. We determine whether we can progress those accounts the way we expect. And we can do all of that in a matter of weeks, not months, which allows us to stay ahead of the competition.

You can look at the data and say definitively, "Yes, there's enough opportunity here to make it worthwhile," or "No, we'd be better off focusing on North America—the APAC market just isn't there." And then you can let your competition spin their wheels all they want while you prioritize your resources and attention where they'll have the most impact.

The Unified Pipeline Model

We've talked about a lot of ways that data-backed, AI-powered decisioning bolsters alignment across the board. One of the most high-impact ways this alignment plays out in successful revenue teams is with a unified pipeline model.

When I talk about pipeline, I'm not just talking about marketing-sourced pipeline. I'm talking about all pipeline. In fact, Latané and I really don't care who gets credit for the pipeline since we're both focused on the same goal: revenue. That's why you'll see that we work together to plan and run spiffs to get AEs prospecting regularly. We have a culture in which *everyone* is expected to prospect. AEs are expected to own their book of business, not just wait for marketing to hand them accounts to work.

This isn't to say that the marketing team isn't accountable for producing pipeline. They absolutely are. But we just want to make sure they're held accountable for the right things. And just as a reminder, the MQL is *not* the right thing. MQLs may be one demand signal, but they're not an effective way to measure marketing's goals and success—at least not if you want to align on revenue. What's truly important for marketing to contribute is the stuff that improves average sales price, the sales velocity formula, and conversions throughout the funnel.

For three years, Latané and I worked on perfecting our unified pipeline model. Our goal was to create true co-ownership and a shared understanding of the underlying revenue assumptions. We wanted to make sure that our conversations were productive and that we were all playing from the same sheet of music. That's the only way we can identify issues in the pipeline and deal with them. After all, if we're each looking at different metrics, or if we're calculating our metrics differently, we can't see patterns together.

Our vice president of revenue operations, Kory Geyer, laid out the steps we used to align on pipeline.

Step 1: To implement a unified pipeline model, define the following:

- Which accounts to target

- Who is responsible for each stage of the buying journey

- How to measure the performance in each stage of the funnel

Step 2: Define funnel stages in an account-based model, such as the following:

- Marketing-qualified accounts

- Sales discovery

- Sales-qualified accounts

- Closed/won

Step 3: When aligning marketing and sales to focus on the right accounts:

- Define your ideal customer profile (all accounts marketing and sales jointly target) by analyzing past performance and future GTM strategy

  ° Past performance includes where you have success based on firmographic and technographic characteristics

  ° Future GTM strategy includes product, sales territory coverage, and revenue plans

  ° Define behaviors that trigger sales activity

Step 4: When setting account-based pipeline targets and measuring performance:

- Revenue, stage duration, stage velocity, and average deal size inputs are needed to determine targets for each stage. Bring revenue leaders together regularly to review pipeline metrics and decide on early stage, mid/late stage, and sales behavior actions to take.

This is the process we used to get aligned on pipeline at 6sense. Here's what it looks like in practice.

Together, our sales leaders and marketing ops folks work backward, starting with the closed-won revenue they're aiming to create. With that final goal in mind, they look at historic conversion rates and velocity throughout the funnel, as well as the average deal size, to determine how much pipeline they need to create at each stage—or stage 0, stage 1, and stage 2.

(Note: The numbers in the following charts are based on hypothetical examples for context, not actual figures.)

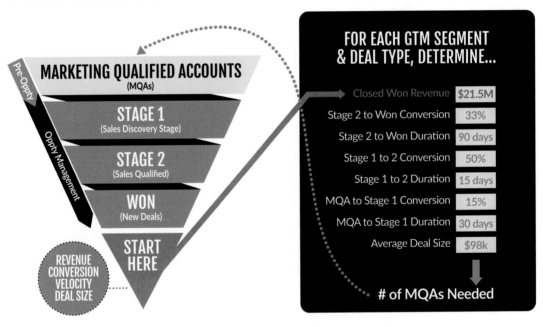

We break down these goals by go-to-market segment, by month, and then by new business versus upsells. So from the very beginning, marketing and sales are on the same page in terms of what our specific goals are and how we'll know if we're on track to create enough pipeline at each stage to meet our final revenue goal.

Until recently we used a spreadsheet like the one on the next page to track all of these things, but we've since made vast improvements on the process, which I'll tell you about next.

SETTING TARGETS FOR EACH GTM SEGMENT

MARKETING QUALIFIED ACCOUNTS
- Pre-Oppty
- STAGE 1
- Oppty Management
- STAGE 2
- WON

	CLOSED WON SALES TARGET	AVERAGE SELLING PRICE	MQA TO STAGE 1 VELOCITY (DAYS)	MQA TO STAGE 1 CONVERSION (%)	STAGE 1 TO STAGE 2 VELOCITY (DAYS)	STAGE 1 TO STAGE 2 CONVERSION (%)	STAGE 2 TO WON VELOCITY (DAYS)	STAGE 2 TO WON CONVERSION (%)	MQA MONTH	# OF MQAS NEEDED	STAGE 1 MONTH	# OF STAGE 1S NEEDED	STAGE - 2 MONTH	# OF STAGE 2S NEEDED	STAGE 2 PIPE AMOUNT NEEDED
FEB-21	$1,249,615	$98,000	40	14.0%	18	45.0%	118	32.0%	Previous Yr.	n/a	Previous Yr.	n/a	Previous Yr.	n/a	n/a
MAR-21	$1,249,615	$98,000	40	14.0%	18	45.0%	118	32.0%	Previous Yr.	n/a	Previous Yr.	n/a	Previous Yr.	n/a	n/a
APR-21	$1,249,615	$98,000	40	14.0%	18	45.0%	118	32.0%	Previous Yr.	n/a	Previous Yr.	n/a	Previous Yr.	n/a	n/a
MAY-21	$1,380,547	$98,000	40	14.0%	18	45.0%	118	32.0%	Previous Yr.	n/a	Previous Yr.	n/a	Feb-21	40	$3,905,047
JUN-21	$1,380,547	$98,000	40	14.0%	18	45.0%	118	32.0%	Feb-21	632	Feb-21	89	Mar-21	40	$3,905,047
JUL-21	$1,380,547	$98,000	40	14.0%	18	45.0%	118	32.0%	Mar-21	632	Mar-21	89	Apr-21	40	$3,905,047
AUG-21	$1,859,162	$98,000	40	14.0%	18	45.0%	118	32.0%	Apr-21	632	Apr-21	89	May-21	44	$4,314,209
SEP-21	$1,859,162	$98,000	40	14.0%	18	45.0%	118	32.0%	May-21	699	May-21	98	Jun-21	44	$4,314,209
OCT-21	$1,859,162	$98,000	40	14.0%	18	45.0%	118	32.0%	Jun-21	699	Jun-21	98	Jul-21	44	$4,314,209
NOV-21	$2,412,372	$98,000	40	14.0%	18	45.0%	118	32.0%	Jul-21	699	Jul-21	98	Aug-21	59	$5,809,881
DEC-21	$2,412,372	$98,000	40	14.0%	18	45.0%	118	32.0%			Aug-21	132	Sep-21	59	$5,809,881

Our Next-Gen Pipeline Model

What I've described so far explains the fundamentals of how we have created a pipeline model that aligns the entire revenue team, clearly defines assumptions, and keeps us all accountable. It has allowed us to notice when a conversion or cycle time slips below an assumption so we can focus our effort there.

But overall, this approach had one important flaw: It didn't use AI. Instead, it used the spreadsheet on the left. And that meant it not only required a lot of manual effort, but also that it was based on a fair number of educated guesses (and hand-wringing) from very smart humans. These guesses were occurring on two sides. Let me explain.

When we think about *sales* forecasting, that's a matter of forecasting what is going to happen based on activity. We already have the goal; it's provided by our board or our CEO.

With *pipeline* forecasting, on the other hand, we don't even start with an established goal. Everything I just walked you through has to happen to even determine what our goal is. So that's the first place where we're relying on educated guesses.

The second challenge is in forecasting what will be created based on those goals.

In the spreadsheet model we had been using until recently, Latané looked at how much pipeline we created every week and see what that looked like for the quarter. The first week of every month she saw how we were looking for the month. And then she'd ask herself, "Is this even the right goal? What if we overachieved last month? Does the goal change?"

Now we forecast pipeline using AI, and it has changed our world. AI solves both of the problems we were facing. First, we can put in our bookings target, and the AI gives us a rolling, accurate goal. And second, it looks back at all our historical patterns to see our underlying performance and project where we'll be at the end of the quarter.

This is critical because accurate pipeline projections are the key to future-proofing bookings. If you're going to get bad news, you want it as early as possible. AI identifies pipeline issues quickly and early so we have time to fix them. And, importantly, it points to exactly *where* we should invest—including which go-to-market segment needs the most attention (upsell, EMEA, commercial, manufacturing, etc.). Do we need more BDRs? ABX managers? Events? The AI tells us where to focus our joint efforts, and then tells us whether we're having our desired effect.

You can see in the sample image below that we can all work off the same dashboard, and no one is worrying about whether the pipeline is sales sourced or marketing sourced. We are simply looking objectively at where we're seeing challenges and then making the best decisions early on to correct them.

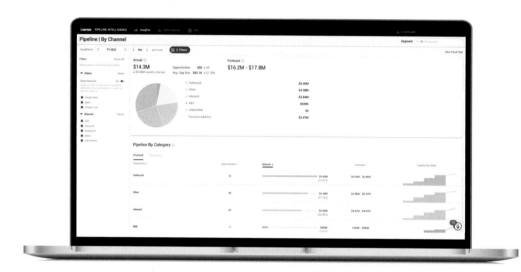

By aligning across the revenue team from the beginning of the pipeline forecasting process and carrying that collaboration through planning and inspection, we achieve a truly unified pipeline forecasting model. And that's important since if you're confident in your pipeline, you can be confident in your revenue.

Marketing + Sales = More Personas Engaged

Mike Weir, CRO at G2, has seen the evolution of marketing-sales alignment, and he's 100% on board:

The CRO position has evolved, and part of the evolution is we need to understand marketing's role and how they can help.

I love working on account-based marketing (ABM) programs with our CMO. It helps us expand the relationship, because frankly the productivity of my team gets better if marketing can help me engage with more marketers, and with more sales leaders at our clients.

There are a lot of people we want to have conversations with. If marketing can help carry that conversation, can help find the individuals who are ready and have detailed questions that we can help answer, it makes us more productive and helps keep us focused on the urgent conversations.

I'm always looking for how we can engage with people beyond just the five or 10 people we already talk to every week. Marketing helps keep them informed, lets them know about product updates, invites them to the events, shares our thought leadership ... but they also help me meet that 11th, 20th, 30th person at an enterprise that I would love to have a relationship with and I just haven't met them yet.

Why we plan together is we're looking at those optimization points. How are we doing in engaging the market, opening them up to consideration, getting them into lead flow, scoring and qualifying to then get them ready for a salesperson?

It's for the benefit of the client because we don't want to waste their time either by reaching out until they're ready to have a conversation. And it's beneficial for our time, too. We want to optimize that time.

We are reeducating a lot of folks who are from the more old school, who say, "I'm just going to make more calls, get more meetings, get more pipeline, and go from there." But no, you have to work smarter, and you have to engage the folks who are ready. Marketing helps educate and warm up an audience to say, "Okay, now I'm ready to have a conversation. I've done my research."

As we all see, buyers are in control of the journey. They do their own research. They're typically far along in their research journey before they want to talk to somebody. Marketing plays a huge role in this educational outreach process.

Peeking Into Marketing's Black Box

A lot of the CROs I talk to don't even have visibility into the pre-sales funnel. They have no real understanding or input when it comes to the section of the TAM that is in early funnel stages. They're not part of the conversation about how marketing engages with prospects to get them ready for sales. It feels like a black box.

That's not the case for me and Latané. She and I look at the same dashboards. I see not only the accounts that I want my sellers to work right now, but also the ones in the earlier stages that are in Latané and her team's court. I can see what the marketing team is doing to warm those accounts and get them to the point where they're ready to talk to a rep. And, importantly, I can see how those efforts are affecting buyer behavior.

That means we can see what's working and keep on doing it. We can also collaborate to "find the red"—the areas where we can improve across the entire funnel to build predictable pipeline.

Steve Fitz, CRO of Sumo Logic, takes a similar collaborative approach with his CMO. He shared his thoughts on modern revenue team alignment in a recent webinar:

> *Candor matters. Execution along with that candor matters more. It's not about finding everything that's working. It's tracking, metricking, and being in that game together. You've gotta create harmony between the two organizations.*

> *It all starts with pipeline. We review that on our weekly leadership sales forecast. So it's about the opportunities, but also the pipeline and what are we doing now that's going to help in the next quarter and the following quarter. That's an evolution of how we prosecute the opportunities across those stages and are we getting the right conversion rates across those stages.*

I couldn't agree more. Getting aligned on metrics and goals and addressing them with candor and a spirit of collaboration, has been key to the revenue team's success at 6sense and to the success of our company as a whole.

Hiring + Retention

Everything we've talked about so far in this chapter is about putting reps in the position to have repeatable success while working more efficiently. While they'll still need to be talented sellers who work hard, the tools we're giving them shorten the distance between them and their commission check or an invitation to Club.

Those are things that make for happy, enthusiastic, and loyal sellers. And that makes the job of hiring and retaining top talent much easier. Especially these days, when the job market is tighter than I've ever seen it, the best sellers have their choice of places to work. If we can't prove to them that we'll put them in the best position to win, they'll go elsewhere. It's that simple.

If, on the other hand, we can show that we give our sellers the technology, tools, and support they need to prioritize their time and start making good money fast, we have a leg up on the competition when it comes to hiring and retention.

As managers, the insights we use for territory planning also give us the confidence to hire the right number of people to work the right segments and territories. We know the exact number of accounts that are in market at any given time, meaning we can know with certainty how many new sellers we can support when we're getting ready to hire.

For the sellers we're recruiting, that message really resonates. We're able to tell recruits, "I can get you ramped and winning faster than the other companies you're considering. Here are our sales numbers and attainment rates, and here's why I know the territory I'm giving you will net you that same level of success." Knowing that they can start hitting and exceeding their quota fast is a huge motivator for sellers, and it helps us immensely in the recruiting process.

A few years ago when we were still pretty small, we decided to start a commercial team from the ground up. Without access to the information we had available, we might have started small and tested the waters by hiring one or two reps. But our technology showed us that we had a surprising number of commercial accounts visiting our site and not raising their hands—probably because we didn't have product pricing or packaging to accommodate them.

We dug further into our in-market data and found that not only was there huge potential here, but our competitors weren't serving that market. So we jumped in with both feet. Our revenue team worked together to make sure we could onboard and support the commercial segment and make them successful in a cost-efficient way—and then we poured gas on the fire. We promoted one of our enterprise account executives, Mac Conn, to head up a new team, and he hired a whole team of new reps to break into the commercial segment.

Was it risky? Well no, not really. We had the data in front of us to show us that as soon as we turned on this tap, we'd have enough accounts to keep all of our new reps fed. And we did—even as Covid hit just weeks after they came on board.

At a time when many sales teams were struggling with how and whether to reach out to people, we could use our technology to see who was still in-market and actively researching. So they were able to reach out without being insensitive—and in fact, they found they were providing a crucial service at a critical time. By having a direct line of sight into which commercial accounts were searching for ways to make up for lost pipeline, our brand-new team was able to continue smashing attainment goals, even in the midst of a once-in-a-lifetime economic upheaval.

What this experience showed me is that whether we're operating in a business-as-usual environment or breaking into new markets in the midst of a pandemic, we can be confident in our ability to make our reps successful as long as we're making data-driven decisions. And that's the secret to hiring and keeping the best sales talent around.

Enablement

Attracting the best talent is, of course, the foundation of building a rock star team. But once you have that talent under your wing, how do you make sure they are set up to do their best—not just in the honeymoon phase, but for as long as they're with you?

I believe that the secret is to foster a culture of learning and growth, from the top down. That means that as leaders, we need to learn out loud. We need to share the positive experiences that are helping us grow, but maybe even more importantly, we need to be transparent about our tough learning experiences. Because our sellers are also going to experience those difficult times, and it's important that we set them up to learn from them.

That's the first step. From there, our job is to commit to providing effective, thorough, and ongoing enablement for our teams. I'm not talking about the occasional training where your team is passively watching, probably checking sports scores while a video plays. I'm talking regular, hands-on training that gets super detailed about what to do and how to do it in different scenarios.

Look at what your deal progressions look like and get very specific about what your sellers should do, each step of the way. Don't assume that they know the basics. They might not have ever learned what you think of as a basic. Or they might have learned and forgotten or grown rusty. Be super explicit about enabling the process, structure, and skills needed to progress deals.

But bear in mind what the famed sales trainer David Sandler tells us: *you can't teach a kid to ride a bike at a seminar.* Same is true for selling. We learn by doing, not by watching slide presentations and filling out worksheets. We help our sellers put their lessons into practice with roleplaying. A lot—weekly, even. The idea is to really activate the learning to prevent that passive, box-checking participation I mentioned earlier.

Of course, there's no one better to learn from than the people who are doing it. So at 6sense, we have our top-performing sellers share what they're doing and help lead the roleplay exercises. But again, we don't just focus on their wins. We play out what happens when things go sideways as well. For each situation, we train for the best, worst, and in-between scenarios.

I see a lot of companies underestimate and underinvest in enablement. But the fact is that these exercises build muscles. And as with any sort of exercise, commitment and consistency are key.

Clearly, I'm a big believer in also enabling sales teams with the best tech. But it's only with this culture of learning that that tech is going to be successful. Providing your reps all the right tools is only one step in the journey toward data-driven, predictable, and repeatable success. You also need to enable them to use the tools at their fingertips.

In order to get sellers to adopt any new tool, technology, or strategy, it's important to start with the "what's in it for me" message.

Toby Carrington, executive vice president of global revenue operations at Seismic, explained at a recent customer conference how their sales team adopted new technology that soon became ingrained in its day-to-day sales motions.

"We of course didn't sell this as some new draconian regime for me to measure what people were doing. We said, 'You're going to win more, you're going to make more money, and here's how you're going to do it'"

You have to think about this when you're thinking about implementing a new strategy. "You've got to think about it down to the really granular level of how you're going to actually make sure that all this good stuff is used," Carrington says. "You've got to get them to really understand what needs to be done for successful adoption."

Meeting your sales team where they already are

We're all creatures of habit, which is why we sometimes resist new systems and processes. To improve adoption, it's important that the information you want sellers to see shows up in the places they're already spending their time.

Alerts can be very helpful, but they should be implemented thoughtfully. Carrington suggests "breaking it down into digestible chunks where people work—certain things on email, certain things on Slack, however they want to receive the information. You need to be where people are when they're doing their daily work, and it needs to be easy. You need to give it prime real estate."

Call on customer success

When you bring on a big new piece of tech, there's generally a customer success team ready and willing to help you drive adoption and enablement. Take advantage of that. The fact is, no two are the same, so tailoring enablement to your specific situation is the best way to drive adoption. Sit down with the technology's customer success reps and dig into your particular strengths and challenges so you can get the product set up in a way that makes your reps see the value, fast.

Consider a tiger team

In some organizations, it makes sense to kick off a new tech purchase by enlisting a few early adopters. This should be a hand-picked team of top reps who have proven a willingness to try new things in pursuit of success. This tiger team can help you fine-tune your new processes before rolling them out to the entire team.

Share wins

Track your tiger team's results and share their successes with the rest of the team. Collect wins, collect stories, and then figure out the best way to get those in front of your whole team—maybe in your all-hands calls, a dedicated Slack channel, or a weekly email. Correlating adoption to success will give the rest of the team a clear path to the same wins.

Steve Fitz, CRO at Sumo Logic, has used this approach with his own team. "The best person to tell that story is the seller who got the benefit from it. That's the poster child of success," he says. "You can tell that story 100 times, and adoption becomes immersive."

These wins have a cumulative effect. While our research shows that adoption starts to pick up in the first two quarters of implementing the account-based go-to-market strategy I'm describing here, it's really in quarters three and four that wins start to rack up and adoption spreads more quickly. By the fourth quarter, our customers see a 2.2x effectiveness rate, on average. And when sellers see their peers achieving more with less effort, they're willing to shake up their old systems to yield the same results.

Track adoption

Once you've proven the value of your new technology, it's reasonable and necessary to expect your team to adopt that tech. As a leader, it's your job to invest in the tools that will put your sellers on the fastest path to success. But as modern sellers, it's their job to leverage the tools that they're given. So set that expectation with your team, and then track adoption. That way, you can celebrate the sellers who are taking advantage of the tools you're investing in while working to remove the barriers for those who are not.

How to Get an (Almost) Instant Spike in Pipeline + Bookings

I talked earlier about how AI factors in variables like seasonality when projecting pipeline for us. That helps us prevent gaps in pipeline based on historical data and current trends. And one of the things we do when we anticipate late-stage pipeline dips is to plan Sales Program Incentive Funds (affectionately known as *spiffs*).

I know spiffs are a hot topic. A lot of CROs avoid them because they think they incentivize the wrong things—like waiting until there's an extra bonus on the table to put forth your best effort. But when used judiciously, I believe a spiff can be a way to rally the team to amp up efforts to achieve a goal with the help of some healthy competition. Spiffs can be effective—but they can also be a massive flop if they're not planned and executed well.

Our BDR manager, Ernest Owusu, is a spiff genius, so I asked him to describe what it takes to run a spiff that has the kinds of results that can turn a lackluster quarter into a record-breaking one. Here are some of his pointers.

Get clear on your goals

Figure out the specific business goals you're trying to accomplish or gaps you're trying to fill. For instance, we ran the July 2021 spiff to account for seasonality and prevent a Q4 dip. Then we worked backward to decide what specific metrics we should incentivize in the spiff to reach that goal. For this one, and for the one we ran in January, we incentivized creating pipeline and progressing early-stage pipeline to the next stage. So we tasked the teams with (1) getting meetings and (2) looking up all their open opportunities and getting meetings with additional people in those accounts (i.e., upping their multithreading game).

Decide: Team or individual spiff?

The July and January spiffs were both team spiffs. In each of our different segments, we created teams with both AEs and BDRs. The reason for mixing it up? It's no secret that AEs aren't always excited to prospect and get meetings; they'd rather focus on closing deals. But we are firm believers that AEs should own their book of business and have an entrepreneurial outlook, so we put them on teams with their BDRs and tasked everyone with prospecting. We then measured both individual and team achievements.

The July and January spiffs were sort of a big deal—a heavy lift with big prizes, lots of teamwork, and plenty of coordination. But small-scale, individual spiffs can be really effective too. The BDR team has a fast-start spiff every month to see who can generate the most meetings early in the month, since we know that the more meetings they generate early on, the more likely we are to hit our revenue goals for that month. Small spiffs can also be a strategic way to address specific gaps you're seeing in your month or quarter—for instance, if your connect rates are looking anemic. They're a good tool for getting people excited to start addressing gaps and doing it fast.

Offer an incentive people will care about

Latané likes to joke that salespeople are so competitive, they'll take each other out at the knees for a free mousepad. But in reality, she knows (and so do I) that having a killer incentive is the difference between a spiff people obsess over and one they forget about on day three. We've found that nothing motivates people as well as the promise of an experience. If you can swing it, a trip (almost like a mini-Club) will fire people up. For the July spiff, the prize was a trip to Vegas, and our sellers went crazy for it. You know your sellers and what will motivate them, so have fun and get creative with ideas that you think will light the fire. If a big trip isn't feasible, you could look into an experience they'd never plan for themselves, like a yacht party. If that's not possible? Cash is always a failproof fallback plan.

Keep it short and sweet

Don't prolong the spiff or you risk fading into the background. We've determined that two weeks is the perfect length for a bigger spiff. Smaller ones can be shorter—just a week or so.

Designate a cheerleader

Keeping enthusiasm high for the duration of the competition is very important. And for that, you need a dedicated cheerleader who is going to keep the energy up, foster healthy competition with daily updates, and rally the teams to do their best. And most importantly, the cheerleader can keep everyone—from BDRs to AEs to sales managers—focused on *why* they're doing this. For the bragging rights, sure. But also for the bigger business goals that inspired the spiff in the first place.

Foster the team mentality

When assembling your teams, think about what you want to accomplish in terms of team-building. Sometimes it makes sense to bring together people in different regions who don't normally talk to each other to build relationships. Other times, you might want to keep people with whom they already work to strengthen those bonds.

Then give teams three days to come up with a team name. In addition to setting the spiff off on a fun note, this also ensures they'll start meeting, engaging, collaborating, and competing right from the start.

Ensure engagement

As the competition starts, it's important to ensure that everyone is participating. One way to do this is to engage leadership. Make sure sales leaders are aware of how the competition is going by sharing the leaderboard and asking them to make sure their sellers are at least earning some points.

Another way to encourage engagement? Cash. With our most recent spiff, we offered individual prizes to the members of the winning team—but only if they crossed a certain point threshold themselves. Each member of the winning team who earned 5 points or more would get $1,000. If they didn't earn their 5 points? That money would get distributed to the members of their team who did.

Double-down on in-market accounts

In-market accounts convert more quickly and at a higher rate. So when we run our spiffs, we make sure to really hammer that message home: spend your time where it'll have the greatest value. On our weekly standups, we are sure to note how many in-market accounts are available to be worked, as well as what their average conversion rate is. The idea is to give our sellers straightforward ways to execute a plan—as well as a fast path to success.

Communicate, communicate, and then communicate some more

Deliberate, engaging, and consistent communication is very important. Plan to give regular updates in the places your sellers already hang out. For us that's Slack and email. I send regular updates to drive competition and keep the spiff at the top of people's minds so it doesn't fade into the background. First thing in the morning, I call people out on Slack for top performance, remind them of the rules, and share the leaderboard so everyone can check their daily standings.

The payoff?

Each of our spiffs has been a success, but the most recent one stands out among all of them. AEs and BDRs were energized and engaged. AEs booked three times the meetings they usually do. We've set ourselves up to meet or beat our pipeline goals for the quarter. And we had a lot of fun along the way.

I know spiffs are controversial. You certainly don't want to abuse them or make them so frequent that sellers wait to put in maximum effort until a spiff comes along. But when used strategically, they can energize the team, build camaraderie, and drive toward revenue goals.

Alignment Across the Revenue Team

The approach laid out in this book has countless benefits, both tangible and intangible. But the most significant change that comes from this modern sales leadership philosophy is true alignment—across the sales team, yes, but also across the entire revenue team.

It's no secret that alignment between sales and marketing is something between an aspiration and a pipe dream at many organizations. That's a huge problem, because when revenue teams are not aligned, they inevitably (and quickly) hit a ceiling in terms of what they can accomplish. Without true alignment, strategy suffers. Revenue suffers. The whole company suffers.

So if alignment is so important, why is it so elusive? A big reason is that sales teams don't trust the leads that marketing provides. And that's with good reason—as Latané explained earlier in the book, marketing-qualified leads are often useless—they're either arbitrarily scored and not actually based on real signals of interest or intent, or they come to the sales team so late that even if we act on them right away, we're too late to get into the deal.

Our sellers know this. They see that MQLs don't convert, and so they start to ignore them. That frustrates marketers, who begin to feel like their efforts are wasted. And from their perspective, it looks as if sales is just being lazy and not working leads the way they should.

A cycle of distrust and division is born.

Another issue is that at the highest levels, CROs and CMOs can't agree on goals, metrics of success, or even which data to use to inform decision-making. This is a major impediment to success, since research[3] shows the most important thing successful, high-growth companies do is to get aligned on things like total addressable market, ideal customer profile, and so forth.

These walls between the different parts of the revenue team are real, but modern technology is starting to break them down. Part of the change we're seeing in tech is that there's more of it and it's better than it used to be. But another way tech is changing is that much of it serves the entire revenue organization. Data that used to flow to Marketing Operations or Sales Operations—and, more often than not, stop there—can now flow throughout the marketing, sales, and customer success teams. And thanks to AI, the same data can be turned into insights and action steps that are uniquely useful to people in different roles.

---

3   https://6sense.com/resources/c/strategies-tactics-and-tech-of-top-performing-b2b-organiza-tions?x=n0_3by&lx=qfqeVx

Revenue technology allows us to leave behind the MQL hand-off that has plagued marketing and sales teams. Instead, it offers a way for the entire revenue team to prioritize the best accounts to pursue, gain deep insights into those accounts, and work jointly to move those accounts through the buying journey. This is possible because of objective and trustworthy data that show what our buyers are doing, what they care about, and where they are in their journey.

That's a big step up from the arbitrary guesswork and lead scoring that has caused so many headaches in the past.

With this single source of truth, we can focus on the metrics that matter. In other words, not marketing-qualified leads. Instead, we want to work with our marketing counterparts to focus on metrics like conversion rates, deal size, overall qualified pipeline, win rates, and revenue.

Aligned revenue technology enables us to share a common set of metrics. And that leads to continuous conversation and collaboration between the departments on things like the following:

- Ideal customer profiles
- Go-to-market motions
- Segmentation
- Account prioritization
- Account nurturing
- Pipeline planning

As a CRO, your collaboration with the CMO is critical for all of these areas. Here is what has worked well for Latané and me:

- *Collaboration around territory planning.* When spinning up a new territory, Latané and I look at data to determine best places to add AEs based on previous success and business objectives.

- *Consider the pod needed to support a territory.* We also make sure that Latané has the team and resources to support this new territory so the AEs are set up to be successful. We've always thought about this in terms of pre-sales, but the pod also needs marketers—an ABX marketer, as well as market development representatives (MDRs) and/or BDRs.

- *Use segmentation to inform ABX strategy.* By creating segments and looking at their behaviors and interests, we can work together to inform our go-to-market strategies for those segments. For instance, when running a competitive takeout for big strategic accounts, we set up a segment to include the top 20 strategic accounts we wanted to book meetings with, and then monitored their activity. Were they looking at us or our competitors? What keywords and topics were they interested in? Then sales and marketing worked together to use that data and create an account-based experience that would most effectively engage these high-stakes prospects. This strategy is also very useful for renewal and retention.

- *Work together on pipeline targets.* Latané and I work backward from the bookings number by segment to create our pipeline targets. It doesn't matter if it's sales-sourced or marketing-sourced; we just want to feed the AEs. What *does* matter is the assumptions and how those are trending. We look at each segment *every quarter* and use the underlying trends to create targets for the next quarter.

- *Account for seasonality.* Historical data shows us when we can expect to see seasonal slowdowns, so we account for those in advance by working together to plan sales and marketing spiffs. For instance, we did a spiff over the summer to get us set up with enough pipeline in Q4 (more on that in the sidebar).

- *Aligning our teams.* Latané and I make sure our teams are working together with the same level of collaboration she and I are committed to. We have a monthly all-revenue team call, and in our sales meetings, the ABX team is aligned to an RVP. I also make sure to hold AEs and managers accountable for holding up their end of the collaboration.

- *Hold ourselves accountable.* We all need to be stewards of the pipeline, and each AE and manager needs to be accountable for their book of business. The best sellers think of themselves as entrepreneurs. They take advantage of everything marketing offers to help them hit their goals. But at the end of the day, they understand that it's their responsibility to hit their numbers—no one else's. As chief revenue officer (CRO) it's important to model this spirit of accountability and support for marketing's efforts and expertise.

To get accounts to the point where they're ready to cross the finish line and produce predictable revenue growth, it's essential that the entire revenue team be on the same page. And revenue technology makes that possible in ways that it never has been before.

In my experience and in our research, this collaborative approach creates a flywheel effect. As the revenue team starts to align on metrics that matter and implement a coordinated, data-based, AI-supported strategy, they start to see wins, fast. And as those early wins accumulate, trust improves. Sales and marketing teams see that their collaboration is working, and so it happens more. We develop the kind of high-level trust and collaboration across the entire revenue team that's necessary to deliver long-term, predictable revenue growth.

Tech + Strategy + Hard Work = Payoff

The ideas I've outlined here explain my take on what it means to be a modern sales organization. But sales is *always* going to be hard. There's not a single thing I've discussed here that is magic. There is no waving a wand and watching revenue pour in. Successful sales teams still depend on all those elements they've always relied on: hard work, talented sellers to do that hard work, and a smart strategy to keep them working in the right direction.

The difference is that we now have some pretty incredible technology to add to the tool-belt. It's one part of the equation, but it can make a huge difference in helping a talented and hard-working sales team maximize their success.

CHAPTER 6

ARE YOU READY TO BREAK THROUGH?

Between weekly coffee talks with other CMOs, spending tons of time talking with our customers, taking part in The Revenue Collective, and joining in on prospect meetings, I probably talk to thousands of marketing and sales professionals per year. I'm constantly awed by how smart and hardworking they are. They teach and inspire me every single day.

So when I saw the results of our predictable revenue growth survey, it was a bit of a shocker. I was surprised and, honestly, disappointed to see that as a profession, we were not as far along in transforming sales and marketing as I thought we would be.

Here are some of the more troubling trends the survey identified:[1]

- *Sales and marketing are misaligned on metrics.* Most sales and marketing teams rely on different datasets, work in different platforms, and track different metrics to measure success, making it nearly impossible to coordinate engagement with the right accounts throughout the customer journey.

- *They disagree about target accounts.* Half of all sales and marketing leaders only somewhat agree (or don't agree at all) on their target account list. Even 42 percent of successful organizations lack consensus.

---

1   https://hub.6sense.com/welcome/state-of-predictable-revenue-growth-report

- *Content delivery is guesswork.* One in three organizations believe content is the most valuable way to generate demand, but only 48 percent can deliver personalized content experiences, and even fewer have a content hub on their website.

- *Organizations still rely on lead scoring, even though it's a suspect way of prioritizing accounts.* Nearly 60 percent of account-driven organizations are still most focused on generating leads (MQLs or SQLs). Half of the respondents believe their lead scoring processes don't even surface the best leads accurately or consistently. That means salespeople spend too much time working junk leads and marketing wastes budget and time on campaigns and events that don't deliver results.

- *Tech stacks are bloated and hard to manage.* From marketing automation platforms (MAPs) to point solutions, tech stacks are too bloated, too complex, or too expensive, according to half of all respondents.

Maybe it's because our study included only non-6sense users, but still, I thought our industry would have made more progress based on all the engagement I've had with so many brilliant, uplifting, and dedicated sales and marketing professionals.

So what's up? Why are we not breaking through and implementing modern sales and marketing strategies when there's a clear game plan for how to do it (remember those five steps?), the technology is available, and the results are real. Plus, it just makes sense—treat prospects like humans and provide a more engaging experience, and you'll have better results. It seems so simple.

But the truth is, we all have reasons (some might say excuses) for why we're not able to make big changes—even though we know they're important. Here are just a few of the reasons I've heard people give for why they keep sticking with the same systems that aren't working for them, instead of shifting to ones that do:

- My company is too big.

- My company is too small.

- It sounds like more work than my team can handle.

- We already have a lot of technology.

- We can't attribute it all, and even though my attribution isn't perfect, at least I understand it. (I'll get into my take on attribution in the Demand Generation section of this chapter.)

- I'm a "relationship seller," and it works just fine.

- My executive team will never go for it.

Then there are all those people who *say* they want to make the change, but they're just not ready yet. They have a checklist of things they need to do, and once their ducks are in a row, they'll get started. But let's get real … It's like having kids. If you wait until you're ready, you'll never take the leap.

The brilliant Mariana Prado Cogan, former senior vice president of digital marketing strategy and operations at PTC, explains the urgency in terms all sales and marketing folks will understand: "You have no choice at this point—you have to do it. There was a time when if you didn't have a CRM, you could still get by. But at some point, you realized that if you're the only one without one, you're going to get left behind. That's how I see this. You have to decide which side of the movement you want to be on. Do you want to be one of the ones with a competitive advantage, or do you want to be left behind?"

Change isn't just coming, it's here

As Mariana said, change isn't a choice anymore. The old ways of selling and marketing are gone, and a new reality is forming, like it or not. I, personally, love it. As I've laid out in this book, the new ways of selling and marketing—with deep customer insights brought to you by AI and big data—are *way* better than the old ways, for both us and our customers.

So the change is happening. We can ignore it and be left behind. Or we can seize this opportunity to shape the future. As we undergo this transformation, I believe we'll see difference-makers emerge across organizations to lead the change.

What is a difference-maker, and how do you know if you are one? I reached out to our CEO Jason Zintak to get his take on this, because he has a knack for recognizing difference-makers from miles away. It's one of the things that makes him such a great leader—the ability to recognize and cultivate leadership traits in others.

Jason says that difference-makers are people who take real risks to advocate for the changes they see as necessary. "There are plenty of people who are armchair quarter-backs. They're happy to point fingers in the stadium, but they won't actually get on the field. Great companies are built by people who get on the field and take risks. They put up an argument for what has to change," Jason explains. "Change is not easy on people. In order to effect change, you have to campaign for it. A difference-maker campaigns, with unabashed waves of courage."

Jason points out these traits of difference-makers:

- They have grit and tenacity.

- They have a high work ethic.

- They're not afraid to provoke, in a professional manner, for the greater good or whatever change they're trying to effect.

- They're curious.

- They're not comfortable with the status quo, or with being conventional.

- They're not clock-punchers—they measure their contribution based on outcomes, not the time or effort it took to get there.

If you recognize yourself in this list, guess what: We need you right now. And I'm not just talking to the people in senior leadership positions. Yes, difference-making CMOs and sales leaders will be key in forging the path forward. But regardless of your role, if you're a difference-maker, it's your time to shine.

You'll remember that Chapter 1 is based on the presentation I gave at our big customer conference, "Breakthrough." At that conference, we looked for the difference-makers— and lucky for us, our customer base is chock full of them. At the conference, I took their pictures and put them up on a wall as inspiration and as a reminder that *people* are going to be the difference in shaping our future. And at the end of my presentation I asked, "Who's in?"

So here's the moment of truth. I'm asking you, *are you in*? If so, I'm dedicating this chapter to you. Read on to learn about what the future could look like for your role—and how to use your difference-maker mentality to stage your own breakthrough!

The Bigger the Goal, the Bigger the Breakthrough

When I was prepping for our big customer conference, Breakthrough, at the end of 2019, I started researching what it is that allows some people to smash goals while others plod along, making only incremental progress.

I was inspired by the research of Edwin Locke, a psychologist who has done groundbreaking work in the fields of work motivation, job satisfaction, and performance, studying the work of top athletes and CEOs. He developed his Goal Setting Theory in the 1960s, and it's still influencing leaders today. The premise? That the difference between those goal-smashers and the plodders is as much about *how* people set their goals as it is about the people themselves.

From my perspective, these are the golden nuggets of Goal Setting Theory:

1. Goals should be difficult. You want big goals. Easy goals are less likely to motivate people. The bigger the goal, the better the performance.

2. The act of goal setting has benefits in and of itself. Setting a goal influences people's effort, their choices, and their likelihood of sticking with it.

3. Committing to goals is key to achieving them. In order for people to want to achieve a goal, they need to understand the why behind it.

A lot of these sound familiar, don't they? These are some of the "whys" behind the ideas and tools I've shared in previous chapters—think back to V2MOM, revenue operating models, and go-to-market plans, for example. Whenever you're setting a goal, either in one of those contexts or elsewhere, try to apply these golden nuggets and see if you experience what I have—the

BREAKTHROUGH

You are the keeper of the Virtuous Cycle. You have the systems and data to make sure everyone is focused on providing your customers a stellar experience.

Revenue Operations

Revenue operations (RevOps) is where sales, marketing, and customer success meet to drive, you guessed it, revenue. Whether it functions as its own official department within an organization or more loosely as a meeting-of-the-minds between sales, marketing, and customer success, the goal is the same: To create a unified approach to all things revenue.

RevOps ties directly to the Virtuous Cycle—the initiative I worked on at Appirio that I told you about in Chapter 1. This was one of my foundational breakthroughs: that it's only by focusing on both customer and employee experience that you can achieve great things. And to create amazing customer and worker experiences, you need the right technology, data, insights, and alignment—all things that fall under the purview of RevOps. That's why I believe RevOps needs to be the keeper of the Virtuous Cycle.

How RevOps drives—and benefits from—the Virtuous Cycle

Study after study has shown that profit and growth are predicated on having satisfied, loyal, and, ultimately, amplified customers. Improved customer experience boosts:

- Customer retention[2]
- Customer loyalty[3]

---

2   https://www.salesforce.com/blog/2018/06/digital-customers-research

3   https://www.gartner.com/document/3899777?ref=solrAll&refval=242242534

- Customer satisfaction[4]

- Cost to serve[5]

- Revenue growth[6,7]

But reaping these revenue rewards requires sellers and marketers to have meaningful insights into what customers want. And in turn, those insights allow us to create the breakthrough digital moments that are personalized and consistent across the brand. Customer experience thrives, and the Virtuous Cycle continues.

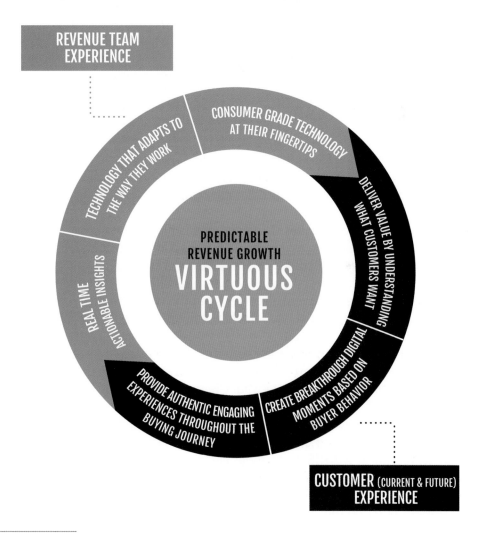

4   https://www.mckinsey.com/business-functions/marketing-and-sales/our-insights/
    improving-the-business-to-business-customer-experience

5   https://www.mckinsey.com/business-functions/marketing-and-sales/our-insights/
    improving-the-business-to-business-customer-experience

6   https://www.mckinsey.com/business-functions/marketing-and-sales/our-insights/
    improving-the-business-to-business-customer-experience

7   https://www.qualtrics.com/docs/xmi/XMI_ROIofCustomerExperience-2018.pdf

"Customers want their partners, vendors, and companies to know them," explains Glenn Weinstein, one of the co-founders of Appirio and current chief customer officer at Twilio. "It's one of the most basic human instincts, wanting to be heard. The only way to know your customers is to have clean, simple, accurate data about them. If you create a simple system that allows your frontline personnel, your sales reps, your support reps, your inside sales, to know the customers in 10 seconds, that reflects in how we talk to them."

So with good systems and data, RevOps can help everyone across the revenue team provide stellar customer experiences—including designing those breakthrough digital experiences (after all, 70 percent of the buying cycle happens in the Dark Funnel™). But digital experience and great insights alone are not enough. To fully realize the Virtuous Cycle, you need productive, loyal, and energized employees. That means that RevOps needs to give marketing, sales, and customer success teams the tools, technology, and data to make them more successful.

RevOps supports, aligns, empowers

Positions that specifically mention the term "revenue" in the title are on the rise and with good reason.[8] SiriusDecisions found that organizations with revenue operations grew revenue around *three times faster* than those that didn't.[9] That's amazing and such a good illustration of how crucial RevOps is for predictable revenue growth!

In practice, revenue operations makes sure everyone is playing from the same sheet of music—or reports and dashboards, as it were. That goes a long way in preventing embarrassing moments like the one that still haunts my dreams, when in a previous job the head of sales and I showed up at a high-stakes meeting and started talking numbers … and they were different numbers. The data were all correct, but the way we reported on it was different, and it sounded like we were at worst making shit up, and at best totally misaligned.

At 6sense, we don't run into these issues because the head of sales and I decided to establish RevOps to standardize data from day one. We were lucky to be able to align on the data from the beginning so that we could create what Glenn calls the "democratization of data."

When RevOps is operating well, data are consistent, shared, and understandable across the organization. And that does a lot more than prevent embarrassing moments—it also opens up the possibility for real growth. "Smart people, given access to good data, will figure stuff out," Glenn explains. "They'll find their own insights and make you a better company."

Most organizations don't do this. Instead, they funnel data through IT or BI teams. And in cases where people know the information they're looking for, that works. "But if you don't know what you want, if you just want to explore, that doesn't work," Glenn cautions. Imagine going to Amazon to look for a good book and getting just a single suggestion. It'd never work because we want options. We want to see reviews, understand why these books are suggested, and have a chance to read the sample chapter.

---

8   https://www.clari.com/blog/the-rise-of-revenue-operations-infographic

9   https://www.siriusdecisions.com/blog/revenue-operations-and-cmos

RevOps difference-makers create an environment in which people can have self-serve access to data. It's this direct access, without a gatekeeper, that allows for real breakthroughs.

But that doesn't mean reporting and sharing insights from the data isn't still a fundamental role of RevOps. In fact, Glenn says that while plenty of companies go 90 percent of the way—creating a data warehouse—they miss that last 10 percent of making the data meaningful and delivering it in formats people can use. As Glenn explains it, "It's the difference between information and news. You can get mountains of information by reading Twitter and blogs. We rely on journalists, the news profession, to make sense out of that information and tell us what's important, to give it context." Within an organization, those "journalists" are the difference-makers in RevOps.

Enabling Teams With Data

Here at 6sense, we've seen first-hand the positive impact of making data and analytics available in a self-service fashion—and how difficult life can be when they're behind a locked door.

When we started as a predictive analytics company, our AI models determined which accounts were in-market for a customer's products or solutions, and we delivered those predictive scores to customers within the CRM. But the why behind the scores was missing. All our users saw was a raw predictive score on account records, and they had no idea how we arrived at those scores—or if they could be trusted.

Today, we fondly refer to that period of company history as the blackbox years. While our predictions were just as on the money back then as they are today, the lack of visibility we provided into scores didn't net the results we wanted.

Fast forward to today, where we've opened up the hood by developing an application layer that allows users to understand the why behind our predictive scores. The benefit to our customers is evident, as customer usage continues to march up and to the right month over month.

The lesson learned is that visibility, explanations, and the ability for users to explore in a self-service manner is critical to success when selecting and implementing new technology—especially AI-driven tech.

Calling all RevOps difference-makers

Marketing and sales operations are huge jobs in their own right, each owning critical systems like CRM and MAP as well as a suite of additional technologies—plus a never-ending demand for reports, dashboards, and training. And the job of selecting and managing tech gets harder by the year; there are more than 7,000 sales and marketing solutions out there today!

With so many responsibilities already on sales ops' and marketing ops' plates, the idea of combining these roles might sound crazy. It may not even be feasible within your organization for any number of reasons, and that's okay. As I said at the beginning of this section, revenue ops is all about sales, marketing, and customer success aligning on all things revenue.

When RevOps teams operate with these big-vision ideals in mind, they have the opportunity to unearth end-to-end customer insights that light up that Dark Funnel™. Remember, only 13 percent of sales and marketing teams have confidence in their data. You can change that by bringing together known and anonymous data from first- and third-party sources, even if ownership of these capabilities is shared by separate sales and marketing ops teams. Layer on easy-to-use segmentation, and suddenly everyone is exploring data and making data-based decisions.

You have the tools, insights, and skills to enable teams throughout the organization to provide amazing customer experience and break through to their full potential. If you are passionate about data, people, technology, and experience, you've got what it takes to be a RevOps difference-maker—and we need you to help mobilize this customer and employee experience revolution!

MODERN REVOPS CAN ...	BECAUSE THEY KNOW ...
Provide revenue teams with powerful insights that create a competitive advantage	How to light up the Dark Funnel™ and make data consistent, shared, and understandable across the organization
Drive operational and cost efficiencies throughout the customer lifecycle	Where revenue teams should prioritize their time and money: ICP accounts, and more importantly IICP accounts
Deliver a more predictable revenue operating plan	How to create an account-based revenue operating model and shift from lead scoring to meaningful account-based metrics
Set every seller up for success	How to automate data enrichment and implement dynamic territories for sales
Put customer and future customer experience front and center	How to orchestrate campaigns and outreach based on AI-driven predictions and buyer intent to drive engagement and ROI
Confidently enable teams and drive adoption of the modern account engagement stack	How to provide insights in a digestible, actionable way for frontline teams

Digital marketers transform the digital experience

If you're like most digital marketers, you love to generate impressions, clicks, and web traffic from your campaigns. We live for it. Throw some creative content and a healthy budget into the primordial soup that is the Internet, and life emerges. It's sort of like playing blackjack—you may bust a few hands, but eventually, you'll hit a winning streak.

BREAKTHROUGH

You create demand through branding, thought leadership, and digital experience. Your goals and measurements need to be tied to pipeline. Understanding your IICP will take your efforts to the next level.

I'll never forget the time I was advising a company, and they were so excited about all of the advertising experiments they had run, each with its own set of metrics: impressions, cost per 1,000 impressions (CPM), click-through rate (CTR), cost per click (CPC), views, shares, likes, share of voice (SOV), content engagement scores, and so on. They asked me which program I thought was best, which one they should put the real money behind.

The honest answer was that I had *no* clue, so I asked some basic questions: What were they trying to accomplish? What accounts did they want to reach? Did they get any of those who liked, shared, or even clicked to genuinely engage with their brand? And what about pipeline?

© marketoonist.com

Unfortunately, understanding the true pipeline and revenue impact of campaigns is easier said than done for most digital marketers, but it's not their fault. Every platform has specific metrics designed to make us believe we're about to win—and win big. And there's no lack of case studies where you can read about how other teams are killing it on some platform and think, "We'd better do that, too."

The phrase "data-driven marketers" has duped us into grasping at any fragment of data that can be measured, even though it may or may not have meaning. It's like being-hyper focused on the bark of a tree when trying to understand forestation. Tree bark can tell you something about what's growing in the woods, but it isn't even a whole tree, much less the entire forest.

Here are some notes from a recent meeting with a digital marketing executive on their strategy. *Web form is working. Huge fan of PPC. Still getting calls today* ... Basically, this was him saying he's not at all focused on the pipeline. So, how did we get to the place

- Web Form is Performing
- SEO Working Well
- Still Getting Calls Today
- A Free Tool That is Working → Blog 50% YoY Growth
  - Optimize and Make More Lead Focused
- Huge Fan of PPC and Wants to Optimize
- Webinars Work Very Well
* Lead Follow-Up is Very Important
  - Some Reps Do it Well & Some Do Not

where a head of digital marketing is thinking about everything but the pipeline, much less customer experience!?

At this point you are probably tired of me talking about the ICP and the IICP, but these are *the* breakthroughs for digital marketing.

1. When everything you do is derived from your ICP, it's like having guardrails in bowling; it's impossible to throw a gutter ball. From paid advertising and social, to content syndication, to outbound programs, you're always targeting the best accounts and never wasting resources on spray-and-pray assumptions.

2. By specifically tracking web activity from accounts in your ICP, you get a clearer picture of how you're influencing the accounts you're most interested in. Take our recent funding announcement, for example. We had a huge traffic spike, as we would expect, on the day of the announcement. We could literally sit on Google Analytics live and watch the numbers tick up. It was kind of mesmerizing. But then we had to ask ourselves: Who were all these site visitors? Were they just industry and investor types? Our competitors? By being able to specifically measure web visits from accounts in our ICP, we could see that indeed we were seeing increased engagement from ICP accounts, meaning the announcement worked from the standpoint of driving interest from accounts we care about. This brings new meaning to "performance-based" digital marketing.

3. Sales teams no longer really *create* demand. Demand is created by prospects in ICP accounts conducting research long before they engage with a salesperson. So digital markers must now *uncover* that demand and turn it into opportunities (remember the Dark Funnel™?). Uncovering this demand—and lighting up your Dark Funnel™—takes more than just driving loads of clicks. It requires a deep understanding of brand positioning, earned media, influencers, and an eye toward personas and the buying jobs they need to complete through the end-to-end digital journey. Advanced digital marketing provides engagement and progression of ICP accounts throughout the entire funnel.

4. Engagement is the name of the game. And engaging ICP accounts to move them through the buyer journey is not a straight line, so we'll need to help them along the way as accounts advance and retreat through their journey. Which leads me to the next big part of digital marketing ... the website!

Ah yes, the website. The most controversial part of marketing. Find me a CMO who's happy with their website, and I will give you my entire shoe collection. The website is a constant work in progress: It's never done, and it's never exactly what you want. Let's look at examples on extreme ends of the spectrum so we can find a better path.

Company A: The "demand gen website." Looking at their website you have no idea what they do. It's like a word randomizer. Clearly, their SEO consultant convinced them to string every search term together over and over again. Not to mention the carnival of bots, flashing lights, and "helpful" pop ups. Please, make it stop. No, I actually don't want to take a meeting or talk to your bot. I literally just got here. All demand, no brand.

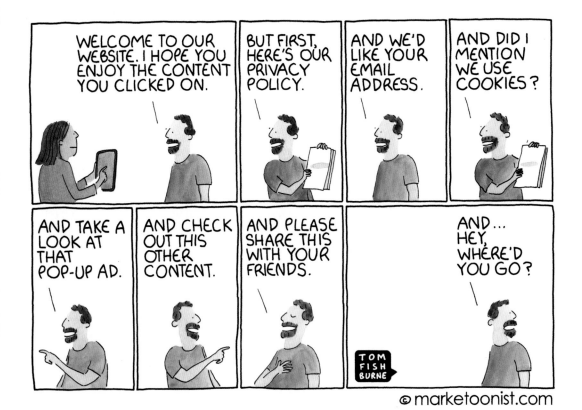

© marketoonist.com

Company B: "The brand/corporate website." This one has a great company vision and mission—that's nice. I can also see they have offices all over the world. Swanky. And I can tell they have a strong executive team. I mean *look at these awesome bios!* Amazing, but ... how does any of this help your customers/future customers navigate a complex B2B purchase decision?

Gartner research reveals that B2B buyers must complete six distinct activities—or "jobs"—to successfully complete a purchase today (see image on page 197).[10] Most B2B buyers will revisit nearly every buying job at least once before they make a purchase. The result: a customer buying journey that resembles more of a maze than a linear path.

This is an incredibly important and eye-opening moment if you're thinking about how to use your most valuable digital asset to shepherd accounts through their buying journey.

---

10   https://www.gartner.com/smarterwithgartner/
     gartner-keynote-the-new-imperative-for-b2b-sales-and-marketing-leaders/

ACCOUNT–BASED BUYING JOBS

B2B SELLING TODAY IS NO LONGER ABOUT PROGRESSING A CUSTOMER THROUGH A LINEAR BUYING JOURNEY.

BUYING JOB	DIAGNOSTIC/TOOL EXAMPLE	CONTENT EXAMPLE
1. PROBLEM IDENTIFICATION How do I rank against my peers? What is the cost/benefit of action/inaction? What am I missing?	**DIAGNOSTIC/TOOL** Industry Benchmark, Survey, Report Cost/Benefit Calculator	**SUPPORTING CONTENT** Analyst Report Blog: The 10 Questions We Wish Prospects Would Ask Us Blog: Plea to the Industry: CEO Perspective eBook: Adapting to Industry Changes
2. SOLUTION EXPLORATION What are my options? How would that work here? What are the trade-offs?	**DIAGNOSTIC/TOOL** Solution Comparison Chart (Harvey Balls!) Product/Feature Test Drive	**SUPPORTING CONTENT** Analyst "Magic Quadrant" Report, G2 Crowd Report, Analyst "Wave" Report Solution 1-Pager Solution Buying Guide
3. REQUIREMENTS BUILDING Help me identify solution criteria What am I missing? Help me prioritize what's important for me	**DIAGNOSTIC/TOOL** Build Your RFP Feature Scoring/Ranking Calculator	**SUPPORTING CONTENT** Analyst Report Infographic: Where Are You in the Evolution of B2B Selling (what you need)? Blog: Most Common Mistakes When Building Requirements for ABM
4. SUPPLIER SELECTION Help me compare solutions Let me see it in action Show me how you're different Help me prioritize trade-offs	**DIAGNOSTIC/TOOL** Solution Comparison Chart (Harvey Balls!) Product Demo/Test Drive/Free Trial	**SUPPORTING CONTENT** "Explainer" Videos Buying Guides Competitive Tear Sheets
5. VALIDATION Confirm my research Corroborate things I've learned Let me talk to your customers Connect me with peers Show me third-party expert analysis	**DIAGNOSTIC/TOOL** Content Hub Video Series Reference Builder User Community	**SUPPORTING CONTENT** Meet Your Peers (Video Interviews) Customer Stories Analyst Reports
6. CONSENSUS CREATION Build a shared understanding within my buying group Help me educate stakeholders outside of the buying group Help me identify & resolve disagreements, engage in debate Help me build a business case and secure budget	**DIAGNOSTIC/TOOL** Self-Serve "Tag" a Colleague with Comment Thought Leadership Library User Community Build-a-Business Case Calculator	**SUPPORTING CONTENT** Blog: 5 Steps to Building an Account-Based Mindset Across the Entire Team eBook: What Sales needs Marketing to Understand about ABM

We already talked about using account insights and intent data to develop a more personalized digital experience by aligning the right message and content with what prospects care about and where they are in their buying journey. But layering in the concept of helping B2B buyers complete the buying jobs just listed gives meaning and purpose to those experiences by defining exactly what we want the prospect to *do* to move forward.

This also helps us go beyond creating an endless stream of topical blog posts to developing useful tools like ROI calculators, benchmarks and assessments, comparison guides, business case and budgeting tools, and more. These are the types of persistent CTAs that can turn your website from brochureware to indispensable by providing real value for prospects who need to complete these essential buying jobs at the right time in their journey.

We've used this approach with good success and are now improving the digital experience with our conversational chatbot, which I told you about in Chapter 4. When we first launched Six (yes, we named our bot Six), we had okay engagement with site visitors. But we soon found Six was a little too aggressive—all he wanted to do was meet, meet, meet! Not very helpful at progressing visitors through the buying journey or pointing them to resources that could help them complete a buying job.

But now that we're able to use account insights to drive Six's conversations, we're seeing much better engagement and results. Because we know the topics (based on first- and third-party intent data) site visitors care about, and also where they are in the buying journey, Six can now tailor the conversation to recommend the right resources and tools on our site to help visitors complete those critical buying jobs. And the results speak for themselves. In just 30 days of infusing these insights into our chatbot, we saw a 118 percent increase in conversations.

I share this as a reminder that as a digital marketer, *you* create the digital experience. In many cases, digital marketing sits in demand gen. For us, it's under brand, because we believe creating a world-class digital experience is so important to the overall brand.

With every ad impression, every page view, and every chatbot conversation, our customers and future customers are making a judgment about us. And digital experience is like your favorite restaurant. They can deliver amazing food again and again, but one bad meal, or even one bad experience with a server and that's it, you're never going back. And why would you? There's a great place right down the street. In fact, there are lots of great places, just like there are lots of great places to do research online, so users aren't likely to stick around for lousy food and crappy service.

Your role as digital marketer is more important than ever. In fact, 70 percent of the sales cycle (and 100 percent of the judging about your brand and solution) is going on under your roof. As our vice president of brand, Michael George, likes to say "pressure is a privilege."

Breakthrough moves for digital marketers

- *Understand buyer intent.* Now more than ever, you must shape your digital experience strategy based on what buyers care about, not what you want to promote.

- *Measure engagement.* It may seem like another vanity metric, but it's not. Engagement is everything, so it's critical for you to understand how many and which accounts are newly or increasingly engaging with your brand, along with which personas across the buying team are engaged and which are not.

- *Focus on the experience.* Your creativity might be amazing and your email might be perfectly crafted, but if you don't offer a friction-free, meaningful experience at every single touch point, visitors will just move to the next result in their search.

- *Develop content and tools* to help future customers complete essential buying jobs.

- *Make friends.* There's a good chance you're the smartest banana in the bunch, but you're going to have to help the broader marketing team and sales team get set up and on board. I once had a digital marketing leader tell me, "Just give me my money so I can generate a ton of leads and not talk to anyone." Yes, you may have to explain how the Internet works for what feels like the 200th time, but such is life. Part of your job is rallying your team and communicating your vision.

Yes, this is all possible

I can see you over there freaking out over all these responsibilities being thrown at you. And if you're in the old-school marketing paradigm, I bet it feels like I'm telling you to climb Everest while also curing cancer and maybe juggling a couple of chainsaws.

But the fact is that once you make the mindset shift, you'll see that you can provide all of these amazing, customer-first digital experiences with *far less effort* than you're currently spending on less-effective marketing campaigns.

Here's a stellar example of this. Grace Kleaveland Kupzcak, our marketing coordinator, told me recently about a project one of her colleagues at another company was working on. They wanted to create personalized content hubs for 100 top accounts in multiple verticals, but they didn't have the same game-changing integrations and dynamic segments we have at 6sense.

"They had *so many* spreadsheets," Grace recalls. "My friend had to get all the BDRs to do research on all of the accounts. Then from there, she compiled a bunch of different Google Docs and created 100 different landing pages, all of them static, with a logo she had to go find, and she had to manually create all of the copies. Then as accounts moved throughout the buying stages, she had to continually refresh." Grace's friend rose to the challenge—but it took her two months of nonstop work to make it happen.

I asked Grace what it would look like if her colleague were to create a similar campaign with all the amazing tech Grace has at her fingertips. Her answer? "It would literally cut the amount of effort to 1/100th. So that alone … it's a game changer for a practitioner in terms of time, effort, and scalability."

Ultimately, everything digital in the new world starts and ends with dynamic segments, which can be activated through any channel via native capabilities, integrations, or open API. And with dynamic, continually updated audiences ready-made for use, you're free to focus on developing and testing creative campaigns and experiences to drive engagement. Plus, you can personalize in a more granular way than ever before since you know where buyers are on their journey and what they care about, and it's easy to maintain that level of personalization across channels.

The reality is that the future is here, and it's yours for the taking.

Let's take a look at some other things that modern digital marketers can do, and how.

👍 MODERN DIGITAL MARKETERS CAN	BECAUSE THEY KNOW
Deliver superior digital experiences across channels throughout the account lifecycle	An account's buying jobs, where they are in the buying journey, and how to deliver engaging experiences that help buyers progress in their journey
Increase ROI across all tactics—Google, content syndication, display ads, and other media	How to ensure their dollars are spent on the best audiences: in-market ICP accounts!
Uncover early-stage interest (even in the Dark Funnel™) and create demand through multi-touch programs	What topics accounts and personas are researching and care most about
Deliver hyper-personalized digital experiences at scale	How to create targeted segments based on where each account is in the buying journey
Maintain consistency in brand and message, across digital channels	How to orchestrate multi-channel campaigns both on and offline by connecting engagement channels to dynamic segments
Be a hero to sales by accelerating the velocity of accounts through the purchase journey	How many accounts are at each stage, how long they've been there, and which content and tactics are most effective at moving buyers forward

Demand generation leader: You're the chief operating officer of the marketing department

Demand generation leaders are some of the most skeptical when they hear about my plan for the future of account-based engagement. And I get it. I really am moving your cheese—off the plate, across the table, out the window, and onto the lawn. No MQLs? No forms? No spam? I get how it might feel like I'm taking a system that "works" and breaking it—but the truth is that the system is already broken. (Saying this makes me feel like Will Ferrel in *Elf* when he finds out the department store Santa is a fake. You sit on a throne of MQLs!)

But still, it's a heavy lift for demand gen. Revenue operations gets to light up the Dark Funnel™ and therefore be a hero to sales and BDR teams. Digital marketing gets to deliver amazingly personalized digital experiences and creatively target and reach the best accounts. So what does demand gen get? Well don't fear—I'm about to tell you all the ways this new approach is going to make your job a million times better than it is now.

But before we get to that, let me just say that demand gen is a tough gig. I know how hard you work, and I realize that you often hear more complaints than praise. More than anyone else in marketing, demand gen folks constantly have to address the never-ending chorus of "these leads suck" coming from sales.

Part of the problem is that the role itself often isn't well defined or supported, leaving you to answer a barrage of questions like, "Why did we go to that useless event?" And, "Why don't we have our content here, or there?" And, "Why are you emailing my prospects?" or its close cousin, "Why *aren't* you emailing my prospects?" The questions and comments go on and on.

The fact is, the demand generation role is incredibly diverse, and there is no standard job description that clearly defines the edges of it in any marketing organization. In fact, what the DG'er does varies considerably from company to company. The role can include digital, content, field marketing, marketing ops, and more. And if you lead demand gen, you know that even if it's not your "job," you're going to be involved in all areas of marketing. DG'ers really are the decathletes of marketing.

In seeking our first demand gen leader at 6sense, I fondly called it our "search for a purple squirrel," because the Swiss Army knife of a demand gen leader we needed likely didn't exist.

Fortunately for us, we found Susan Peterson Schatschneider, one of the smartest demand gen marketers I've ever met. Susan's breakthrough—and the one she instilled in us—was the realization that it's really not about demand generation once you light up your Dark Funnel™ and you can see all the demand in front of you; it's really about *demand capture*.

This creates a paradigm shift in arguing over what's a lead and what's not because it's not an arbitrary marketing score; it's a backtested algorithm that statistically shows which accounts are going to open an opportunity. The only question is whether that opportunity will be with us or our competition.

This is how it occurred to Susan that we needed to move from static to dynamic territories. She saw the game is not about generating *more* MQLs; it's about fast tracking in-market accounts and ensuring they're worked as effectively and efficiently as possible. Remember, in Chapter 1 I recounted how we realized we were throwing in-market, ready-to-engage accounts (6QAs) on the floor because they weren't part of assigned AE territories.

This "capture" ah-ha moment even became the basis for a new product feature: DG'ers can now see in real-time how many accounts 6QA'ed in the last X days but are not yet an open opportunity. Our team looks at the past 30, 60, and 90 days, and it's what now keeps us up at night. The last thing anyone wants to see is 2,000 accounts that have 6QA'ed, and no open opportunities to show for them.

But isn't that what forms and spam are all about—capturing demand so we can convert it to opportunities? Well, we took those away because they have the opposite effect, and the reality is that buyers are in charge of the journey. It's now about generating engagement with multiple personas to the point that they *lean way in* with you and convert—not just in terms of moving them to the next stage in the buying journey, but also in terms of buying into your brand.

So what does one need to do that? Well, to begin with, you need multiple tactics. Because some people will respond to direct mail while others will respond to a webinar invite, and still others just want to get straight to the point with a chatbot.

In other words, in addition to working with a variety of channels, we also have to multithread. This is a sales term that means ensuring you have multiple personas involved in a deal—or in this case engaged pre-opportunity. As marketers, we want to do the same thing with qualified accounts.

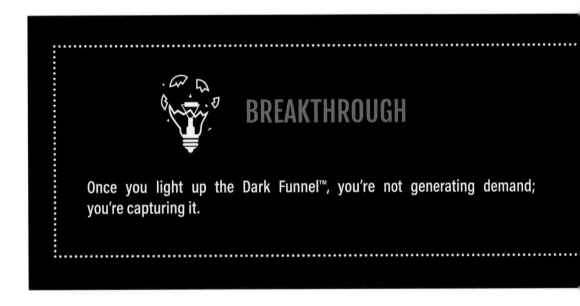

BREAKTHROUGH

Once you light up the Dark Funnel™, you're not generating demand; you're capturing it.

Multithreading with key personas

A brilliant analyst I've worked with a ton talks about research they've done on the importance of multiple engaged personas. He points out that a standard "lead" or single person showing **activity converts less than 1 percent of the time.** However, if a second person is engaged, the research found that the activity is statistically way less random. Furthermore, if a third person is engaged, it's even less random and likely to become an opportunity. As DG'ers, we need to be able to track and enhance that buying group engagement so we can pass really high-quality accounts to sales.

Sounds really sophisticated, but you don't have to be sophisticated to use sophisticated technology. You just have to be creative and know how to think through the *ifs* and *thens* that come with the key capabilities outlined in Chapter 3, like dynamic segmentation.

Dynamic segments are at the core of how DG'ers use buyer journey logic to hyper-target specific audiences across channels. For example, a segment might be created for strong ICP fit companies that have visited my product page, researched a competitor within the last seven days, and also attended our recent webinar.

With this segment in hand, we can then use it to orchestrate engagement through any channel at our disposal—such as chat, direct mail, content stream, and cadence—and they can all be connected and ready to rock. The segment determines the accounts we're targeting, and it's always updating as accounts meet or stop meeting the criteria.

Ultimately, the goal of orchestrating engagement is to meet the buyer where they are on their journey, follow them to the channels they prefer, and deliver highly personalized, consistent, and relevant experiences. In other words, it's all about customer experience. And it's achievable because today we have technology that allows for seamless integration across systems—without having to download and upload tons of spreadsheets and manually align data.

When you see the difference in practice, it's mind-blowing. Here are some examples of what this new, AI-driven orchestration can look like:

- If an account is a tier-one target and an executive-level persona registers for a webinar, prompt the AE to send a personalized email offering a demo.

- If an account is a strong ICP fit and moves to decision or purchase but then goes silent for 10 days, direct mail a gift to the key persona.

- If a director-level persona attends a demo, automatically invite a C-level persona in a specific job function to connect with one of our executives.

- If an account moves into the decision or purchase buying stage and is a strong fit for my ICP, automatically acquire missing contacts in the buying center and add key personas to a sales cadence for BDR outreach.

If you've ever used a journey builder, I'm sure these types of actions sound familiar. The difference here is that rather than a static, linear series of if/then statements, you have dynamic segments on your side. And if you recall from Chapter 3, AI reveals the buying stage, top keywords for your ICP, and the personas that are engaged. With those types of insights being updated dynamically, the dream of delivering the right message at the right time with the right tactic becomes a reality.

That's pretty cool—and user experience is only going to get better as AI continues to advance. In the very near future the old world of rules will go out the window entirely, and instead you'll simply set a goal, like *increase engagement with accounts in this top-of-the-funnel segment*, and AI will determine how to achieve that goal.

Does this sound too good to be true (or too scary to think about)? Let's double-click into this new demand gen world and take a look at how it works.

Dynamic segments and AI-driven predictions are still at the core of how DG'ers will target key audiences, but rather than building rules around segments, you'll start by setting a goal like the example above. Next, you'll tell the machine what tactics it can consider using to achieve that goal—and what parameters it must adhere to.

For example, for our goal of increasing engagement with a specific segment—say the financial services vertical—we might tell the machine that it can use display campaigns set up in the system, but that it must adhere to a weekly budget of $250 for this goal. We might also tell the system that it can personalize web and content experiences if those accounts visit our website, add leads and contacts to a campaign in CRM or MAP, add leads and contacts to a sales cadence, and purchase missing contacts and add them to specific systems. With the suite of tactics outlined for the machine, it can then choose how to orchestrate engagement in order to achieve the business goal.

In addition to tactics that we tell the machine it can use on its own, we might add other tactics like direct mail that require human approval. If the AI determines that a direct mail should be sent to five contacts tied to accounts in our segment, an admin user is notified and can choose to approve or decline the machine's request.

This is the future of demand gen. If it fires you up and sets your mind whirring with all the possibilities AI-driven orchestration opens up for you, you're probably "purple squirrel" material. And DG'ers like you who embrace these possibilities will be the ones who take control of their pipeline and lead their teams to predictable revenue while competitors are chasing MQLs the same way they always have.

What about attribution?

Leaning heavily on AI to generate demand with accounts you actually care about sounds great, but what about attribution?

Purple squirrels know that it's not the white paper download that generated the seven-figure deal that closed last quarter. It's also not the LinkedIn ads that generated the deal, nor was it the webinar series. It's a mix of all of these tactics because really great marketing is like an amazing craft cocktail: it has lots of tasty ingredients that need to be mixed in the right proportions and the right way, from muddled mint to high-end tequila to fresh lime. The more buyers and the longer the sales cycle, the more complex the cocktail.

Herein lies the issue with attribution: Most attribution solutions look at the top-of-the-funnel white paper download versus the ROI calculator and determine that the calculator is what converted. But perhaps it was the white paper that lured the account to the website in the first place. If you blindly follow the attribution, you'll end up serving straight tequila shots rather than well-balanced cocktails—and we're a little more sophisticated than that, aren't we?

But I get it. As DG'ers, we want to know which tactics to keep and which to kill, and attribution provides a potential white knight to help. I went down this road at Appirio, spending months coming up with an attribution model in pursuit of the dream of tying every last dollar to a marketing tactic. It's a lot like lead scoring—subjectively picking what gets points. *This piece of content is worth X, that one is worth Y, and an event is worth Z.*

The attribution model I developed was some extremely advanced stuff at the time, but when push came to shove, I found that using basic attribution with the campaign object in Salesforce was more informative than an attribution model and software. Basic attribution with Salesforce campaigns is actually a decent way to measure where people ultimately raise their hand or go from unknown to known, and it can help you create a throughline for an entire campaign.

At the end of the day, though, you still have to use your brain. Back to my cocktail versus straight tequila analogy: You can't compare the tequila to the mint or the fresh lime. Those elements aren't comparable. But if you consistently keep the buying stage at the forefront of your analysis, you can measure a tactic's effectiveness in moving someone to the next step. The Salesforce Campaign object does a good job of measuring the effectiveness of things like tradeshows and other key conversion points. We set up basic rules that require reps to add contacts to opportunities so we can compare and contrast tactics that make sense to measure this way. For example, you could ask, *Is this a show we go to again or should we go to another show?* You wouldn't ask *Should we do another tradeshow or redesign the website*, because those questions are not comparable.

Ultimately, attribution is not only about getting credit. Remember, we're always finding the red and looking for ways to improve. This approach is about putting future customers and their experience first. When sales and marketing collaborate, they're working together to find and fix problems so they can deliver great experiences to ideal accounts—and maybe mix some amazing cocktails along the way.

Breakthrough moves for demand generation

- *Focus on in-market accounts.* Determine which campaigns to run in order to capture the most 6QAs, and then etch that GTM plan into your brain. DG'ers should work across the marketing team to design ideal plans each quarter. Ensure your acts of demand gen are not random tradeshows or webinar series, but rather strategic programs designed to capture and progress 6QAs so you continually put the sales team in the best position to win.

- *Co-own the revenue operating model.* It's critical to monitor 6QA conversion and progression from stage 0, 1, and 2—and to adapt if you see shifts.

- *Leverage tech and insights to fix cracks.* Customer experience is our North Star, and we have the tools and data needed to patch leaks and improve opportunity conversion rates. Experiment with how you're orchestrating engagement to find improvements. For example, triggering an informative email to the right persona at the right time can enhance experience in a way purposeless blasts never do. And get ready for the future; AI-driven orchestration is a total game changer. Imagine being able to take 100 accounts that 6QA'ed and provide them highly customized orchestrations to progress them to pipeline—with a fraction of the effort it would take to do it otherwise.

- *Eliminate time sucks.* Implement disqualification and low-touch processes for accounts that aren't a good fit. It's okay to not spend a ton of time and resources on them. But have a plan so they are not hanging out to dry. Implementing an AI assistant tool like Conversica can be a great way to handle low-priority inbounds. On-demand or self-service demos and content and disqualification nurture programs are also effective.

- *Mobilize the broader GTM team.* Nothing is more important than really working in-market accounts. Our customer Impartner uses their "time well spent" dashboard to monitor key metrics for 6QAs, and our own BDR team here at 6sense relies on "Ernie's dashboard" to ensure in-market accounts are worked. Remember, the goal is to replace cold calls with warm calls that are perfectly timed based on buying center analytics and in-market predictions. This is what sets teams up for successful calls—and part of how we put customers first.

As the demand generation leader, the marketing team looks to you to define the path to pipeline success. Get ready for the future—and for greatness.

Managing Change

Change is hard. Convincing others to get behind big change? Even harder. With the kind of change we're talking about here; you're going to need buy-in—so start laying the groundwork early. If you've ever read *Moneyball* or seen the movie, you'll remember how Billy Beane had to justify his new mathematical approach to scouting and selecting players to both the owners and fans of the Oakland Athletics. As the leader of demand generation, you'll have to do the same with this new data-informed approach.

From the CEO down, everyone in your organization is likely accustomed to measuring marketing's success through the lens of MQLs. As you know by now, MQLs are an arbitrary measurement of success. But in some organizations, they're the only measurement you've got. When you're making the case for ditching them, you need to be ready to explain why they're not serving you, why you're better off without them, and how you're going to measure your success instead.

One of the scariest aspects of making this move is that when you get rid of MQLs, lead volume will decrease. But *that's a good thing*—and as the change-maker, it's your responsibility to help people understand why.

In part, it comes down to basic math. In the lead world, every contact who downloads something is deemed a lead, even though they're actually part of a buying team. With an account-based approach, the focus shifts to qualified accounts that may consist of several individuals. So what may have registered as three or six or nine leads will now register as one account. You'll still be working with all those individuals (and more effectively), but you need to prepare your team to expect the numbers to decrease once you're counting accounts instead of leads.

Plus, when your focus shifts away from nurturing and following up on every lead conversion, you no longer have to worry about the interns, consultants, job seekers, and other junk leads that forms inevitably capture. And on the flip side, you also don't have to waste time chasing that chief financial officer from a three-person company who could never afford your solution to begin with. You're only working in-market accounts and not junk leads, so again, numbers will go down. And, again, that's a good thing.

But most importantly, moving away from the arbitrary MQL metric allows you to start measuring *real* impact—in other words, things that grow revenue. The key is going back to the revenue operating model you developed thanks to Chapter 4 and looking at the most important revenue-influencing metrics: deal size, cycle time, and win rate.

When you show your executive leadership the cohort analysis that compares deal size, cycle time, and win rates from those MQLs to the same metrics for accounts that are qualified based on your new data and insights, jaws will drop. That's what happened with one of our customers, who did this and was able to show a 68 percent faster time to close, 77 percent increase in win rate, and nine time increase in average deal size after shifting away from MQLs and toward 6QA'ed accounts.

This analysis—coupled with the fact that the AI can be backtested so you can see with a high degree of accuracy how the models are performing at any given time—will have CFOs, CEOs, and CSOs jumping on board.

After all, as our friend Mariana from PTC says, "When you show them the money, they're going to get behind you. What executive is going to say, 'You can bring us $10 million with this new tech-driven approach? No, thank you. Just keep using that trusty typewriter.'"

Communicate early and often

A key to change is communicating early, consistently, and transparently with the whole team about your results. Keep examining and reinforcing that, and you'll build confidence in your account-based strategy.

The reality is that every account predicted to be in-market won't turn into an opportunity or revenue. No model will get you a 100 percent win rate. But when you play it out and run the process consistently, there's no question that in-market accounts outperform MQLs by leaps and bounds.

As Billy Bean will tell you, when the team wins, fans, owners, and eventually the entire league takes notice. This is why the job is no easy feat; it's about change management. Counting MQLs is probably easier, but it doesn't actually measure your success. The transition to this approach will require a mindset shift, but the results

MODERN DEMAND GEN CAN	BECAUSE THEY KNOW
Ensure sales and marketing teams are mobilized to work accounts with the highest likelihood to close	The pipeline and revenue impact of focusing on 6QAs
Create customer/prospect-centric experiences that adapt as buyers' behavior changes	How to leverage AI and dynamic segments to reach ICP accounts with the right message on the right channel
Build, analyze, and adjust processes to optimize the revenue team's time and effort to ensure accounts are converting to opportunities.	How to identify engagement stalls, cracks, and leaks, and where accounts are on the buying journey and when/how revenue teams should engage, to ensure BDRs are working efficiently at account and aggregate level
Generate a higher ROI for programs	Which tactics have the greatest impact in moving accounts through buying stages, resulting in pipeline and revenue

Field Marketers: The Future Chief Market Officers

I have so much love for field marketers. You are my people. In fact, a major break-through for me is that field marketers are the future CMOs of the world—you're the on-the-ground experts in your market, the quarterbacks of the go-to-market-plan, the alignment-builders between sales and marketing, and the masters of the mind-blowing moment. The difference-makers in field marketing have what it takes to grow their careers all the way to the top—and to make an incredible impact wherever they go.

Before I go too much further, I should clarify what I mean when I talk about field marketing, since there are so many different interpretations of the role. Field marketers are not event coordinators or party planners. Sure, they may be the masterminds behind killer events, but field marketing is so much more than "menus and venues."

Instead, field marketing is a critical component of the customer experience revolution. Field marketers are the end-to-end creators of the programs that engage our target accounts in meaningful ways—all with their eyes steadfastly trained on the organization's business objectives.

My introduction to field marketing (and marketing in general) came when I was an ambitious account executive in desperate need of pipeline. Since I didn't have a team of field marketers behind me, I took matters into my own hands and started throwing field marketing events all over the country as a way to get in front of my key prospects. I learned a few important things through that experience. First and foremost was that—while it's really fun to plan and host parties—events are about so much more than just getting in the same room with prospects. Getting people together and creating unique experiences to connect, learn, and have fun is a strategic way to make a name for your

NO FORMS. NO SPAM. NO COLD CALLS.

organization, get your customers (and future customers) pumped, and build engagement and alignment among your own team.

I also learned that the event planning aspect of field marketing is a lot of freaking work. Maybe that's why it's listed as one of the top-10 most stressful jobs—right up there with firefighters and airline pilots![11]

But again, breakthrough field marketers know their job is about so much more than event planning. At 6sense, our field marketing team owns the majority of the Tier 1 or "lightning strike" campaigns I told you about in Chapter 4. They are the brains (and the blood, sweat, and tears) behind our critical pipeline-driving programs, taking care of everything from business objectives to budget to overall experience.

They're able to go from event-planning to major campaign design and execution because they have the technology I described in Chapter 3. The segmentation capabilities turn them into consultants instead of task-doers. Everyone in our organization knows that if they want guidance about how to engage with our market, the field marketing team can guide them.

When sales wants to run a dinner series, for instance, they can ask our field marketers which cities will have the best engagement and which accounts they should invite for the highest likelihood of success. The field marketing team can pinpoint the best cities to visit—and they can also equip the sellers with key insights (like personas and what keywords they care about), which allows meaningful engagement. It goes back to what Glenn said earlier—customers just want to be known, and the only way to know them is with good data.

Orchestration capabilities allow field marketers to take programs to the next level, with multi-tactic campaigns rather than just one-off events. Orchestration is also key if you want to be able to create these incredible future-customer experiences at scale.

Modern field marketing is (kinda) like throwing a surprise party

Clearly field marketing is evolving. Standing out in this crazy and loud landscape where everyone is competing for time is hard and scheduling the occasional steak dinner just isn't going to grab anyone's attention anymore. Modern field marketers need data, insights, and more to move the needle. Think of it in terms of throwing the perfect surprise party (because I know you field marketers love a party analogy!)

- *Know your guest of honor (i.e., your segment).* Would you ever try to throw a surprise party for someone you didn't know? Of course not. That would be creepy and weird. So the first step is to know the best accounts to target for your programs, and why. Why are these good accounts for you? Is there

---

11   https://www.cbsnews.com/news/10-most-and-least-stressful-jobs-in-america/

enough in the segment? What successes have you had with similar accounts in the past? Are these accounts in an industry where you can be successful? If this seems hard to know, flip back to Chapter 3 to bone up on all the tools that put this type of information right at your fingertips, so anyone on the field marketing team can slice it and dice it to extract whatever insights they need.

- *Set your budget.* Is this a big-payoff account segment (think 50th anniversary party) or a higher-velocity, lower-revenue segment (think 32nd birthday party)? Consider the payoff and make trade-offs where needed to get the most engagement for the buck. In our world, a 32nd birthday party might get display advertising and business development outreach, while the golden anniversary would get the full monte—display, content, direct mail, and an exclusive experience.

BREAKTHROUGH

You are the future CMOs, the quarterbacks of the go-to-market plan, and the masters of the mind-blowing moment. Understanding the IICP ensures all the amazing stuff you do actually makes a difference.

- *Get your guests from point A to point B.* If you're throwing a party, you're going to need a map to get people where you want them to be. Predictive analytics is the ticket to knowing where each guest is starting from (buying stage) and how far we need them to go to reach the venue (closed-won). Just like any good journey, previously traveled routes are usually the best option to get where you're going. If you make it overly complicated, charting new paths through the marsh, don't expect a full house.

- *Assemble your helpers.* Would you throw a surprise party without a few accomplices? Not unless you want to be pulling your hair out—and dropping a few balls here and there. For our purposes, sales or business development representatives (SDRs/BDRs) are the perfect partners in crime. They understand the logistics and the plan, and they know the end game. They have tools like a sales engagement platform to keep everyone on track.

- *Give the people what they want!* You wouldn't plan a surprise party for a vegetarian at a steakhouse. Likewise, good field marketers don't execute a campaign unless it delivers exactly what their prospects care about. This is where intent data comes in. Knowing the minute details about what their prospects are interested in allows them to deliver relevant, personalized experiences. In ABM, one way we do this is with a content hub where we can serve up personalized content. If you have great intent data and understand their persona and where they are in the journey, your hub can be incredibly tailored for the guest of honor.

- *Check your guest list twice.* What's a surprise party without all your guest of honor's favorite people? As a host, you need to know who their friends and family are—and make sure you're communicating with them about the soiree. The parallel in our world? We need to make sure we're engaging not just one person on an account, but the entire buying team. Look at persona maps to determine key people to invite, enrich your records, orchestrate your engagement, and get those VIPs to the big event!

Are you ready?

I hope that all you field marketers read about what's possible in this new world and feel inspired to reach new heights. You might wonder whether you're really the right person to lead this change. I think you are. In fact, I think field marketers are *exactly* the right people to do it. Here's why ...

You're creative. Field marketers are some of the most creative people I know, and creativity is an underappreciated and absolutely critical skill in marketing. You're the ones who are always asking yourselves the important questions—the ones that will make you stand out and make your potential customers want to engage with you. *What fun or interesting thing can we do to spark conversation? How can we make our direct mailer awesome enough that it gets opened instead of trashed? Does this microsite, content, or creative make me want to take a meeting?* Those are all the insight-seeking, creative questions that make the difference between a ho-hum campaign and one that nets massive amounts of pipeline.

You know the event is only half the story. Your ability to see the whole picture amplifies the impact of the team's efforts. Great field marketers understand that planning a big event isn't just about the event itself. It's about creating a buzz before, during, and after. It's about creating valuable content that will live on long after the event is over. It's about creating a microsite that adds value and creating engaging ads for aircover. The best field marketers are *always* finding ways to differentiate via standout experiences that humanize the prospects. So who better to embrace and champion a bold new approach that's about all those things?

You dig data and technology. Modern field marketers love data and how it can inform and transform the way they do their jobs. They are also perfectly at home with cutting-edge technologies. They can dig into tools like 6sense, Marketo, SalesLoft, LeanData, Sendoso, ON24, and more to get to know their market and create experiences that will blow their prospects' minds—and make them want to take that meeting.

You jive with sales. I said it before, but one of the key ways modern field marketers make a difference is by driving alignment between sales and marketing. A critical aspect of that is aligning on metrics so everyone is pursuing the same goals. At 6sense, our field marketing team sits on all the forecast calls. They know the state of pipeline and bookings. So every program they work on is tied directly to those sales goals—building pipeline, accelerating opportunities, and closing deals.

You've got your eye on the ROI. Sure, creativity, event planning, and blowing people's minds with amazing experiences is fun. But you know that the fun is not the point. Everything you do is rooted in your astute business decision-making skills. You ask yourself the right questions: *What ROI have we gotten in the past? How can we eke out some more? How do I stretch the budget while still pulling off a memorable and engaging event? What non-attributable impact will this event have?*

You can turn on a dime. Your extreme agility—coupled with your ability to put those Chapter 3 capabilities to good use—means that when things go sideways (and they will), you have the ability to pivot. Say, for instance, a global pandemic shuts down all in-person events. You have the temperament and the tools to brush yourself off and create new ways to engage with future customers that make sense to them right now.

You're the face of the brand. Whether it's in-person or in a digital environment, you're the one who is "in the field" with your customers, partners, and prospects. You're building relationships and representing your brand and culture, and you take that seriously. That's why I say that you're the budding chief market officers—you're building the skills, relationships, and knowledge you need to be *the* expert in the market!

Go forth and lead the change!

You may not have mastered all the points above. You may not feel ready. You may feel intimidated by the bold new path I've laid in front of you. But I have faith in you. Here's my advice: Just start doing it. Make the changes you can, and advocate for the changes you want to see. You truly are one of the most powerful positions in the marketing department—so go ahead and lead that change!

MODERN FIELD MARKETERS CAN	BECAUSE THEY KNOW
Drive tight alignment between sales and marketing	Where accounts are in their journey and which tactics to employ to move them forward
Maximize the impact from webinars, trade shows, dinners, and other events	Which accounts, contacts, and personas to prioritize—and what topics they care about
Accelerate pipeline by engaging the right accounts at the right time	How many accounts are at each buying stage and which are the best ICP fit
Orchestrate campaigns that generate a buzz leading up to, during, and after events	Which dynamic segments to focus on and how to leverage everything from high-impact direct mail to digital campaigns
Measure the success of field marketing events	How many accounts progressed through the funnel as a result of field marketing programs

BDRs, SDRs, MDRs: You make the magic happen!

I have such mad respect for business development reps (BDRs), or as you're called in some orgs, sales development reps (SDRs) or marketing development reps (MDRs). Aside from all the built-in awesomeness about you—you're super motivated, creative, and enthusiastic—you also generate boatloads of revenue for your organizations.

That's not just my perception. Research backs me up. Advisory firm TOPO recently published research that shows BDRs/SDRs/MDRs serve a critical function for world-class B2B sales and marketing teams. Their 2019 Sales Development Benchmark report found that you are:[12]

- The most significant pipeline drivers in world-class companies, averaging $415K in pipeline per month, drumming up 57 percent of the pipeline overall.

- The most important channel for successful account-based programs, with 88 percent of account-based marketers citing outbound SDRs as an important channel in their marketing strategy. Because of this success, 41 percent of organizations have built a dedicated account-based SDR team.

But your job is challenging. In spite of how important you are to the success of your organization, less than half of you are consistently hitting quota.

---

12   https://6sense.com/resources/reports/topo-2019-sales-development-benchmark-report/

So what's up? You're naturally driven, you work your tails off, you want to win, and for the most part, you love your job. So why isn't success coming more easily for more of you?

We did our own survey to get to the bottom of that question, and what we found might not come as a surprise to you. First, we found that prioritizing your time is a challenge. About one-third (31 percent) of you are spending your time on unproductive activity instead of activity that allows you to close more deals by engaging the right prospects at the right time. The top timesuckers filling up your timecard? Meetings, administrative work, and bad prospecting.

In addition to that, nearly half of you say the prospects you're working are not an ideal fit. No wonder 57 percent of you get a negative response when engaging with your prospects! If you're not targeting the right personas who are actually in-market (your IICP) at the right time in the buying journey, of course your efforts are not going to land. Plus, if you don't have insights into what your prospects care about, you're bound to miss with your attempts at connection.

Here's what BDRs told us they need to be more effective and successful:

- More relevant accounts and prospects to target
- Clearer buyer personas
- Visibility into where prospects are in the buying journey
- Tighter sales and marketing alignment
- More time to do outreach versus wasting time on research, meetings, and administration
- The ability to scale their efforts

Does this sound familiar to you? It certainly does to me, and I only spent one day as a BDR ...

A mile in your shoes

I was so confounded by our BDRs' struggles to succeed that I wanted to figure out what wasn't working. And when you don't know exactly what's going on, it's easy to assume the worst—that people are not putting in the work or that you hired the wrong people. But rather than jump to conclusions, I decided to spend the day with our BDR team to figure out what was going on. Let's just say, I learned a lot.

I quickly realized that what was going on had nothing to do with work effort or acumen. Our BDRs were talented and working their butts off. But that effort was being misdirected.

What first shocked me on my day as a BDR was seeing how much time and energy our BDRs spent researching accounts. They went through 10-Qs, websites, and articles—so much content!—to try to understand buyers' needs and desires. We dedicated the whole morning to this research, without having any way of knowing if it was even valuable for the prospects we wanted to call.

Even after all this research, the team still struggled to figure out exactly what buyers wanted. Once we got prospects on the phone, it felt like we were missing the mark. We didn't have the right insights to understand what our prospects needed right then and there, so we didn't make great first impressions or hold meaningful conversations.

It was a long day, but it gave me context to understand what was going on. The team *was* putting the work in. But as leaders, we weren't optimizing how we applied that effort. They spent all their time researching and guessing at prospects' needs, and they weren't able to use their creative brains and boundless energy to get meetings.

My a-ha moment

After that day, I felt like a curtain had been opened. Once I struggled through the challenges our BDRs faced every day, it made perfect sense that they weren't hitting their numbers. And that's when I had a *huge* a-ha moment—the one that led to this whole bold new vision (and this book) to begin with.

It started with the realization that as BDRs, your success or failure is not entirely on you. Sure, you're the only one who can control the amount of effort you put in, and you need to give it your all. But it's also on leadership to create an environment in which you can optimize your time. I knew we had to completely change the way we prospect to align with the reality of how today's B2B buyers buy. That meant we had to be willing to flip the script and rethink how we set BDRs up for success.

So we set to work. Our first step was to put an end to guesswork so they could use their time and talents more efficiently. We wanted to give BDRs full visibility into the Dark Funnel™ so their process would be 100 percent powered by real insights. As the CMO of 6sense, I was sitting on top of the best predictive intelligence engine in the world (*in my unbiased opinion*), but we hadn't hardwired the insights into our own process. Sure, we used insights in our outreach, but that's a far cry from hardwiring the insights into our process. I knew that we needed the latter if we wanted to set up our BDRs for success.

Our solution: We began time-stamping accounts the moment they moved from the awareness/consideration stages of the buying journey into purchase/decision. We know that this is the magic moment when accounts transition from just wanting to learn (anonymously) to wanting to engage with vendors. You might remember that at 6sense, we call this a 6QA (6sense-qualified account).

BREAKTHROUGH

You are a big f'in deal. With work ethic, aptitude, and the right insights, you will do great things. Have the confidence to advocate for what you need!

The reason it's so important to start the clock ticking at this exact moment is that we know that when accounts are ready to engage, our likelihood of success skyrockets if we're the first company to engage with them meaningfully.

Being able to provide this information to our BDRs makes it crystal-clear how to prioritize their account outreach. They're no longer spinning their wheels with the accounts that just aren't ready to hear from them. Instead, they're providing valuable communication at the precise moment that prospects want it. And if all goes well and we are, in fact, the first vendor they engage with, our BDRs have an opportunity to develop a personal connection with them—and perhaps even save us from going through the dreaded RFP process. It's the difference between *in-market* and *inbound*. If you wait until an account is inbound, guess what: Every other vendor in your space is engaging with them at the same time, and your likelihood of standing out just drastically decreased.

An end to cold calls

This was when I first made my declaration that our BDRs would not make another cold call. Cold calls aren't just a waste of time; they're also the perfect way to tank a BDR's confidence. I mean, who wouldn't start to take it personally when they get *no* after *no* after *no*?

As I've said, this declaration was met with a high (and understandable) degree of skepticism from the sales leaders who placed a lot of value on phone calls. But when I explained that I wanted to eliminate *cold* calls—not the calls themselves—they were all in.

What I wanted to make sure we were doing, as marketing and sales leaders, was setting our BDRs up for success. So I made it a rule that before BDRs could make a call, we needed to equip them with specific information about who a prospect is, their role, what aspect of the business they are most interested in, and where they are in the buying journey.

These insights would give a BDR far more confidence going into a call because they have the ability to immediately deliver value to the buyer. Meanwhile, marketing would be providing personalized, targeted aircover to ensure the prospects were warm and ready for the BDRs' calls.

Same thing for emails. No more spam does not mean that email goes away. It means that we give our BDRs a clear list of accounts who *want* to hear from them. They focus on that list instead of filling inboxes with unwanted and annoying emails. And they can be sure they're providing value because we tell them exactly what each prospect cares about.

Five Rules for BDR Breakthroughs

Rule #1: Power outbound sales with personalization

As we've discussed, showing your prospects that you understand what they care about is key to forging meaningful connections and providing value. That means you need to know the keywords they're researching, what their role on the buying team is, and where they are in the buying cycle.

But as a BDR, your dance card is jam packed. So it's not realistic to expect you to interpret what each and every keyword means, or how they relate to various personas on the buying team. This is where marketing can support you with well-developed value cards. Here is an example of the value card we use for the search term "CDP." Note that it gives our BDRs immediately applicable information about how to connect with people in different roles based on their interest in CDPs. If you had a tool like that, wouldn't you feel more confident in your ability to quickly and easily deliver personalized value to the different people across a company's buying team?

CDP
CUSTOMER DATA PLATFORM

Packaged software that creates a persistent, unified customer database that is accessible to other systems

HEAD OF DEMAND GENERATION

Outbound Marketing Campaign Support

Create segments using the CDP and feed those segments to marketing systems such as email service providers, marketing automation tools, or built-in multi-channel, personalized campaign orchestration.

MARKETING OPS LEADER

Reporting and Dashboards

Advanced reporting capabilities include customizable drill-down reports and integration with external analytics tools for more advanced reporting.

HEAD OF MARKETING/CMO

Omnichannel & Offline Aggregation

Ability to provide a seamless experience across multiple channels, devices, applications and physical or offline channels like a storefront.

REVENUE/SALES OPS LEADER

Ecommerce Recommendations & Optimization

Includes support for features to handle things like shopping cart abandonment, repeat purchases, next best offers, commerce campaigns, etc.

Rule #2: Use a multichannel strategy with a mix of manual and automatic touches

It's important to create a cadence that incorporates a variety of types of touches, including LinkedIn connection requests and "likes," manual and auto-generated emails, phone calls and voicemail, video, and direct mail. Take a look at this example of one of our cadences, in which we execute the first three steps over the course of the same day. We start with a LinkedIn connection request to put a face with a name, follow up with a personalized email, and finally call or leave a voice message if they don't answer.

1. CONNECTION REQUEST	2. EMAIL #1	3. PHONE CALL (VOICEMAIL)	4. EMAIL #2 (VIDEO)	5. PHONE CALL	6. PHONE CALL (VOICEMAIL)
7. EMAIL #3 (AUTO)	8. EMAIL #4 (AUTO)	9. LINKEDIN ENGAGEMENT	10. EMAIL #5 (AUTO)	11. PHONE CALL	12. ALYCE GIFT
13. LINKEDIN (IN-MAIL)	14. EMAIL #6	15. PHONE CALL (VOICEMAIL)	16. PHONE CALL	17. EMAIL #7	18. NURTURE

If you don't take a multi-channel approach, you're overlooking the fact that prospects respond differently in different channels. Getting comfortable with multi-channel communication may take some learning and practice. But with good support from leadership, it's a skill you can build if you haven't already.

Rule #3: Rely on templates, and personalize them with keywords and persona

Customizable templates are critical for speed and efficiency. An email template, for example, should be 80 percent fixed copy relevant to all buyers, leaving you only 20 percent to customize based on the individual buyer interests, activity, and persona. The same is true for guided scripts for calls, voicemail, and video. Your marketing team should be providing you with these tools to improve your chances of success.

Rule #4: Update materials and cadences quarterly

The last thing you want to do is reach out to prospects with stale or outdated information. That's why it's important that templates, value cards, and other materials are refreshed on a quarterly basis based on success metrics. Work with your team to evaluate what steps of the cadence are strong, what subject lines are successful, and what content is most effective. Optimize the ones that don't perform as well. It's also important to keep things current and fresh by incorporating new content if available, like analyst reports and metrics.

Rule #5: Don't give up on unresponsive prospects

Remember that time stamp? It allows you to see in real time how accounts are moving along. Well sometimes even with the best outreach and intentions, accounts slow down or even stall, and they need an extra boost. This is when direct mail is an ideal extra step. If you have an account that's ghosting you, or if the key persona on the buying team just won't give you the time of day, don't give up. If they made it in-market, it's with good reason. They were showing enough signs of buying intent that you can be confident in taking your efforts to the next level. At 6sense, we use Alyce, which is the service I talked about in Chapter 4. We've seen that giving an extra, personalized nudge to the accounts we're confident in can make a night-and-day difference in terms of engagement and conversion.

Difference-makers in action

So how did life feel once our BDRs weren't wasting their time on cold calls, unwanted emails, and accounts that weren't ready for them? Well, the energy was palpable. Walking into the office, you could feel the buzz. The BDR team wasn't wasting time figuring out what accounts to focus on, slogging through research, or tracking down contact information. Marketing had done all of that, so the BDRs could get to work making the magic happen with energy, engagement, and focus.

Juline Lamusga, who was one of our top-performing BDRs at the time of this change (and is now kicking ass as an AE), shared her perspective.

> *Knowing who to target and basic messaging is great, but the big difference in prospecting is learning WHY the account is in-market and figuring out how to talk to them based on what they care about. I loved being able to be hyper-personalized because I knew keywords, pages they'd visited, where the buying team was located, and more. It provided a lot of direction. It wasn't just raw data or scores, it was a clear picture and timeline of the account that I could use to engage in a meaningful way.*
>
> *I'm pleasantly persistent and felt empowered to not give up. If one channel didn't work, I'd get creative in other ways. I'd almost do more touches. Hearing a no doesn't mean they are not interested ... a no from one person at an in-market account is just that—a no from one person. If one person on the account wasn't interested, I wouldn't stop until I got a no from everyone on the persona map. Because I knew that if the account 6QA'ed, someone was interested.*

Clearly, Juline is a difference-maker. And once she was given the tools and insights she needed to stop wasting her time on unproductive activities, she started to soar. In fact, so did our BDR team in general. Since implementing these changes, our BDR team is empowered to do their jobs efficiently and effectively. Today, 80 percent of our bookings come from 6QA'ed accounts. We went from inconsistently delivering our pipeline goals to overdelivering, increasing BDR quota by more than 50 percent. We exceeded my wildest expectations.

What's more, our CEO is now getting thank-you notes about how awesome and helpful our BDRs are. I'm telling you, that is *not normal.* Usually the only communication you get about the people doing outreach is complaints (and maybe the occasional cease and desist). So for our BDRs to be providing so much value that our customers are proactively thanking us is really just astounding.

It's been amazing to see the team progress and excel. And I'm confident that if you're a difference-maker like Juline, you can do the same.

Rise up and embrace the change!

If you're a sales, business, or marketing development rep and you're ready to ditch the old, ineffective ways of prospecting, it's time for you to embrace your inner difference-maker! Step one is to *advocate for what you need to be successful.*

While I learned a ton about what BDRs need by spending a day in their shoes, not all leaders are going to do that. That means that it's up to you to identify what will make you most successful and ask for it.

It's also important to remind yourself that *you can do great things*. Not just good things, but great. I have super high expectations of BDRs because I've seen what they can achieve when they're hardworking, well-resourced, and inspired. Keep your expectations of yourself high. Don't aim to be a super BDR. Aim to be *the best seller*.

And remember that you are so much more than a "cadence pusher." You are the voice of the brand and the curators of the customer experience. In most cases you're the first impression a customer will ever have—so make sure you're putting forth your best, most brilliant, most customer-obsessed self.

Finally, BDRs, know that you are a BFD! The greatest gift I was given in life was high expectations—and I'm sharing those with you here. I fully believe that you are capable of working harder than everyone else, constantly learning and adapting, and seeking out every single advantage to better yourself.

Now go forth and advocate for this no-spam, no-cold-call vision—and see how it transforms your life!

MODERN BDRS/SDRS/MDRS CAN	BECAUSE THEY KNOW
Deploy outreach cadences to prioritized (warm) accounts, resulting in higher response rates	The identity of accounts showing intent, which ones are an ICP fit, and where they are on the buying journey
Personalize outreach based on the account and contact's unique interests	What topics accounts and contacts care most about and how they've engaged in the past
Engage the entire buying team rather than working leads	The composition of the buying team and each person's current level of engagement with the brand
Improve engagement rates and boost the number of meetings scheduled	Which accounts to reach out to and how to perfectly time outreach sequences
Strategically use tactics like direct mail to generate meetings and engagement	How many days accounts have been in the purchase and decision buying stages

Sales Leader

It's never been easy to be a sales leader, but it seems to be getting harder and more complex by the day. Whereas selling used to be all about relationship building (remember those steak dinners and ball games?), it's now so much more. The pace of selling has exploded, and the expectations on you as a sales leader are constantly increasing. Add to that the new tools, technologies, data, and intelligence now available, and it's clear that being a successful sales leader requires an entirely new set of skills and competencies.

At the same time, sales and marketing can't even agree on which fundamental metrics to use to measure success—so it's no wonder they're misaligned pretty much every step of the way. Here are just some of the disconnects we found in a recent survey we conducted:

- **Accounts engaged:** sales cares, marketing doesn't
- **Deal velocity:** sales cares, marketing doesn't
- **Sales accepted leads:** sales cares, marketing doesn't
- **Accounts in market:** sales cares, marketing cares less
- **MQLs:** marketing cares, sales doesn't

This is a huge problem for sales leaders. After all, your marketing team is supposed to be warming up accounts for you and arming your team with key insights into those accounts that they need to be successful. And yet 50 percent of sales and marketing leaders can't even agree on which accounts to target—which does not bode well for turning those accounts into opportunities and closed deals!

This disconnect—especially at a time when expectations of sales leaders are getting more and more aggressive—is untenable. But here's the good news: The new vision I'm laying out here will abolish the misalignment that's holding you back and set you up to achieve new levels of success for you and your team.

What keeps you up at night?

As a sales leader, your most important job is to put your team in a position to succeed. And if you're like the difference-making CROs, CSOs, and heads of sales I know, this dedication to your team's success drives you to constantly be "looking for the red."

That never-ending anticipation of trouble spots and the constant search for ways to improve are marks of a truly dedicated sales leader—one who will stop at nothing to help his or her team win. If you're in that category, there are probably questions that keep you up at night. In this section, I'm going to walk through a few of the ones I've heard from some of my favorite sales leaders—and offer some insight into how this bold new vision of selling and marketing is going to help you put those questions to rest.

Where do we have leaks and breakdowns?

You know that opportunities are slipping and not getting worked—but why? Sorry to say it, but you have an eff-load of leaks and breakdowns—and a lot of them have to do with the misalignment between sales and marketing that I keep talking about. If you've ever heard the refrain, "These leads suck. Marketing isn't even qualifying them!" from your team, or "Why are tier-one accounts not even getting touched?" from the marketing team, you know you've got leaks and breakdowns aplenty. This lack of alignment doesn't just lead to finger-pointing—it also undermines financial performance, according to 60 percent of sales and marketing professionals.[13]

Step 1 in Operation Plug the Leaks: Get right with your CMO. Align on your metrics, starting by *torching your MQLs*. Just like that scene in *Mr. Mom* when he burns that old flannel shirt that no longer serves him, it's time to burn your breakdown-causing MQLs to ash. Working crappy leads is not setting your team up for success, so stop doing it. Instead, align with your CMO on the operating model (Chapter 4) and embrace an account-based funnel. Work together as a revenue team with your CMO— no defensiveness or territorialism allowed—to agree on metrics, share data, and align on priorities. This move alone will change the paradigm and allow you both to start working to plug those leaks.

> **Old world:** Leaks and breakdowns abound.
>
> **New world:** Sales and marketing align on the revenue operating model and are always working together to plug leaks and restart after breakdowns.

Why does everything take so long?

If you're finding that everything takes forever—from deploying a field program to closing a deal—it could be that your data are inadequate. And in modern selling, data is king. You need to have trustworthy data in order to be able to do your job efficiently, and your team needs it to be able to do theirs. Without reliable, usable data, you're shooting blind and wasting time.

Here's another area where sales and marketing misalignment rears its head. If you're getting your data from an outdated CRM, and marketing is getting its data from a cruddy MAP, you come to the table with different beliefs about what's important and how to prioritize. That's a problem because you have critical decisions you need to make on a daily basis: *What's my addressable market? What accounts should I call today? What's the best way to structure my sales territory? Should I run a competitive campaign this quarter? Do we go after a new vertical? How many new AEs can I confidently add?* If you're not answering those questions with trustworthy data, you're just guessing. And while Ouija

---

13 https://business.linkedin.com/en-uk/marketing-solutions/blog/posts/sales-and-marketing/2018/Sales-and-Marketings-big-challenges-for-2019

boards are fun for middle-school sleepovers, they're not how we should be making decisions in the high-stakes world we play in.

BREAKTHROUGH

Modern tech and seamless alignment with marketing will help you fulfill your promise to give your team every advantage possible to win.

This is where rich, reliable data comes in. And I'm not just talking about that shaky first-party data you have but don't really know what to do with. I'm talking about integrating reliable third-party data so you can see not just known activity, like who's filling out forms, but anonymous activity as well. That includes who's visiting your website and not raising their hands, but it also includes information about what accounts are doing when they're not within your four walls—their research on blogs, competitors' sites, industry reports, and so forth. This kind of rich data allows you to see where your untapped opportunities are.

The customer data platforms (CDPs) I told you about in Chapter 3 are also essential here. They make it possible to break down data silos, de-dupe records, and cleanse data so that when you're making decisions, they're based on a single source of rich, accurate account data that you can take action on.

When you have a clear source of reliable data, debates, and delays go out the window. In their place, you have deft, agile marketing and selling. Our director of commercial sales, Michael (Mac) Conn, has a shining example of what this looks like in practice.

> *We recently heard that one of our competitors was exiting our market segment, and that another one wasn't doing that well. So during my weekly call with our amazing Field Marketing Leader, Courtney Smith, I told her about it. I floated the idea of running a campaign or two in light of the news. She set up a meeting for us to talk more about it the next day.*

At the start of that meeting, we pulled up our platform to look at the number of accounts we could target and see if it was even worthwhile. Within 15 seconds, we had determined that there were workable segments that either had those competitors' technology installed or had been actively researching those competitors in the past 7 days. So right off the bat, we knew it was actually worth our time to pursue. We got to spend the rest of that 30-minute meeting talking about the fun stuff—what the campaign was going to look like. And the next day, the marketing team was already running ads and a LinkedIn campaign against the audience we had defined at the start of the meeting.

Within two weeks, we had five opportunities against accounts in those market segments. If that's not sales and marketing alignment, I don't know what is.

The ability to take the data equation off the table and figure out whether it's worth our time—without debate and delay—is what made this possible. Rallying around an objective data set is key, and usually that's the hardest thing to do.

> **Old world:** It takes forever—and a lot of back-and-forth—for sales and marketing to accomplish anything together.
>
> **New world:** Decisions are made quickly and based on shared, trusted data.

That type of fast, agile, data-fueled decision-making is *only* possible because our sales and marketing teams are so aligned. And that alignment wouldn't be possible without the tech that makes clean and trusted data possible.

Are we missing opportunities or getting into deals too late?

Is there anything worse than working your ass off on an account only to wake up and find out your competitor just closed what should have been *your deal*—and your team didn't see it coming? Or when you hear that your competitor landed a huge deal that you didn't even know was in-market? Or when you bust your butt on an RFP only to learn that you were only column fodder?

I know sales leaders, and I know that there is *nothing* that gets under your skin like losing. But when you don't have the right tech and the right data, you're playing from behind.

One of our customers, Aprimo, ran into this problem after they were the leaders in three Forrester waves. (I know, sounds like a nice problem to have!) But suddenly they found they were being inundated with RFPs—not because these prospects were really considering them, but because the procurement teams at the companies threw them in there based on their wave success. And frustratingly (but predictably), they kept losing these RFPs.

When they took a step back, they realized that when they got into the game so late, they had no chance at winning. "We were finding that 57 percent of the buying process had already happened before we knew about it—there was all this in-market activity that we had no view to," explains Ed Breault, Aprimo's CMO. They knew they had to reach prospects much earlier in their journey if they wanted to influence their decision-making.

How did they do that? With the capabilities we talked about in Chapter 3, they were able to light up the Dark Funnel™. Based on the activity they saw there, they could easily spot which accounts were gearing up for an RFP.

Having this sneak preview meant that sales and marketing could both jump into action—doing their research, creating a microsite for the prospect, and putting themselves in a great position to win— sometimes preempting the RFP process altogether.

I love this story because it's a perfect example of how modern sales leaders can work together with marketing to anticipate possible accounts and pro-actively uncover demand—ensuring that you nei-ther miss opportunities nor come at them too late.

> **Old world: We miss opportunities because we either don't know about them, or we find out about them too late to influence their buying journey.**
>
> **New world: We light up the Dark Funnel™ and begin to influence IICP prospects at the earliest stages of their research.**

Are reps spending their time on the right accounts, and am I setting them up to succeed?

As a sales leader, your only asset is your people, and their only asset is their time. So you need to optimize how they use that time and set them up to be as successful as possible.

I mentioned it in the BDR section, but it bears repeating: Our frontline hunters—the BDRs, the prospectors—are wasting a colossal amount of time on unproductive activi-ties. I'm not talking about sneaking games of Candy Crush at their desks. I'm talking about chasing worthless leads, doing endless research, and reaching out to prospects at the wrong time, with the wrong message. And none of that is their fault; it's because we're not setting them up for success.

And BDRs aren't the only ones we're failing. Our AEs *hate to lose*. But when we give them territories filled with junk, or when they don't have the insights to know what their buyers are doing and thinking, they're bound to have lackluster results.

But fully equipping the entire selling team with these kinds of insights and making it re-peatable and scalable can be a challenge. "It's easy to make one or two reps successful," says Mark Ebert, our head of sales. "But I need to be able to make every rep—including our BDRs, our ISRs, commercial, large enterprise—across multiple territories successful, and I need it to be repeatable and scalable."

Mark explains that given the pace at which they need to perform, modern sales teams expect their leaders to equip them with everything they need to function at a high level. That includes really good tech that can tell you about the buying team, the competitive landscape, the most important challenges your customers are facing, what they have in their tech stack, and how engagement is changing throughout the cycle.

With that tech in place, "It's about calling equipped with the information you need so you have the highest probability of winning," Mark explains.

The right tech, like 6QA insights and dynamic territories, allows you to scale by giving you the tools you need to build proven, repeatable processes. Having those processes in place makes it easier for the sellers to sell and for you to add new people to your team seamlessly—and provides confidence that you can give them good territories.

As a difference-maker sales leader, you know that you can set your sellers up for success when you give them:

- An awesome territory
- Prioritization within their territories so they can make use of every incremental moment
- Prospecting insights to get connected with the best opportunities (i.e., the ones that are actually going to happen)
- Deal insights—including personas engaged and competitors involved—for every interaction throughout the deal

And knowing that all of this is running in the background for every AE is what's going to help you sleep at night.

> **Old world:** Your sellers are flying blind, wasting their time on the wrong accounts with little insight.
>
> **New world:** Your sellers use deep insights to prioritize accounts, multithread deals, and hone their interactions based on what they know about their buyers.

Are we showing up the right way in front of prospects?

The customer experience is at the heart of this revolution we're creating. Are your sellers giving your prospects a stellar customer experience at every touch point? If not, they (and you) are leaving opportunities on the table.

When your AEs meet with a prospect, you want to be confident that every interaction the prospect has had with your brand so far has been a good one. It's the difference between walking into a meeting where the people across the table are already annoyed with you and walking in to find a buying team who's super impressed with what they've seen so far. If your prospects already feel a connection to your brand—and if they feel like your AEs know and understand them (you know, because you've treated them like humans), you have a much greater chance of success.

Every single interaction with a potential customer is a chance to either reinforce your relationship or minimize it (or have no effect at all). There are literally hundreds of these before a deal closes. It's true that 70 or 80 percent of those touches will be orchestrated by marketing (another win for alignment!), but there's still plenty that are in your control as a sales leader: You can control who you hire, and you can control how prepared they are to deliver a killer experience.

Let's start with who you hire. You're a difference-maker, and ideally, you'll hire a team of difference-makers. How do you know if you've found a seller who is going to crush it for you? "I look for aptitude and acumen, which is a great combination of natural ability and the capacity to exercise good judgment and think on your feet," our CEO Jason explains. "If you have those two ingredients, most everything falls into place. The third thing I look for is a bit of an intangible, which is the will to win, willpower." What is one sign that the person you're hiring has these traits? An insatiable curiosity. "If someone is relentlessly curious, they tend to focus on learning and optimizing on the job," Jason says.

With your team of curious and talented sellers, now you need to set up the processes to make sure they thrive. These are the processes I spoke about previously—built on the best insights and repeatable and scalable across the team.

That's when you can focus on making sure your sellers are rocking the customer experience part of the equation. One tool for doing that is the value cards I've told you about. They make it possible for every seller—even the ones fresh out of college—to understand their prospects so they can be consultative and add value. I'm also a big believer in value selling and supporting processes with ROI, constantly improving our skills with tools like Gong, and mapping our cycle to buying jobs.

These are all keys to the no-spam and no-cold-calls parts of this manifesto—if you're providing value at every interaction, you aren't spamming, and you aren't cold calling. You're delivering the right experiences to the right accounts at the right time.

> **Old world:** Sellers are ill-equipped to know your buyers and connect with them as humans.
>
> **New world:** Bring on the X factor! Your prospects feel known and understood—and more likely to buy—because they've been treated well at every touchpoint.

All of this needs to be built into your training process, and it needs to be reinforced daily as part of your team's culture.

The bright new world of sales leadership

For sales leaders who have made the shift to modern selling—bolstered by modern technology—there's simply no going back. They can't imagine trying to lead their teams without the types of insights and tools they have now.

In fact, one of our customers conducted a survey to see just how great of an impact the right tech capabilities have on their ability to sell. Every single respondent—100 percent—said that losing 6sense Sales Intelligence would have a medium to high impact on their ability to hit sales goals.

The results were astounding but easy to believe if you've experienced the transformation that's possible with this technology. It's hands-down the greatest thing you can do to set your team up for success. I've never heard of another investment that gets the kind of buy-in we heard about in this research. There's no CRM implementation, sales training, certification, or coaching that can yield the type of growth that is possible with the right intelligence capabilities.

Being in sales is hard enough. Leveraging cutting-edge technology across the entire process gives every member of your team the greatest chance at striking gold—and that's the goal of every difference-maker sales leader I know!

MODERN SALES LEADERS CAN	BECAUSE THEY KNOW
Help sales reps strategize on deals and prioritize actions to maximize win rates	What accounts and contacts care about, how and when they've engaged, and the composition of the buying center
Scale success while rapidly hiring and growing the team	How to design repeatable processes driven by data, from prioritizing BDR outreach to aligning with marketing for air cover during deal cycles
Manage pipeline to ensure reps hit their number and avoid unpleasant end-of-quarter surprises	How to work with revenue ops to design dynamic territories based on ICP fit and buying stage
Rapidly adjust to changing market conditions	How to partner with marketing to determine the best campaigns to run
Ensure teams are not getting into deals late or missing deals altogether	How to uncover the Dark Funnel™ and ensure 6QAs get worked

Sales and Account Executives

There are a million books out there for sales methodologies, but most of them are written with the average salesperson in mind. You, my friend, are not the average salesperson. You're a top seller—one of the difference-makers. And if you're not there yet, it's certainly what you strive to be.

Over the past 20 years, I've worked with some amazing, awe-inspiring sellers. But the absolute best ones I've ever met are here at 6sense. Our incredible sales culture comes all the way from the top, and it permeates throughout the entire team. Our sales leaders have had noteworthy careers as high performers themselves, and they have a knack for hiring and growing great sales talent. So that certainly contributes to the success of our sales team.

But it's the sellers themselves who put in the hard work day after day to produce jaw-dropping results. They are the ones who hold themselves to sky-high expectations and accountability. For our top sellers, meeting quota is table stakes. If they're not hitting 150 percent or above, they're "finding the red" to do better.

When I think about what sets these sellers apart, what defines them as difference-makers, I realize they're fully committed to their *why*. They ask the big questions about what they want in life. They've determined what they want to do, and they're crystal clear on it. And they're committed to how their sales career is going to get them there. That's why they do the hard work, even when no one is looking. It's an intrinsic motivation to beat their goals that makes them unstoppable.

As I said, this is a culture that permeates our entire sales team. Every single AE working at 6sense is a difference-maker. And you know that the AE who is leading that incredible pack is truly next-level.

A total commitment to winning

When I heard Dasha Vasilyeva's presentation at our field kickoff, I had chills. Dasha—who goes by the well-deserved nickname DashaFierce—is currently our top seller, and she has some advice for modern sellers who want to rise to the top the way she has. She calls it winning by 1,000 cuts: "You have to keep fighting the daily battles," she told our sales team. "At the beginning, you're going to lose more than you're going to win. The more you train yourself, the more you lose, the smarter you get. And eventually, you win."

Like many top AEs, Dasha has the heart and perseverance of a professional athlete. She's totally committed to her craft—and that craft is winning. Like Michael Jordan, she's willing to fail as many times as she needs to in order to get the win. I loved this MIchael Jordan quote that Dasha shared in her presentation:

I've missed more than 9,000 shots in my career. I've lost almost 300 games. 26 times, I've been trusted to take the game winning shot and missed. I've failed over and over and over again in my life. And that is why I succeed.

In basketball, the work to improve entails running drills, training, and taking shot after shot after shot. For AEs, that work is doing the extra research to really understand their prospects, getting in touch with the right people, taking the time to make their prospects feel known, and prepping for every meeting like it's a playoff game.

And there's good news in this new frontier of selling and marketing for Dasha and the top sellers like her: Today's technology makes these game-changing moves possible in ways they never could have dreamed of before.

Top sellers use every advantage

Expectations of sellers are higher than ever, and the way buyers buy has shifted dramatically. We know that they're completing much of the buying cycle anonymously, they buy in teams of a dozen or so people, and they don't engage until their minds are pretty much made up. It's no wonder selling is getting harder by the day.

But again, you're a difference-maker, and you're not going to stop because of new challenges. You are going to find every advantage available to you to help you win. And in the modern landscape, those advantages come in the form of the tech capabilities I described in Chapter 3. Here are just some of the ways modern tools have transformed the ways sellers sell with a competitive advantage.

The timing is right

Dasha remembers a time at a previous job when she warmed an account for months—visiting the office, walking the halls, building amazing relationships with the team—but never closed the deal. A few months after she had moved to a different territory, she learned that the company signed a deal with the rep who took over her territory. She'll never forget what the customer said when she asked why they hadn't bought from her: "Well, Dasha, we didn't have a need for what you were selling. Your timing was off."

Timing is never a problem anymore, now that she has technology that prioritizes accounts based on their readiness to engage. She knows now that the accounts she's working are in-market to buy.

Meeting prep gets even more personalized

Real-time sales intelligence lets us see what accounts are researching, so when we show up to a meeting we can speak directly to the pain points we know they have—not just the ones they're telling us about. For instance, if we know that a team is researching Drift in addition to predictive analytics, we can add a slide to our deck that talks about our seamless integration with Drift, and how our solution can make it an even more powerful tool.

Forecasting is grounded in reality

Having visibility into the engagement of the entire buying committee gives us a really good measure of how likely a deal is to close. Dasha says she won't forecast something as a commit if she doesn't have the entire buying committee engaged. Using the persona map, she will find the gaps in engagement and make meaningful connections with all members of the buying team—thereby improving her chances of closing the deal.

BREAKTHROUGH

You carry a lot of weight in the company and are on the hook to deliver the goods—use your voice to advocate for what you need! Every insight and advantage matters. Insist that they be made available to you.

The teams are aligned

As the AE, you're the quarterback of the deal. You need to be able to rally the whole team together. With trustworthy data that's shared among the entire revenue team, you're able to make sure you're all on the same page and presenting a united front. You can connect the entire buying team with their counterparts at your company and build relationships that will pay dividends.

You have allies in negotiations

Here come those dividends. Because you've been able to align your team to multithread your deals, you have multiple relationships you can lean on to finalize agreements. The different stakeholders you've nurtured across the organization become your champions.

Breathing Life Into a Dying Deal

Dasha talks about how technology helped her breathe life into a deal that was on the ropes. It had been moving along nicely, but then life got in the way for the CMO—layoffs, competing priorities—and suddenly it was radio silence. But Dasha never took her eye off the buying signals and keyword activity in her dashboard. And she could see that some key players on the buying team were researching some of our competitors. But still, she wasn't getting anywhere with her outreach to the CMO.

So what did she do? She got busy multithreading. She reached out to the company's sales leader to introduce him to our sales leader, Mark. Meeting: booked.

Even though this was a marketing-funded project, Dasha knew that the whole buying team would influence the decision. In the meeting with the head of sales, Mark and Dasha were able to explain how our solution would transform not just their marketing, but their selling as well. She created a brand advocate within the company. Suddenly, the CMO resurfaced to start the conversation up again and to schedule a demo for the executive team. The deal got back on track, and they are now a happy customer.

Without the visibility that she had into the account's research activity, Dasha might have assumed the deal was dead. But because she could see that they were still researching our competitors, she knew there were signs of life. And being able to see the engagement of different members of the buying team allowed her to find another avenue by which to revive the deal.

It's about tech ... and so much more

The future of selling *is* going to dramatically shift with the amazing new tech capabilities available to us, and if you use them to your advantage you are going to reach new heights in your career.

But what makes you a difference-maker is about so much more—it's your X factor that pushes you to the head of the pack.

You have off-the charts emotional intelligence, making it second-nature for you to build relationships with people. You set big goals, you embrace change, you have thick skin, you're sharp as a tack, and you are always learning. Add to all those amazing qualities the advantage that technology provides, and you're going to be unstoppable!

MODERN SELLERS CAN	BECAUSE THEY KNOW
Get in deals early by engaging with prospects before the competition	The identity of accounts showing intent, how and when they've engaged with the brand, even before prospects raise their hand
Effectively manage their pipeline to meet or exceed their number	How to prioritize accounts in their territories and coordinate efforts with BDRs based on ICP fit and predicted buying stages
Differentiate themselves by adding value throughout the buying process	How to personalize outreach content, presentations, and demos based on the topics accounts and contacts care most about, and which personas and competitors are engaged in the deal
Win more often	How to engage the entire buying team within accounts, if engagement is trending in the right direction, when new competitors show up in a deal, and the key personas that need to be engaged

Why we need this change, now more than ever

I hope by now I've made my case that embracing this tech-fueled, data-driven approach to sales and marketing isn't just a good idea, it's the only way to stay relevant and thrive in your role.

It's no longer enough to look at our static ICP or persona maps. Customers, industries, and markets evolve constantly, and we must be agile enough to meet them where they are. Nothing put a finer point on this for me than seeing how our teams adjusted and adapted when Covid turned our world upside-down.

You probably remember the moment in mid-March 2020 when it became clear that life as we knew it was about to change dramatically. All of a sudden, schools were closing, professional sports leagues were canceling their seasons, and non-essential businesses were shuttering their offices.

It also became clear that travel was out of the question. Which meant that whatever revenue we were banking on from trade shows, conferences, and customer meetings had just evaporated. Companies across the world suddenly found themselves grappling with how to stay alive as the ground shifted beneath us.

Mac, our director of commercial sales, had it especially rough when Covid hit. He was a new manager with a brand-new team of six in a growth market we had just broken into. They were all just getting their legs under them when suddenly their legs were swept out.

That first Monday after the office shut down, Mac remembers a pervasive feeling of fear. "There was personal fear, there was health fear, there was professional fear. *'How do I do my job? What do I do?'*" For salespeople especially, the climate was confusing and scary. "Every LinkedIn post was blowing up some seller for doing their job in the face of Covid," Mac says. "When you start seeing that, especially if you're doing outbound, you're afraid that anything you do is going to make you a pariah."

There was no roadmap to follow—we were all redefining the rules in real-time. Mac made a prudent decision: hit the pause button for 48 hours and come back together after some thinking and with some perspective.

"I did a lot of deep thinking myself," Mac says, "but I also put it on my team to come up with their own ideas." What they concluded was that their work couldn't stop because the customers they serve don't have the luxury of stopping their work. Instead, they shifted their mindset and decided to double-down.

The second thing they realized, and it kinda brings a little tear to my eye, is that the technology at their fingertips made it possible for them to continue their outreach without being insensitive. They could see who was still in-market and actively researching. And not only would they not be insensitive, but they'd also be providing a crucial service at a critical time. After all, a lot of companies were scrambling to make up for lost event pipeline, so they were out there actively researching solutions—and Mac's team could give them that solution.

"It gave my team the confidence to know that if we focus on in-market accounts now, we not only didn't need to worry about being blasted on LinkedIn, but we were really going to be able to actually help them out."

The approach everyone was preaching—stop sending blast emails, produce your content and let people consume it, sell with empathy—was the exact process we had already set up with our no-forms, no-spam, no-cold-calls strategy. The team took that 48-hour pause and came back with the realization that we'd been preparing for this for months.

© marketoonist.com

Just like on a "normal day," our tech allowed Mac's team to prioritize in real time the accounts that were ready to engage in that exact, bizarre moment. It also told the team what people were interested in so they could tailor their emails and phone calls to make them as relevant as possible—without a single "in these unprecedented times" blast email.

In the end, our insights and technology sustained us through what could have been a devastating time for our business (and that was for many). In fact, our numbers didn't just remain steady, they improved in the weeks after the shutdown took effect. Our pipeline exploded—quadrupling in that first week and at least doubling in the weeks after. In fact, Mac's team ended that quarter at 125 percent of plan.

"Without in-market understanding, there's no way in hell we'd have gotten even close to that," Mac says. "Being laser-focused on going after those in-market accounts allowed us to be successful."

Difference-makers, it's your time to break through!

Whether you're in one of the roles I explored in this chapter or if you're in another part of the revenue team, if you're a difference-maker, we need you. It's time to mobilize and be part of this movement!

I hope this book will serve as a guide to help you lay out your plan for breaking through to new heights in sales and marketing. If any of it feels overwhelming, just remember that you only need to start where you are and keep moving forward. Small changes become habits, and new habits become a way of life. As US Navy Admiral William McRaven said in his now famous commencement speech, "If you want to change the world, start off by making your bed." In other words, monumental changes are made one small task at a time.

You'll make mistakes along the way (I know I sure have). And that's not just okay, it's good. Remember that Michael Jordan quote? Perfection is the enemy of progress, so anticipate mistakes and hiccups. You will accidently send an email meant for 90 people to 900 instead. You will sometimes send a follow-up email that someone considers to be spam. You will forget to take down that one form from five years ago and someone will call you on it. And, if you're anything like me, your skin will crawl and you'll beat yourself up … but you'll learn.

So expect mistakes. Just dust yourself off, learn from them, and move forward. Tune out the naysayers and the critics and carry on.

No forms, no spam, no cold calls is an aspiration, not something you need to succeed at 100 percent of the time. It's a reminder for us all to look in the mirror, check ourselves, and shock our systems into doing better. It's that big goal Edwin Locke told us about—set your sights big, and you can't help but strive for them.

And most of all—have fun. I hope you'll hear this as a rallying cry to bring passion, creativity, and outside-the-box thinking back into your professional life. The fun factor is so important, and this new approach helps you achieve it. I always tell my team that if they're not having fun at least 8 out of every 10 working days, we're doing something wrong.

Now's a good time to start laying the groundwork with your V2MOM. Get clear on your vision (deliver predictable revenue growth through a customer-centric prospect experience), values (no forms, no spam, no cold calls), and methods (strategy, process, technology, and people). It'll keep you focused not just on how you're doing this, but why.

It's time. Get up, make your bed, and get started on changing the world!

AFTERWORD

In the time since launching this book, I've had the opportunity to meet with thousands of marketing and sales leaders who have read it. The response has been overwhelming. It's been exciting and humbling to hear about all the ways in which these professionals have been putting the book's ideas into practice.

It certainly hasn't been a small undertaking. I know I'm asking you to shake up the way you've been doing things for years—maybe decades—and I get how hard that can be. But now that the book has been out in the wild for a couple of years, I can say with more certainty than ever that this approach really works. It does take commitment, openness to change, and a sharp focus on the outcome you're trying to achieve. But it pays off. I've seen it again and again with colleagues, peers, and customers who have implemented it since the book was first published.

In this edition of the book, I want to add a chapter that will help you overcome obstacles to implementing the strategies the book presents. In following the journeys of all these revenue professionals for the past two years, I've heard some common questions about how to go from old-school to new-school revenue. I thought it would be useful to address those questions here, in case they're on your mind too.

How do I know (and show) that marketing is successful?

I know I told you that MQLs aren't worth a dime. They're not a reliable or data-driven way to measure marketing's success for all the reasons I've already explained ... but you can't measure *nothing*, right? So what should take the place of the MQL in accounting for how well marketing is doing its job?

The short answer is that modern marketers measure their success by how they're contributing to revenue. So we use KPIs that track to revenue. These are not vanity metrics—I hope we've moved beyond all of those. These are the metrics that indicate whether the business is moving in the right direction.

In our organization, marketing tracks pipeline, and we look at it every day. There are two different ways to look at pipeline. First is with a sales mindset: Sellers look at how much pipeline they're sitting on that's closeable at the beginning of a quarter or month. The second is with a marketing mindset: I look at raw pipeline produced month over month, quarter over quarter. The reason is that it tells us whether we're on track to meet revenue goals while we still have time to do something about it. For instance, if pipeline is off in Q4, we might have a Q1 revenue gap. So we can take steps now to right the ship.

In addition to the entire pipeline number, we also drill down into the makeup of the pipeline (e.g., new business versus upsell, inbound versus outbound versus ABX, strategic versus commercial versus enterprise, EMEA versus APAC versus AMER). Each of these areas could impact my pipeline assumptions, and I need to be able to see how each is performing against expectations so we can address any issues that come up.

This all ties back to being a chief *market* officer. When you're focused on your ideal customer profile and really understand it, the market lens affects everything you do—including how you look at how you can influence metrics that matter. There are a number of other revenue-driving metrics marketers should track, including average selling price (ASP), cycle time, win rates, and customer retention. These are all things that come together to create a revenue cycle. Here's how marketing can affect each.

Cycle time + ASP

Marketing has a major role to play in accelerating cycle time and increasing ASP. And a key part of doing that is to only serve up the most winnable opportunities to sales. I think of sales as our most expensive channel. And just like you wouldn't send a bottle of Dom Perignon to everyone who fills out a form on your site, you shouldn't have sales dedicate time and resources toward an account that's not ready. Instead, marketing can play a role in engaging multiple stakeholders on the account and making the most strategic marketing plays possible so that by the time the account is ready for sales outreach, the sales process will be faster and more successful.

Win rates

Tracking both competitive and non-competitive win rates helps marketers understand how our efforts are contributing to closed deals. And by looking at both subsets of win rates, we can see how we're completing two big jobs: differentiating from the competition and creating new projects. There are a lot of ways marketing can contribute to each.

Competitive win rates show how well we're making the case that we are a better choice than our competitors, and we can do that through thought leadership, a compelling value story, high customer satisfaction scores, and partnership with enablement to make sure sellers are delivering the most effective messaging.

Non-competitive win rates show how well we're persuading buyers that indecision is costlier than action—and specifically action that leads to buying from us. Marketing contributes to non-competitive win rates by providing earlier-stage education to create problem and solution awareness, by creating urgency, and by setting the stage for buyers to select our solution when they do decide to buy.

Customer retention

For too long, SaaS economics have meant marketing pours all its resources into customer acquisition, not retention. But keeping current customers happy is essential for predictable revenue. It's far more expensive to replace a customer than it is to retain them. And don't forget the upsell and cross-sell opportunities that disappear when a current customer walks.

Marketing has a huge role to play in retaining customers, and we can measure our success by tracking our net revenue retention (NRR) score. NRR tells us how much revenue is generated from existing customers, and it's a measure of a company's health that investors and markets obsess over. In fact, one survey of private equity firms and strategic buyers[1] found that NRR is the most important metric for the overwhelming majority of investors when evaluating a company. Another measure we should track is gross retention, which doesn't factor in upsell.

CMOs can influence both of these by rethinking customer marketing. Customer marketing is far more than just case studies and reference management. It's about analyzing the entire customer life cycle and running plays proactively to keep customers happy and engaged at each stage. That means making sure we're creating the right programs for customers, knowing our audience, and knowing what they're going to show up for. All in the purview of the chief market officer.

One of the things we do at 6sense is to look at what percentage of our customers have engaged in marketing programs each quarter. If no one is showing up, maybe our programming needs help, or maybe we're not marketing and communicating about the programs effectively. Another thing we do is to partner with the product team to understand how people are experiencing our product and improve the in-app experience.

Ultimately, your brand is not what you say it is. It's how people experience you. And dissecting the overall customer journey through that lens will allow you to positively influence every one of the metrics I've outlined here.

This is an especially high-level view of metrics that matter. I could probably write an entire book about it. Who knows, maybe there's a Volume 2 in our future ....

---

1   https://softwareequity.com/the-impact-of-net-retention-on-valuation-for-public-saas-companies/

Moving from reporting to forecasting: Be a financier, not an accountant

Accountants make decent money, but they don't make Wall Street money. So why do the folks on Wall Street get paid so much more? It's because they look forward and project or forecast future profits to figure out where to place bets. Accountants, on the other hand, add up what has already happened and report on it. They're focused on the past.

For marketers who want to elevate their game, I'd suggest a mindset shift: Think of yourself as a financier, not an accountant. Your value to your company increases exponentially when you can start to look at trends and underlying data, make assumptions, and then forecast what's to come.

That's what financiers do every day. They do due diligence on a company, consider historical trends, and build a model for how that company is going to fare in the future to decide whether or not to bet on it.

For marketers, our big bets are the programs and resources we invest in. We're forever asking ourselves whether we are investing in the right things. And we can get a certain amount of validation with accounting-style assessments, like looking at what programs worked in the past. But it's infinitely more useful to be able to understand what programs are going to work in the future. And that's where marketers can apply the financier approach by making predictions about pipeline.

If you're just reporting on pipeline, you're too late to do anything about it. But if you start forecasting pipeline instead, you can see where you're going—and influence it while there's still time.

Sales already has tools to accurately forecast, but I consider marketing's forecast to be the first line of defense in future-proofing bookings and revenue. And we need to be able to predict two things: First, what our pipeline needs to be to meet revenue goals, and second, where we'll end up based on what's currently happening.

A lot of marketers have wanted to do this for years. But we've been held back by the sheer amount of data analysis and predictive capabilities we'd need to make accurate forecasts. We've done our best with spreadsheets and guesswork, but we're only human. Even using good data sets and updating our forecasts quarterly, our forecasts haven't been as accurate as we'd like. What we really need is AI baked into our revenue platforms that accurately adjusts to real-time data and makes predictions based on that.

These dashboard images show hypothetical examples of the kinds of at-a-glance insights that are possible with AI-fueled pipeline prediction. You can easily see not only how you're doing by month, by channel, for the year, etc., but how you're projected to do in the future.

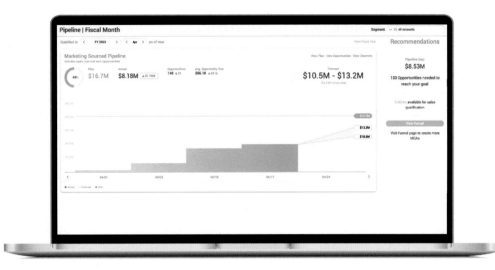

Do I *really* have to give up my MQLs?

I'm firm in my belief that MQLs are the wrong gauge of marketing success. But they're entrenched in so many revenue organizations that giving them up altogether is a non-starter for some marketers. And that's okay. I'm not saying you need to completely scratch the MQL if it's serving a purpose for you and your organization.

If the idea of giving up entirely on MQLs makes you nervous, then go ahead and keep tracking them. But I would challenge you to change the way you use them. As I just explained, modern marketers need to be focused on pipeline and the metrics that drive it. So instead of focusing on reporting on MQLs as a measure of success, look at them as one of many signals of how you're progressing toward your pipeline goals. Rather than thinking of MQLs as a target, think of them as an indicator and be sure to look at them in the context of ICP, web traffic, meetings booked and completed, and of course the metrics I mentioned earlier.

One of our customers who implemented the *no-forms, no-spam, no-cold-calls.* approach put it succinctly when she said, "We're not going to miss our revenue targets because we're not going to miss our pipeline targets." Which sounds obvious, right?

But if you start to think in those terms, and you still want to track MQLs, go for it. It's a signal. That's all. Just like an SQL is a signal. Just like if you're in product-led growth, a free trial download is a signal.

By keeping your success metrics focused on pipeline, you'll notice that people stop asking you about MQLs. They'll start asking about pipeline.

That means that instead of obsessing over MQLs, you can start looking for and optimizing revenue moments that will increase pipeline. For instance, when accounts are researching your competitors. Or, more broadly, when accounts are researching companies that are in the same ecosystem as you. For us, when someone is researching sales outreach tools, we know they're looking for ways to make their BDRs more efficient and effective. They're actively looking to solve a problem that is related to the problems we solve. So that's a revenue moment for us.

Likewise, when a company is actively hiring or has just recently hired key roles, that could be a revenue moment. For us, that might mean when a new CMO comes on board, or when the sales department is ramping up its hiring.

Or for publicly traded companies that file reports laying out their strategy, do they mention problems your solution solves? If so, that's a revenue moment.

These data are all available ... but you need to seriously consider what constitutes revenue moments for your organization so you don't miss them. Of course, you also need AI that sorts through all those mountains of data to identify the moments you care about. But the first step is to understand that these are the ways you drive pipeline and revenue.

I have also heard from some people who are nervous that if they switch to 6QAs they'll have fewer leads. The 6QA applies a pretty rigorous scoring model to ensure qualification, after all.

But having fewer leads can actually be a good thing. I want to share a story I remember from back when I was a sales leader. It's all about focus, and it perfectly reflects the journey I see so many people going through: First there's a decrease in leads, then there's a freak out, then there's a change of heart, then there's success.

When we opened our office in EMEA, we staffed it with one seller to start. And that meant he had a massive universe of potential customers to sell to—every vertical every product, every geo within EMEA. And at first we thought there was no way he wasn't going to blow his numbers out of the water. After all, look at all those possible opportunities!

But pretty quickly we realized that too much of a good thing was leading to overwhelm—the poor guy was traveling constantly and going after every shiny new opportunity. He didn't have the time or focus necessary to get each account to the finish line. And B2B buying is hard! Buyers need a lot of support and attention to make a purchase. Not surprisingly, he was soon missing his numbers.

Finally, I asked him to try a new approach. I explained to him that it's better not to work an account at all than to work it just a little bit. So instead of selling everything to everyone, I suggested he narrow his focus to just one product line and only sell to companies within 50 miles of his home.

He initially bristled. I was suggesting he give up roughly 90 percent of the accounts he was working on to focus on one product in a postage stamp-sized area. But he humored me. He started to work fewer opportunities, but he worked them with renewed focus and attention that hadn't been possible previously. He committed to the process. And almost immediately, things started to turn around. He made his numbers and then some. And the best news is I got to celebrate with him at President's Club.

This was an important lesson for him and for all of us. There's no trophy for working the most accounts. There's no prize for working the hardest. The rewards (like Club) come when you use every tool in your toolbelt and you focus fully on the deals that

The mentality of working an account, not a lead

Once people get comfortable reporting on pipeline instead of MQLs, there's still a hurdle to clear: how to get a 6QA to pipeline. I think that's actually the core of the biggest transformation that has to be made when shifting from lead-based to account-based.

This comes back to what I was talking about earlier about the MQL just being a signal. What we do, and what we see our successful customers do, is to say that we don't care what the underlying intent signal is. It could be a hand raise, it could be an SQL (one of the revenue moments I told you about earlier), it could be a 6QA. When we see a signal that's ideal for us, we start working the full account—not just the contact who raised their hand or showed intent.

Contrast that to how lead-based sales and marketing works. In that scenario, a lead comes in with an email attached to it. A BDR or SDR follows up with that lead, books a meeting with that individual, and moves on. But we know that engaging only one person on a deal is a recipe for disappointment. It's just not how B2B buying works. In B2B purchases, there's a buying team of 6 to 10 people or more. So we need to be working as many of those individuals as possible in a coordinated effort—not just the first one we identify.

Sales leaders know that single-threaded deals don't work. If you ever sit on a forecast call with a sales leader, you'll hear their frustration when a seller is only talking to one person at a company because those deals just don't close.

We can apply that same mentality to the entirety of the customer journey. If we don't want a single-threaded deal, why would we want a single-threaded lead? When we start thinking in those terms early on, we see the lead as a signal. And we start multithreading right at the beginning by identifying who's on the buying team and then engaging multiple stakeholders.

To determine who you want to engage, you can take a historical look at deals that have closed and learn from those. If you have good AI, it will tell you which personas have to be involved in a deal for it to be successful. And then you have your game plan: It's not just, "Follow up with this lead, book a meeting, and be done." Now it's, "Get contact data for these two, four, or six people and book meetings with all of them."

This is a hugely important change in both philosophy and procedure. And some key things need to happen in order for it to work properly.

First of all, think about how you structure your SLAs for BDRs and SDRs. We're all familiar with the SLA for a hand raiser (i.e., inbound). Typically the expectation is that the rep will respond within minutes. That's a good expectation—and it should be the same for 6QAs, since just like with inbound, every minute you wait decreases the likelihood of response. But the difference in our model is that we don't incentivize reaching out to just one individual, either for inbounds or for 6QAs. Our SLA sets the expectation that for inbounds, the rep will reach out to three people within six minutes. For 6QAs, we still expect outreach to three people, but the time frame is 20 minutes.

Of course, once you identify the personas you need to connect with for a successful deal, you need to know how to contact them. And this is an area people have told me they struggle with—finding current and accurate contact data for the people they want to engage. This is actually what led 6sense to acquire a leading contact data provider. Because the easier we can make it for BDRs and SDRs to do their jobs, the more likely they are to do them well. And if we're shifting expectations on them and requiring them to reach out to multiple key personas, we need to make it as simple as possible for them to do it.

Making the switch from lead-based to account-based requires changes across the board. What I've outlined here alters the way frontline teams operate, as well as how they're comped. It calls for new systems and better data to help you orchestrate it. It's not a small undertaking—but it is where the rubber meets the road in this modern B2B sales and marketing approach.

No 6QA left behind

As leaders, it's up to us to set the right expectations for our teams and to provide them with the resources they need to meet those expectations. But then it's on them to put in the effort and meet them. And the next step in this process is to put systems in place to make sure people are doing what we expect them to do.

As JZ says, you need to "inspect what you expect." We need to have the right measurements in place to ensure that (1) our BDRs and SDRs are working all the qualified accounts on their lists and that (2) they're working entire accounts, not single leads.

To inspect that first expectation, we need to make sure that we're capitalizing on those revenue moments I described earlier. For us, the best proxy of that is the 6QA. Are our BDRs, SDRs, and sellers working all their 6QAs, and are they working them in a timely fashion? We have dashboards and reports that show us that at a glance, and I am hyper-focused on them. We know statistically that 6QAs convert 30 percent better at two times the deal size, with a 30 percent faster cycle time than non-6QA accounts. So not working them is like leaving money on the floor.

Every Friday I get a report that flags any unworked 6QAs so we can inspect and improve. I also look at the quality and quantity of activity to make sure that not only is our SLA met, but also that we're personalizing and reaching out through multiple channels.

To address the second concern—whether outreach is happening in the right way—we've implemented something called the Quality Outreach Score. That shows us not just whether the accounts are being worked, but *how* they're being worked. Are we engaging all the right personas? Are we personalizing well and working a variety of channels? In addition to emailing, are we utilizing social, calling, and gifting when appropriate? Each of these factors into the quality of the outreach and implementing this scoring system has allowed us to make sure that we're providing the level of personalized engagement that our customers deserve.

With these systems and our tech at our disposal, it's pretty easy to stay on top of 6QAs and make sure they don't sit untouched. But the nature of the BDR and SDR roles is that they're prone to turnover—either because people do so well that they advance and become sellers, or they don't work out and they move on. Either way, average tenure in the role is 1.8 years, according to research from the Bridge Group. That means we are perpetually training new people in this role. And the systems, tech, and processes—along with a robust enablement program—ensure that we maintain our standards even as the teams change.

Of course, even with the best team, tech, processes, and enablement, stuff happens. People get sick, go on vacation, or just have a bad day. Whatever the reason, there will be times when plan A doesn't pan out. It's essential to anticipate that and to have a safety net in place so that even when there's a gap in coverage, no 6QA gets left behind.

This is another place where AI comes to the rescue. We have our AI configured to take over when humans aren't following up on 6QAs fast enough. The first touch in any sale is incredibly important, and we know that there's no second chance to make a first impression. So we don't use canned emails; our AI is sophisticated enough to personalize and give that five-star first-touch experience. Of course the first preference is to have a human doing the outreach, but our backup plan truly helps me sleep at night because I know it means we'll never have 6QAs sitting there untouched, no matter what life throws at us.

The "No Spam Nurture"

To be clear, AI-powered outreach is not spam. After all, I can't write a book with "No Spam" in the title and then send out a bunch of junk emails. We follow the basic rule: If you know nothing, do nothing. In order to not spam, we need data that allow us to be timely and personalized, such as persona, role, timing, keywords, and industry. And, of course, contact data.

Now while all that data are critical to sending personalized and timely emails, data orchestration is equally important. If you just rely on occasional mass updates of your data, your outreach and messaging will quickly be outdated. Data orchestrations allow you to use up-to-the-minute data to set up real-time plays.

With the right data and tailored orchestration, we can send automated emails or nurture sequences that are not spam.

With this in mind, I challenged our team to create what I call the No Spam Nurture. We started with these key data points: persona, role, and timing. Persona and role can be hard data to get, but we've been able to automate this process just as soon as an account starts to show early signs of interest. We have set up a play that acquires the contact data for the account and enriches the record in Salesforce. We have gotten to the point now where 98 percent of our active contacts in Salesforce have persona and role data. That's the only reason we can do this No Spam Nurture.

This rich, clean, and fresh data are the key to putting all our creative ideas in motion. With our No Spam Nurture, priority number one is that the outreach needs to feel authentic. And priority number two is that it needs to be pure give. Again, that first touch is *so* important, and the last thing we want to do is start off a relationship by asking for something. So there is no call to action or anything. We simply provide resources that we believe will be genuinely useful based on persona, role, and timing.

So a CMO, for instance, might receive a series of emails from me letting them know about CMO Coffee Talk, the networking group I help run for other CMOs. The group has been an amazing community for me and the 1,700+ other members who currently take part in it, and I am always thrilled to bring new CMOs into the fold. So when we see an account starting to show interest in 6sense, the CMO is entered into this No Spam Nurture to receive communications directly from me, CMO to CMO.

The marketing ops person will receive a similarly value-oriented nurture from our marketing ops person, Chris Dutton. His emails talk about things that keep him up at night in his role and offer some resources that have helped him.

And so on. We have a set of very tailored, very helpful email nurtures that allow us to engage positively and genuinely with people we can each relate to. It's a real relationship-builder ... even if it includes some automation and is powered by AI.

With this nurture in place, we can be sure that our first touch with every contact is on brand, helpful, and engaging. And, most definitely, *not spam.*

You gotta wanna

It was only a few years ago that the name of the game—the only game you had—was spam, forms, and cold calls. But technology has come such a long way since then, and you don't have to operate in that old way anymore. You now have the opportunity to gather volumes of data, and volumes of signals, about your buyers' behavior.

AI is so advanced now that it can recognize patterns in data that no human could ever hope to pick up on. Those patterns tell you what your buyers are interested in, whether it's the time to reach out, and what channels you should use to do it most effectively.

This new tech is making it possible to innovate in ways we never could have before. And it couldn't come at a better time because we know that customers are fed up with the experiences we've been providing. According to Gartner's research, 64 percent of B2B buyers say they're so underwhelmed by the digital experiences companies are providing that they can hardly tell them apart.

So it's no surprise that the companies that are embracing this new technology—the data and the AI that can turn it into actionable intel—are completely changing the game. They're engaging with prospects and customers in new and exciting ways, and it's setting them on a path to unbelievable success.

That's a choice they're making, and it's paying off for them. And that success is available to you too. The tools are here. They're available to you *right now*. *Right now*, you can have visibility into your Dark Funnel™. *Right now*, you can revolutionize how your sales and marketing teams create, manage, and convert pipeline to revenue. *Right now*, you can generate an experience that's meaningful, with no forms, no spam, no cold calls. And with this opportunity, you can create a competitive advantage for your organization and yourself.

I wish I could tell you that you could flip a switch and the change would be made, and you could go sip a margarita on the beach while your pipeline fills. But the reality is that creating and maintaining a competitive advantage takes work—and will. As I tell my sons all the time, you can have all the resources in the world in front of you, but in order for those to make a difference in your goals, *you gotta wanna*.

You gotta wanna change the game. *You gotta wanna* add value for your buyers. *You gotta wanna* tear down silos between sales and marketing. *You gotta wanna* provide real insights and stop with the guesswork. *You gotta wanna* believe that it's possible. And *you gotta wanna* put in the work to make it a reality.

I'm a big believer in professional and personal breakthroughs. Breakthroughs call on us to commit to something that's big and a little uncomfortable. Making that commitment to something audacious—and then putting your back into it—is how you create the change you want to see.

The good news for you is that most of your competitors are not doing that. They're not embracing change and setting their sights on what's possible. But you are, which means that competitive advantage is yours if you want it. You've read this book, which tells me you're ready for a breakthrough. Now lean into it, and make your big, bold vision a reality.

LATANÉ CONANT

As CMO of 6sense, Latané is passionate about empowering marketing leaders with effective technology, predictive insights, and thought leadership so they can confidently lead their teams, company, and industry into the future. As a "recovering software saleswoman," she is keenly focused on leveraging data to ensure marketing programs result in deals, not just leads.

Prior to 6sense she was the CMO and a sales leader at Appirio. She was instrumental in aligning sales and marketing under a consistent and relevant message—resulting in increased bookings, average deal size, and win rates. Latané is creative, charismatic, and competitive. Her high energy, positive attitude, and sense of humor are contagious, and it's hard to find a customer, partner, audience, or employee who doesn't want to work with her.

INDEX

NO FORMS. NO SPAM. NO COLD CALLS.